World Hunger

World Hunger: 12 Myths

Second Edition fully revised and updated

Frances Moore Lappé, Joseph Collins, and Peter Rosset

with Luis Esparza

Grove Press
New York

The original edition of this book was written by Frances Moore Lappé and Joseph Collins in 1986. Revisions and updating for this second edition were the work of Joseph Collins and Peter Rosset, with the assistance of Luis Esparza.

Published simultaneously in Canada
Printed in the United States of America

SECOND EDITION

Library of Congress Cataloging-in-Publication Data
Lappé, Frances Moore.
    World hunger : twelve myths / by Frances Moore Lappé, Joseph Collins, and Peter Rosset
      p. cm.
    Includes bibliographical references and index.
    ISBN 0-8021-3591-9
    1. Food supply.   2. Agriculture and state.   3. Nutrition policy.
4. Poverty.   5. Social policy.   I. Collins, Joseph, 1945–   .
II. Title.
HD9000.5.L33   1998
363.8—dc21   98-29927
                                                                  CIP

Design by Laura Hammond Hough

Grove Press
841 Broadway
New York, NY 10003

98 99 00 01   10 9 8 7 6 5 4 3 2

To the memory of our friend Harry Chapin,

who believed that ordinary people could overcome hunger

once we free ourselves from the myths that entrap us.

Contents

Preface and Acknowledgments
to the Second Edition

I t has been twelve years since we published *World Hunger: 12 Myths* here at The Institute for Food and Development Policy, better known as "Food First." Even more years have passed since an earlier edition was called *10 Myths*. Over the years we have heard from dozens and dozens of people who told us this book literally changed their lives. Many first read it as students, changing their career goals as a result. Others read it as part of a church social action or study group, while still others picked it up in a bookstore or were given it by a friend. Almost all those who contacted us said they were moved to personally take some kind of action, changing something about their own lives, in many cases becoming activists. We are proud yet humbled to have that impact: proud because we have made a contribution to the fight against hunger, yet humbled by the knowledge that it is ordinary people who must, and will, bring about the changes that our world so desperately needs.

The time has come for a new edition of *World Hunger: 12 Myths*. Since the last edition came out, we have seen big changes in the world: the end of the Cold War; accelerated economic globalization; the imposition of budget cutting and free-trade initiatives on third world countries; severe cuts in social programs here in America; and the recognition that human population growth rates are falling worldwide, to name a few. Remarkably, in researching this edition, we found that despite these new developments, our basic arguments are as valid today as they were a dozen years ago. Yet the context has changed, and there is new evidence to support our viewpoints. We think this edition will be as important for readers of earlier versions as for people who are reading it for the first time.

We wish to deeply thank the following research interns at the Institute for Food and Development Policy–Food First, whose work contributed immeasurably to this edition: Gavin Post, Simon Mui, Annette Blau, Marc Herbst, Abikök Riak, Nandita Jhaveri, David Silverberg, Li Kheng Poh, Jennifer Bagnell, Fuyuki Kurasawa, Michael Mace, Xochitl Alvarez-Ponce, Kathy Yoo, and Shauna Olson. Staff members Marilyn Borchardt, Deborah Toler, Anuradha Mittal, Martin Bourque, and Martha Katigbak also made significant contributions, as did María Elena Martínez.

Needless to say, we remain solely responsible for any errors that remain in the final version of the book.

None of Food First's work, including this new edition, would be possible without the support of its members. We thank each of you. We also thank all of the foundations and churches who have supported our work over the years.

Thank you.

World Hunger

Beyond Guilt and Fear

For over twenty-five years we have sought to understand why there is hunger in a world of plenty. For us, learning had to begin with unlearning. Cutting through the simplistic and scary clichés about hunger, we arrived at some surprising findings:

- No country in the world is a hopeless case. Even countries many people think of as impossibly overcrowded have the resources necessary for people to free themselves from hunger.
- Increasing a nation's food production may not help the hungry. Food production per person can increase while more people go hungry.
- Our government's foreign aid often hurts rather than helps the hungry. But in a multitude of other ways we can help.
- The poor are neither a burden on us nor a threat to our interests. Unlikely as it may seem, the interests of the vast majority of Americans have much in common with those of the world's hungry.

Our book explains these surprising findings and many more that have freed us from a response to hunger motivated by guilt and fear. But first we must ask the seemingly grade-school question, just what is hunger? Many people assume they know—they've felt it, they've read about it, they've been touched by images of hungry people on television. But the greatest obstacle to grasping the causes and solutions to world hunger is that few of us stop to ponder this elemental question.

What Is Hunger?

Television images haunt us. Stunted, bony bodies. Long lines waiting for a meager bowl of gruel. This is famine hunger in its acute form, the kind no one could miss.

But hunger comes in another form. It is the day-in-day-out hunger that almost 800 million people suffer.[1] While chronic hunger doesn't make the evening news, it takes more lives than famine.

Every day this largely invisible hunger, and its related preventable diseases, kill as many as thirty-four thousand children under the age of five.[2] That's 12 million children per year—more than the total number of people who died each year during World War II. This death toll is equivalent to the number killed instantly by a Hiroshima bomb every three days.

Statistics like this are staggering. They shock and alarm. Several years ago, however, we began to doubt the usefulness of such numbers. Numbers can numb. They can distance us from what is actually very close to us. So we asked ourselves, what really is hunger?

Is it the gnawing pain in the stomach when we miss a meal? The physical depletion of those suffering chronic undernutrition? The listless stare of a dying child in the television hunger appeal? Yes, but it is more. And we became convinced that as long as we conceive of hunger only in physical measures, we will never truly understand it, certainly not its roots.

What, we asked ourselves, would it mean to think of hunger in terms of universal human emotions, feelings that all of us have experienced at some time in our lives? We'll mention only four such emotions, to give you an idea of what we mean.

A friend of ours, Dr. Charles Clements, is a former Air Force pilot and Vietnam veteran who spent a year treating peasants in El Salvador. He wrote of a family he tried to help whose son and daughter had died of fever and diarrhea. "Both had been lost," he writes, "in the years when Camila and her husband had chosen to pay their mortgage, a sum equal to half the value of their crop, rather than keep the money to feed their children. Each year, the choice was always the same. If they paid, their children's lives were endangered. If they didn't, their land could be repossessed."[3]

Being hungry thus means anguish. The anguish of impossible choices. But it is more.

In Nicaragua some years ago, we met Amanda Espinoza, a poor rural woman, who until then had never had enough to feed her family. She told us that she had endured six stillbirths and watched five of her children die before the age of one.

To Amanda, being hungry means watching people you love die. It is grief.

Throughout the world, the poor are made to blame themselves for their poverty. Walking into a home in the Philippine countryside, the first words we heard were an apology for the poverty of the dwelling. Being hungry also means living in humiliation.

Anguish, grief, and humiliation are a part of what hunger means. But increasingly throughout the world, hunger has a fourth dimension.

In Guatemala we met two poor highland peasants who, with the help of World Neighbors, an Oklahoma City–based voluntary aid group, were teaching their neighbors how to reduce erosion on the steep slopes onto which they had been pushed by wealthy landowners monopolizing the flat valley land. Two years later, we learned that one had been forced into hiding, the other had been killed. In the eyes of the wealthy their crime was teaching their neighbors better farming techniques. Guatemala's oligarchy feels threatened by any change that makes the poor less dependent on low-paying jobs on their plantations.

Often, then, a fourth dimension of hunger is fear.

Anguish, grief, humiliation, and fear. What if we refused to count the hungry and instead tried to understand hunger in terms of such universal emotions?

We discovered that how we understand hunger determines what we think are its solutions. If we think of hunger only as numbers—numbers of people with too few calories—the solution also appears to us in numbers—numbers of tons of food aid, or numbers of dollars in economic assistance. But once we begin to understand hunger as real people coping with the most painful of human emotions, we can perceive its roots. We need only ask, When have we experienced any of these emotions ourselves? Hasn't it been when we have felt out of control of our lives—powerless to protect ourselves and those we love?

Hunger has thus become for us the ultimate symbol of powerlessness.

3

The Causes of Powerlessness

Understanding that hunger tells us that a person has been robbed of the most basic power—the power to protect ourselves and those we love—is a first step. Peeling back the layers of misunderstanding, we must then ask, If powerlessness lies at the very root of hunger, what are hunger's causes?

Certainly, it is not scarcity. The world is awash with food, as chapter 1 will show. Neither are natural disasters to blame. Put most simply, the root cause of hunger isn't a scarcity of food or land; it's a *scarcity of democracy*.

Wait a minute! What does democracy have to do with hunger? In our view—everything. Democracy carries within it the principle of accountability. Democratic structures are those in which people have a say in decisions that most affect their well-being. Leadership can be kept accountable to the needs of the majority. Antidemocratic structures are those in which power is so tightly concentrated that the majority of people are left with no say at all. Leaders are accountable only to the powerful minority.

In the United States, we think of democracy as a strictly political concept, so it may seem contrived to apply it to the economic questions of land, food, jobs, and income. Political democracy helps us as citizens to protect certain rights—to reside where we will, to vote, to have our civil liberties upheld, and so on. Unlike many societies, here such universal political citizenship is taken for granted.

But along with many other societies, we lack a concept of economic citizenship. To parallel our universal political rights, we have not yet established universal economic rights, such as the right to life-sustaining resources or the right to participate in economic decision making.

What we hope to show in this book is that as long as this fundamental concept of democracy—accountability to those most affected by decisions—is absent from economic life, people will continue to be made powerless. From the family, to the neighborhood or the village, through the national level, to the level of international commerce and finance, we will witness the continued concentration of decision making over all aspects of economic life, including what it takes to grow and distribute that on which all life depends: food. Poverty and hunger will go on destroying the lives of millions each year and scarring the lives of hundreds of millions more.

Let us look briefly at how antidemocratic decision making robs people of power over their lives on each of the levels mentioned above.

First, within the family, who controls food resources? Women are responsible for growing at least half the world's food. The resources women have to grow staple foods largely determine their family's nutritional well-being. But many women are losing authority over land use—the result of the privatization of land ownership and a focus on export crops that began under colonialism. Credit for growing cash crops goes overwhelmingly to men, and food crops have stagnated. This dynamic within the family helps explain growing hunger.[4]

Second, at the village level, who controls the land—and how many families have none at all? In most countries, a consistent pattern emerges: Fewer and fewer people control more and more farm and pasture land. With fewer families controlling an ever greater share of the land, more and more people have none at all. A 1993 study reported alarming percentages of rural families who are landless or have insufficient land to support themselves. In Peru the number of landless or land-poor was 75 percent, in Ecuador 75 percent, 66 percent in Colombia, 32 percent in Kenya, and 95 percent in Egypt, among many others.[5]

Third, at the national level, how are public resources allocated? Wherever people have been made hungry, power is in the hands of those unaccountable to their people. These antidemocratic governments answer only to elites, lavishing them with credit, subsidies, and other assistance. With increasing brutality, such governments fight any reform that would make control over food-producing resources more equitable. The Landless Workers Movement (*Movimento dos Trabalhadores Rurais Sem Terra*, or MST) in Brazil is struggling to turn over land left idle on huge estates to landless families. In 1995 and 1996 at least eighty-six landless workers, family members, and MST activists were assassinated, most by the military police acting at the behest of wealthy landowners.[6]

There is yet a fourth level on which democracy is scarce—the international arena of commerce and finance. A handful of corporations dominate world trade in those commodities that are the lifeblood of third world economies. Efforts by third world governments to bargain for higher commodity prices have repeatedly failed in the face of the preeminent power of the giant trading corporations and the government trade policies of the industrial countries. Industrial countries import $60 billion a year worth of food from the third world,[7] but traders, processors, and marketers reap most of the profit. For every dollar a U.S. consumer spends to buy cantaloupes grown in El Salvador, less than a penny goes to the farmer, while traders, shippers, and retailers receive eighty-eight cents.[8]

Heavily indebted to international aid agencies and private banks, third world nations are also at the mercy of policies decided upon in the capitals of the industrial nations, policies leading only to further impoverishment.[9]

In attempting to capsulize the antidemocratic roots of hunger, we have traveled from the level of the family to that of international commerce and finance. Let us complete the circle by returning to the family.

As economic decisions are made by those unaccountable to the majority, insecurity deepens for millions of people. Economic pressures tear family bonds asunder as men are forced to leave home in search of work, and joblessness leads to family violence and dissolution. More and more women shoulder family responsibilities alone; worldwide, perhaps as many as one-third of all households are now headed by women. On top of the weight of poverty, they confront barriers of discrimination against women. The breakdown of the traditional family structure does not bring liberation for them; it simply means greater hardship. Most of the hungry in the world are women and the children they care for. Most of those who die from hunger every year are children.

In our effort to grasp the roots of hunger, we have identified the problem: the ever greater scarcity not of food or land but of democracy, democracy understood to include the life-and-death matter of economics. But we must dig deeper. Why have we allowed this process to happen at the cost of millions of needless deaths each year?

How We Think about Hunger

Especially in troubled times, people seek ways to make sense of the world. We grasp for organizing principles to help us interpret the endlessly confusing rush of world events. It's a natural human process—perhaps as natural as eating itself. But living effectively depends on how well our organizing principles reflect reality.

Unfortunately, the principles around which many of us have come to organize our thinking about world hunger block our grasp of real solutions. This entire book is structured around such organizing principles. We call them myths, to suggest that the views embodied may not be totally false. Many have some validity. It is as organizing principles that they fail. Not only do they prevent us from seeing how we

6

can help the hungry, they obfuscate our own legitimate interests as well. Some fail us because they describe but don't explain, some are so partial that they lead us down blind alleys, and some simply aren't true.

What we want to do is to probe the underlying assumptions people have about world hunger's causes and cures. For we've come to believe that the *way people think about hunger is the greatest obstacle to ending it.*

After reading our book, we hope you will find that you no longer have to block out bad news about hunger but can face it squarely because a more realistic framework of understanding—to be repeatedly tested against your own experience—enables you to make real choices, choices that can contribute to ending this spreading but needless human suffering.

Our book may shake your most dearly held beliefs or it may confirm your deepest intuitions and experiences. Most of all, we hope that it convinces you that until humanity has solved the most basic human problem—how to ensure that every one of us has food for life—we cannot consider ourselves fully human.

CHAPTER 1

Myth 1:
There's Simply Not Enough Food

MYTH: With food-producing resources in so much of the world stretched to the limit, there's simply not enough food to go around. Unfortunately, some people will just have to go hungry.

OUR RESPONSE: The world today produces enough grain alone to provide every human being on the planet with thirty-five hundred calories a day.[1] That's enough to make most people fat! And this estimate does not even count many other commonly eaten foods—vegetables, beans, nuts, root crops, fruits, grass-fed meats, and fish. In fact, if all foods are considered together, enough is available to provide at least 4.3 pounds of food per person a day. That includes two and a half pounds of grain, beans, and nuts; about a pound of fruits and vegetables; and nearly another pound of meat, milk, and eggs.[2]

Abundance, not scarcity, best describes the supply of food in the world today. Increases in food production during the past thirty-five years have outstripped the world's unprecedented population growth by about 16 percent.[3] Indeed, mountains of unsold grain on world markets have pushed prices strongly downward over the past three and a half decades.[4] Grain prices rose briefly during the early 1990s, as bad weather coincided with policies geared toward reducing overproduction, but remained well below the highs observed in the early sixties and mid-seventies.[5]

All well and good for the global picture, you might be thinking, but doesn't such a broad stroke tell us little? Aren't most of the world's hungry living in countries with food shortages—countries in Latin America, in Asia, and especially in Africa?

Hunger in the face of ample food is all the more shocking in the third world. According to the Food and Agriculture Organization (FAO) of the United Nations, gains in food production since 1950 have kept ahead of population growth in every region except Africa.[6] The American Association for the Advancement of Science (AAAS) found in a 1997 study that 78 percent of all malnourished children under five in the developing world live in countries with food *surpluses.*[7]

Thus, even most "hungry countries" have enough food for all their people right now. This finding is based on official statistics even though experts warn us that newly modernizing societies invariably underestimate farm production—just as a century ago at least a third of the U.S. wheat crop went uncounted.[8] Moreover, many nations can't realize their full food production potential because of the gross inefficiencies caused by inequitable ownership of resources. We will discuss this in chapters 4 and 6.

Finally, many of the countries in which hunger is rampant export much more in agricultural goods than they import. Northern countries are the main food importers, their purchases representing 71.2 percent of the total value of food items imported in the world in 1992.[9] Imports by the thirty lowest-income countries, on the other hand, accounted for only 5.2 percent of all international commerce in food and farm commodities.[10]

Looking more closely at some of the world's hunger-ravaged countries and regions confirms that scarcity is clearly not the cause of hunger.

India. India ranks near the top among third world agricultural exporters. While at least 200 million Indians go hungry,[11] in 1995 India exported $625 million worth of wheat and flour and $1.3 billion worth of rice (5 million metric tons), the two staples of the Indian diet.[12]

Bangladesh. Beginning with its famine of the early 1970s, Bangladesh came to symbolize the frightening consequences of people overrunning food resources. Yet Bangladesh's official yearly rice output alone—which some experts say is seriously underreported[13]—could provide each person with about a pound of grain per day, or two thousand calories.[14] Adding to that small amounts of vegetables, fruits, and

9

legumes could prevent hunger for everyone. Yet the poorest third of the people in Bangladesh eat at most only fifteen hundred calories a day, dangerously below what is needed for a healthy life.[15]

With more than 120 million people living in an area the size of Wisconsin, Bangladesh may be judged overcrowded by any number of standards, but its population density is not a viable excuse for its widespread hunger. Bangladesh is blessed with exceptional agricultural endowments, yet its 1995 rice yields fell significantly below the all-Asia average.[16] The extraordinary potential of Bangladesh's rich alluvial soils and plentiful water has hardly been unleashed. If the country's irrigation potential were realized, experts predict its rice yields could double or even triple.[17] Since the total calorie supply in Bangladesh falls only 6 percent short of needs,[18] nutritional adequacy seems an achievable goal.

Brazil. While Brazil exported more than $13 billion worth of food in 1994 (second among developing countries), 70 million Brazilians cannot afford enough to eat.[19]

Africa. It comes as a surprise for many of us to learn that the countries of sub-Saharan Africa, home to some 213 million chronically malnourished people (about 25 percent of the total in developing countries),[20] continue to export food. Throughout the 1980s exports from sub-Saharan Africa grew more rapidly than imports,[21] and in 1994, eleven countries of the region remained net exporters of food.[22]

The Sahelian countries of West Africa, known for recurrent famines, have been net exporters of food even during the most severe droughts. During one of the worst droughts on record, in the late 1960s and early 1970s, the value of the region's agricultural exports—$1.25 billion—remained three times greater than the value of grain imported,[23] and such figures did not even take into account significant unreported exports.[24] Once again, during the 1982–85 drought food was exported from these countries.[25]

Nevertheless, by 1990, food production per person had apparently been declining for almost two decades,[26] despite the productive capacity suggested by Africa's agricultural exports, and in 1995 over one-third of the continent's grain consumption depended on imports.[27] We use the word "apparently" because official statistics notoriously underreport, or ignore all together, food grown for home consumption, especially by poor women, as well as food informally exchanged

10

within family and friendship networks, making a truly accurate assessment impossible.[28] In fact, the author of the AAAS report referred to earlier argues that hunger is actually *less* severe in sub-Saharan Africa than in South Asia.[29]

Repeated reports about Africa's failing agriculture and growing dependence on imports have led many to assume that simply too many people are vying for limited resources. Africa's food crisis is real, as evidenced by moderately high rates of childhood malnutrition, but how accurate is this assumption as to why the crisis exists?

Africa has enormous, still unexploited, potential to grow food, with potential grain yields 25 to 35 percent higher than maximum potential yields in Europe and North America.[30] Beyond yield potential, ample arable land awaits use. In Chad, for example, only 10 percent of the farmland rated as having no serious production constraints is actually farmed. In countries notorious for famines—Ethiopia, Sudan, Somalia, and Mali, for example—the area of unused good-quality farmland is many times greater than the area actually farmed,[31] casting doubt on the notion that there are simply too many people for scarce resources.

Many long-time observers of Africa's agricultural development tell us that the real reasons for Africa's food problems are no mystery.[32] Africa's food potential has been distorted and thwarted as follows:

- The colonial land grab that continued into the modern era displaced peoples and the production of foodstuffs from good lands toward marginal ones, giving rise to a pattern by which good land is mostly dedicated to the production of cash crops for export or is even unused by its owners.[33] Furthermore, colonizers and, subsequently, national and international agencies have discredited peasant producers' often sophisticated knowledge of ecologically appropriate farming systems. Promoting "modern," often imported, and ecologically destructive technologies,[34] they have cut Africa's food producers out of economic decisions most affecting their very survival.
- Public resources, including research and agricultural credit, have been channeled to export crops to the virtual exclusion of peasant-produced food crops such as millet, sorghum, and root crops. In the 1980s increased pressure to export to pay interest on foreign debt further reinforced this imbalance.[35]
- Women are principal food producers in many parts of Africa, yet both colonial policy and, all too often, ill-conceived foreign aid and

11

investment projects have placed decisions over land use and credit in the domain of men. In many cases that has meant preferential treatment for cash crops over food crops, skewing land-use and investment patterns toward cash crops.[36]

- Aid policies unaccountable to African peasant producers and pastoralists have generally bypassed their needs in favor of expensive, large-scale projects. Africa has historically received less aid for agriculture than any other continent, and only a fraction of it has reached rain-fed agriculture, on which the bulk of grain production depends.[37] Most of the aid has backed irrigated, export-oriented, elite-controlled production.

- Because of external as well as domestic factors, African governments have often maintained cheap food policies whereby peasants are paid so poorly for their crops that they have little incentive to produce, especially for official market channels.[38] The factors responsible for these policies have included developed-country dumping of food surpluses in African markets at artificially low prices, developed-country interest in cheap wages to guarantee profitable export production, middle-class African consumer demand for affordable meat and dairy products produced with cheap grain, and government concerns about urban political support and potential unrest.[39] The net effect has been to both depress local food production and divert it toward informal, and therefore unrecorded, markets.

- Until recently many African governments also overvalued their currencies, making imported food artificially cheap and undercutting local producers of millet, sorghum, and cassava. Although recent policy changes have devalued currencies, which might make locally produced food more attractive, accompanying free-trade policies (discussed in chapter 8) have brought increased imports of cheap food from northern countries, largely canceling any positive effect.[40]

- Urban tastes have increasingly shifted to imported grain, particularly wheat, which few countries in Africa can grow economically. Thirty years ago, only a small minority of urban dwellers in sub-Saharan Africa ate wheat. Today bread is a staple for many urbanites, and bread and other wheat products account for about a third of all the region's grain imports.[41] U.S. food aid and advertising by multinational corporations ("He'll be smart. He'll go far. He'll eat bread.")[42] have played parts in molding African tastes to what the developed countries have to sell.[43]

12

Thus, beneath the "scarcity diagnosis" of Africa's food situation lie many human-made (often Western-influenced) and therefore reversible causes. Even Africa's high birth rates are not independent variables but are determined by social realities that shape people's reproductive choices, as we will see in chapter 3.

A Future of Scarcity?

A centuries-old debate has recently heated up: Just how close are we to the earth's limits?

Major studies have arrived at widely varying conclusions as to the earth's potential to support future populations. In a 1995 book Professor Joel Cohen of Rockefeller University surveyed estimates put forth over four centuries.[44] Always a slippery concept,[45] estimates of the earth's "carrying capacity," or the number of people who could be supported, have varied from a low of 1 billion in a 1970 study to a high of 1,022 billion put forth in 1967. Among studies published between 1990 and 1994, the range was from "much less than our current population of 5.5 billion," according to Paul Ehrlich and others, to a high of 44 billion estimated by a Dutch research team, with most estimates falling into the 10 to 14 billion range.[46] By contrast, the 1996 United Nations forecast, generally considered to be the best future population projection, predicts that the world population will peak at 9.36 billion in the year 2050 and stabilize thereafter[47] (projections of the maximum future population have been coming down over the past few years). This is well within what most experts view as the capacity of the earth.

In view of today's abundant food supplies, as well as the potential suggested in this chapter and in chapter 6, we question the more pessimistic predictions of demographic catastrophe. Only fifty years ago, China pundits predicted that that famine-ridden nation could never feed its population. Today more than twice as many people eat—and fairly adequately[48]—on only one-fourth the cropland per person used in the United States.[49]

Not that anyone should take the more pessimistic predictions lightly; they underscore the reality of the inevitably finite resource base entrusted to us. They should therefore reinforce our sense of urgency to address the root causes of resource misuse, resource degradation, and rapid population growth.

Lessons from Home

Finally, in probing the connection between hunger and scarcity, we should never overlook the lessons here at home. More than 30 million Americans cannot afford a healthy diet; 8.5 percent of U.S. children are hungry, and 20.1 percent are at risk of hunger.[50] But who would argue that not enough food is produced? Surely not U.S. farmers; overproduction is their most persistent headache. Nor the U.S. government, which maintains huge storehouses of cheese, milk, and butter. In 1995, U.S. aid shipments abroad of surplus food included more than 3 million metric tons of cereals and cereal products,[51] about two-thirds consisting of wheat and flour. That's enough flour to bake about six hundred loaves of bread per year for every hungry child in the United States.[52]

Here at home, just as in the third world, hunger is an outrage precisely because it is profoundly needless. Behind the headlines, the television images, the superficial clichés, we can learn to see that hunger is real; scarcity is not.

Only when we free ourselves from the myth of scarcity can we begin to look for hunger's real causes. That search is what our book is about.

CHAPTER 2

Myth 2:
Nature's to Blame

MYTH: Droughts, floods, and other events beyond human control cause famine.

OUR RESPONSE: On January 22, 1994, the *Chicago Tribune* ran the following story: "Man Dies; Found in Unheated Home." The article called it "the fourth fatality of the week's cold wave." Surely the reporter who wrote the story didn't really believe that the weather caused the four deaths. The man was probably poor and unable to pay his heating bills. Maybe the others couldn't even afford a home. In 1985, four hundred homeless people died on the streets of Chicago.[1] Yet who could really blame the weather? In the United States people are vulnerable to bad weather only if they are too poor to afford heat or shelter.

The "great potato famine" killed over a million Irish people between 1845 and 1849 and caused another million and a half to emigrate to America. In official histories it is described as a natural disaster, an epidemic of potato blight, that caused the famine. Few people know that Ireland was a net exporter of food throughout those years. The same blight devastated potato crops across Europe, but mass starvation occurred only in Ireland.[2]

In an 1846 letter to the prime minister, an observer remarked, "For 46 years the people of Ireland have been feeding those of England with the choicest produce of their agriculture and pasture; and while they thus exported their wheat and their beef in profusion, their own food became gradually deteriorated . . . until the mass of the peasantry was exclusively thrown on the potato."[3] The majority had become vulnerable to the blight because their impoverishment under British rule had reduced their diet to potatoes alone.

Many of us assume that things are somehow different in today's third world. Those who die in famines there are victims of this or that natural event—most often the weather in the form of a drought or flood.

But if we take a closer look, we find that things are not really different. A major study of droughts, floods, and other natural disasters carried out by the Swedish Red Cross and the international public interest organization Earthscan brought the question of vulnerability to the fore for today's third world as well. The researchers found that the annual number of victims of natural disasters jumped sixfold in the 1960s and 70s, much greater than the increase in disasters.[4] A similar pattern held during the last decade.[5] Clearly, rather than disasters becoming more common, people had become more *vulnerable*.

Human-made forces make people increasingly vulnerable to nature's vagaries. Pushed onto marginal, drought-prone lands or deprived of land altogether, in debt to moneylenders or wealthy landowners who claim most of their harvests, unemployed or so poorly paid that nothing is left to fall back on, and weakened by chronic hunger, millions die. Natural events are not the cause. They are the final blow.

Lessons from the Bangladesh Famine

In the autumn of 1974, international attention turned to one of the worst famines of modern times. The mass media readily accepted the Bangladesh government's claim that the famine taking over 100,000 lives was caused by harvest-destroying floods.

But many workers on the scene as well as later researchers argue that despite the floods, at no point was Bangladesh short of food. One peasant described what happened in her village: "A lot of people died of starvation here. The rich farmers were hoarding rice and not letting any of the poor peasants see it." Asked whether there was enough food in the village, she replied, "There may not have been a lot of food, but if it had been shared, no one would have died."[6]

The 1974 Bangladesh famine was not exceptional. Widely recognized for his studies of modern famines, Harvard University's Amartya Sen

16

has found that famines have occurred not because of a shortage of food but because people's claim to food is disrupted.[7] When people are denied the resources to grow or retain enough of their own harvests to meet family needs, and when only buying power—money—gives people claim to additional food, many will go hungry and even starve if their income falls or food prices dramatically rise.

People's income may fall precipitously because they lose their means to produce. Poor people might have to sell their land or animals because of a death in the family, for instance, or mounting debts might mean that they lose their land after a single bad harvest. Many such distress sales lay behind the famine deaths in Bangladesh.[8] Often the price of what the poor produce suddenly drops, leaving them unable to buy enough food. Or if the income of better-off groups suddenly increases, food prices may soar beyond the reach of the poor, even with no major harvest failure.

Rumors of a future shortfall, whether true or false, can prompt well-to-do farmers and merchants to hoard food, guaranteeing a shortage for others and windfall profits for themselves. As two longtime observers of rural Bangladesh commented on the 1974 famine, "While to most people scarcity means suffering, to others it means profit."[9]

One large farmer in Uganda explained candidly how she had amassed over five hundred acres. "The 1980 famine helped," she said. "People were in need. For the first time, they were willing to sell land, cows—things they wouldn't dream of selling in normal times."[10]

Recurring Famine in Africa's Sahel

In the early 1970s, the much publicized famine in the Sahelian nations of West Africa helped move us to found the Institute for Food and Development Policy. The common assumption, reinforced by media coverage, was that the famine resulted from prolonged drought. But we learned that even during the famine years, surveys by the Food and Agriculture Organization of the United Nations—squelched by displeased aid-seeking governments—documented that all but one Sahelian country in West Africa produced enough grain to feed its total population.[11] Moreover, water was adequate to grow vast amounts of cotton, vegetables, peanuts (for cooking oil and livestock feed), and other agricultural goods for export. In fact, during the drought many agricultural exports from the Sahel—largely to well-fed consumers in Europe—actually increased.[12]

17

In the mid-1980s, drought and famine once again struck the Sahel. Poor farmers were among those who suffered most. In debt to rich farmers and merchants, they were forced to sell their crops at harvest time at rock-bottom prices and were left without enough food to survive the "hunger season." Nor did they have enough money to buy food, since merchants eagerly hiked their prices to take advantage of crop shortfalls.[13] Because bad harvests leave ordinary farmers so much deeper in debt, they have little cause to rejoice even when good rains fall. Debt, not the weather, is the real killer of Sahelian peasants.[14]

Desertification in the Sahel is a problem that has exacerbated the vulnerability of agricultural and pastoral peoples.[15] Yet desertification is itself a human-made process stemming from the misuse of fragile lands. Beginning with the colonial period and intensifying in recent decades, the drive for export crop cultivation has exhausted cropland and displaced food producers into fragile drought-prone areas, where natural vegetation is destroyed by overgrazing and the cultivation of inappropriate soils.[16]

West Africa's food merchants ensure that no one with reasonable financial resources goes hungry. Due to drought in 1984, Mali's grain harvest was 400,000 tons below what had been expected, but the four major private merchants had no trouble bringing almost that much into the country from neighboring Ivory Coast for anyone who could pay for it.[17] "There's always food in the market, but we have no money," one West African peasant told University of California geographer Michael Watts.[18]

Starvation is not directly linked to drought, for people starve even though enough food is near at hand. While crop failure devastates one area, in another not far away farmers may reap a bumper harvest, observes John Scheuring, an American agricultural scientist with years of experience in the region.[19]

Too sophisticated to simply blame nature, many Western observers point to what they believe is a deeper cause of hunger in West Africa: Increased numbers of people and their livestock have simply overrun the capacity of the land. You can't blame nature for that, they tell us.

But this effort to probe deeper begs as many questions as it answers. In chapter 4, we explore the many human-made forces generating this imbalance with nature. None of the human-made forces evident in the Sahelian famine of the 1970s were adequately addressed in subsequent years. Little wonder that famine—striking the poor most heavily—recurred with a vengeance in the 1980s.[20]

A close look at foreign aid programs also helps to explain the recurrence of famine. Most of the dollars have gone to expensive (and often technically dubious), large-scale irrigation schemes, mostly to grow commodities for export,[21] thus failing to affect food production or reach the majority of peasants.

So it is not surprising that during the 1982–85 drought a number of Sahelian countries increased farm exports as their food production fell.[22] During the drought year of 1984, a record quantity of cotton was exported.[23]

During the 1980s, Cold War super-power rivalries exacerbated tensions dating from colonial times, driving war and conflict in various African countries. These conflicts, which have spilled over into the post–Cold War period, have contributed to the deterioration of an already complex web of social and economic phenomena, multiplying vulnerability to hunger and famine.[24]

Ethiopia's Human-made Tragedy

In the early 1980s media coverage of starvation in Ethiopia reinforced the notion that drought is to blame for famine. We visited Ethiopia's highland villages in January and February of 1985, seeking out the causes of the widespread human suffering we had seen on television.

First, we learned how wrong we were to assume that the Ethiopian drought prevailed over the entire country or even most of it. As our jeep wound over mountain roads, we saw one valley in which the rains had brought a good harvest, followed by a valley where obviously little rain had fallen. The next valley had only enough rainfall to grow drought-tolerant sorghum. Ethiopia's sheer size (twice the area of Texas) and its varied geography (a splintered highland massif surrounded by lowland areas) make it highly unlikely that a drought or any other climatic condition would be nationwide.

Several agriculturists confirmed our impression, estimating that the 1982–85 drought affected at most 30 percent of Ethiopia's farmland.[25] An agricultural specialist within Ethiopia told us that with drainage, rich but waterlogged valley bottom lands could be planted, perhaps doubling the cultivated land area.[26] Traveling through the relatively well-watered Awash River valley, we saw vast acreages of prime land producing cotton and sugarcane for export. We also learned that for eight years prior to the drought, food production in many villages had already deteriorated—perhaps as much as 20 percent per person as a nationwide average.

If much of the country was unaffected by drought, and if food production had already dropped before it began, clearly drought cannot explain shortages that contributed to 300,000 deaths by 1985.[27] How can we understand such a tragedy?

When a military uprising overthrew Emperor Haile Selassie in 1974, the young rebel officers correctly charged that feudalistic landlordism, hoarding, and governmental indifference—not the years of drought—had caused the famine of the early 1970s. Peasant hopes soared soon thereafter when the new government decreed a sweeping land reform ending landlord-tenant relationships. Unfortunately, peasant-based rural development soon dropped off the agenda as the government sank into a quagmire of military conflicts with separatist groups. Colonial powers had imposed arbitrary borders in the region without respect to the geographical organization of local societies, guaranteeing decades of post-independence uprisings for self-determination.[28] The new government ended up spending almost half of its entire budget on the military.[29]

Between 1976 and 1980, the government imported more than $2 billion worth of weaponry from the Soviet Union.[30] The heavy interest payments on the foreign debt thus generated, further pressured the government to concentrate on exports rather than food crops. At the same time, in the East-West race for influence in the Horn of Africa, the United States greatly stepped up its arming of neighboring Somalia, with which Ethiopia, for all practical purposes, had been at war since 1978. U.S. policy provided the Ethiopian military with the perfect rationale for funneling resources into weapons rather than rural development. Government-run farms, considered a secure source of food for the armed forces, were the main repositories of the government's vastly disproportionate investment in agriculture.[31]

Meanwhile, the mainly conscripted army—over 300,000 strong and by far the largest in sub-Saharan Africa[32]—drained the countryside of the able-bodied young men needed for plowing and other heavy agricultural work. In 1985 the government forcibly relocated between 700,000 and 800,000 peasants from areas sympathetic to rebel forces.[33] The civil war eventually ended in 1991 with the overthrow of the Mengistu regime and the independence of Eritrea.[34]

Just as the war, grounded in external interests not drought, was at the root of the suffering in Ethiopia, so is it in other famine-stricken countries in Africa. Of the thirty-one drought-affected countries in sub-

Saharan Africa in the early 1980s, only five experienced famine: Mozambique, Angola, Sudan, Chad, and Ethiopia.[35] Each famine occurred in the context of war, and in each case the origin of the conflict can be traced to superpower geopolitics and/or the influence of former colonial powers.

Throughout history, human societies have worked to protect themselves against the vagaries of nature. Especially in large areas of Africa, periodic droughts have always challenged human survival. Precautions against their consequences have invariably been part of human culture. In the Old Testament, we read of the seven abundant years followed by seven lean years. So in much of Africa, farmers traditionally assumed that they should build up reserves to prevent famine. Also, for centuries in the semiarid areas of Africa, farmers and herders fashioned methods to cope with times of drought and other natural hardships. Life was never easy. Hunger was probably common, but not mass starvation, except—tellingly—in feudalistic Ethiopia. But the precautions and sound agricultural practices that had prevented famine were overturned in the short-term interests of European colonial powers.

Rwanda: Human Nature and Ethnic Conflict?

The appalling events that put Rwanda in the spotlight during the 1990s—genocide, civil war, and starving refugees[36]—illustrate the destructive power of war, a thoroughly human-made disaster.

Nevertheless, the conventional wisdom that posits drought-related famine as the direct product of "natural disasters" saw the Rwandan situation as the product of another kind of "natural" force: human nature, in the form of ethnic conflict among tribal peoples.[37] Not to deny the importance of ethnic factors, whose conflictive nature was dictated by colonial politics similar to those that generated conflict in Ethiopia,[38] but the forces that triggered the catastrophe were anything but natural.

Until the end of the 1980s, Rwanda had been described as a small and poor, but economically healthy and self-sufficient country. Traditional farming systems based on crop rotation and intercropping according to a highly sophisticated set of decision-making rules had been capable of sustaining farmers and their families for decades.[39] However, the fragmentation of small farms by inheritance—within a land-tenure pattern monopolized by a small number of wealthy land-

21

owners—was pushing the system to its limits, and few families could still survive from farming alone.[40]

A rural country traditionally combining subsistence agriculture with cash crops for export,[41] Rwanda had become increasingly dependent on coffee in the period leading up to the disaster.[42] Coffee prices began to fall in the mid-eighties, and by 1992 they were 75 percent below the 1986 level,[43] plunging the economy into crisis.

The earlier performance of Rwanda's economy had been regarded as comparatively successful by international observers.[44] With the coffee crisis, however, mounting balance-of-payments problems and heavy pressure from Western governments forced the government to sign a so-called "structural adjustment" program with the IMF and the World Bank in September 1990.

The program, whose ostensible aim was to achieve "macro-economic stabilization and improved international competitiveness,"[45] began with the devaluation of the Rwandan franc by 15 percent in 1992 (on top of a 40 percent devaluation it had undergone in 1990). Also mandated were massive government cutbacks and the withdrawal of subsidies for farmers and the urban poor, higher domestic interest rates on credit for farmers and small businessmen, the drastic reduction of barriers to imported goods, the elimination of price guarantees for coffee producers, and the selling off of state enterprises.[46] The impact on the economy and on living standards was abrupt and drastic.[47]

The proportion of people living below the poverty line, which had increased from 9 percent in 1982 to 15 percent in 1989 (with partial famine in the south),[48] leapt to 31 percent by 1993, while food production plummeted and the country became dependent on food aid.[49]

In this context the outbreak of war was but a more obvious and radical expression of the many forms of quiet violence inherent in a rapidly deteriorating situation, an extreme event in a series of other less obvious events that had led to growing desperation among a substantial portion of the population.

In January and February 1993, a rebel group called the Rwandan Patriotic Front moved to overthrow the thoroughly discredited government. They attacked in the most fertile part of the country, causing mass flight and the displacement of fully 13 percent of the country's population, as well as a 15 percent drop in agricultural products marketed.[50]

The outbreak of rebellion and war triggered ethnic tensions left by the legacy of colonialism and reinforced by powerful interethnic class differences.[51] Incipient ethnic conflicts were immediately seized upon

22

by the now desperate government, which manipulated them in an attempt to create a last-ditch ethnic base of support. The slaughter and deprivation that ensued took the lives of over a half million people.[52]

For all the complexity of the ethnic question, it is clear that rapid impoverishment of the population radicalized ethnic relations.[53] It also drove the government bureaucracy to manipulate a potentially explosive situation in a futile attempt to save itself.[54]

As a result of the war, the Rwandan economy completely collapsed along with the nation's principal institutions and social fabric. Coffee and food production plummeted due to the displacement of peasant farmers.[55] One out of seven Rwandans fled from the areas containing the most fertile soils;[56] and conflict disrupted communications, industry, and other economic activities everywhere.[57] The armed forces grew as well, further reducing the resources available for other purposes.[58]

This is a story not of "natural" and inevitable ethnic conflict, but rather of a country literally driven crazy by the vagaries of the world coffee market and externally imposed economic policies. As the social fabric of a country is pulled apart during times of crisis, it will tear along the lines of previously created "difference," in this case laid down by the colonial legacy.

Reflections on Famine

Famines, it turns out, are not natural disasters but social disasters, the result of human arrangements, not acts of God. Blaming nature, we fail to see that *human* institutions determine:

- *Who will have a claim to food.* As long as people's only claim to food is through the market—and incomes and prices remain volatile—people will die in famines no matter how much food is produced.
- *Who will be chronically vulnerable.* Famines are generally a disaster for the poor but an opportunity for the rich. When good rains finally return or when floodwaters recede, in most societies people's access to food-producing resources doesn't return to what it was before. Poor farmers and poor herders who were vulnerable before are likely to have been made more insecure.
- *The vulnerability of the agricultural system itself—soil, drainage, seeds— to drought and other natural adversities.* As long as people are forced by economic pressures to abuse the soil and to forgo time-tested conservation practices, poor harvests will become more common.

- *Who will use hunger against whom.* Food is often used as a weapon of war, and hunger is always a product of it [59]

If we believe that famines are caused by nature's vagaries, we will feel helpless and therefore excused from action. Learning that famines result from human-made forces, we discover hope. No one can change the weather, but we can take responsibility for establishing more stable farming systems and altering the economic rules so that people's claim to food may never be denied.

Only in this direction can we further humanity's age-old quest for food security.

CHAPTER 3

Myth 3:
Too Many Mouths to Feed

MYTH: Hunger is caused by too many people pressing against finite resources. We must slow population growth before we can hope to alleviate hunger.

OUR RESPONSE: In all of our educational efforts during the past twenty-five years, no question has been more common than Do too many people cause hunger? We've answered no, but in the eyes of some this is tantamount to irresponsibly dismissing population growth as a problem.

We do not take lightly the prospect of human numbers so dominating the planet that other forms of life are squeezed out, that all wilderness is subdued for human use, and that the mere struggle to feed and warm ourselves keeps us from more satisfying pursuits.

The question of population is so vital that we can't afford to be the least bit fuzzy in our thinking. So here we will focus on the three most critical questions this myth poses. Is the human population of the world growing "out of control"? Are population density and population growth the cause of hunger? And what is the nature of the link, if any, between slowing population growth and ending hunger?

Is Population Growth Out of Control?

On November 23, 1997, the *New York Times Magazine* proclaimed in a headline: "The Population Explosion Is Over."[1] The author of the article summed up what demographers have known for some time: human fertility and population growth rates are falling as quickly as they once rose. In fact, the secondary headline read in part, "the prospect of an emptier planet is creating its own set of problems."[2]

Since we published the last edition of this book, it has become clear that human fertility and population growth rates are dropping rapidly around the world. In the early 1950s, when we began to hear echoes of Thomas Malthus in warnings of an impending population explosion, the global total fertility rate (the number of children per woman) was five, more than double the replacement rate of 2.1 (the number that gives a stable population size over time).[3] By the late 1970s the total fertility rate had fallen to four, and by the mid-1990s it was 2.8 and dropping.

European and North American fertility rates peaked in 1955, dropping steadily since, and in Europe are now well below replacement. In Asia and Latin America, fertility has fallen steadily from about six in 1950 to below three in 1995. In Africa, fertility peaked at 6.75 in the early 1960s, dropping slowly through the 1960s, 1970s, 1980s, and 1990s. In 1995 it stood at 5.7, about where South Asia and Latin America were twenty years earlier, and precisely the fertility level at which those regions then experienced accelerated fertility declines.

The Demographic Transition

All of this neatly fits the concept of the "demographic transition," first observed in the two centuries preceding 1950 in what are today's developed countries.[4] Prior to the transition, these northern countries experienced high death rates matched by high birth rates, resulting in a relatively stable population size over time. But then improving living standards and public health measures caused death rates to drop, followed by a gradual drop in birth rates, which by the 1970s once again matched death rates. Between the onset-of-mortality decline and the drop in birth rates, population surged in northern countries, actually quadrupling. But that is long over, and most developed countries are now projected to experience population shrinkage in the future.[5]

Demographers long posited that today's third world countries would undergo a similar transition. Indeed, in the period following World War II, mortality decline accelerated in developing countries.[6] As the demographic transition model would predict, that led to a surge in population growth. And as expected, the death rate decline was later followed by a compensatory drop in birth rates. Instead of taking two centuries for the process to complete itself, this time it appears it will happen in less than one century.

Based on new data on fertility decline, the United Nations projection of the size the human population will reach in the year 2050 is now 9.37 billion, about 50 percent larger than today's population.[7] While that may still seem large, the new estimate is down from the 11.16 billion that was projected just twenty years ago.[8] The population is projected to stabilize shortly thereafter, most likely below 11.5 billion.[9] As noted in chapter 1, that is within the levels that most experts estimate the earth could support.

If that is so, then why all the fuss? It seems that many nondemographers either lost sight of, or never really understood, the nature of the demographic transition. Terrified by the apparently exponential growth of third world populations, which they assumed would continue to grow explosively until checked by massive famine and epidemics, these analysts generated alarmist predictions. In his 1968 best-seller *The Population Bomb* Paul Ehrlich wrote: "The battle to feed all of humanity is over. In the 1970s the world will undergo famines—hundreds of millions of people are going to starve to death. . . ."[10] Similar treatises have been written over the years by others, such as Lester Brown of the WorldWatch Institute.[11] Though starvation on the scale predicted by Ehrlich has not occurred, he repeated the warning in 1990 in *The Population Explosion.*[12]

Ironically, these warnings came just as demographers were announcing that fertility was starting its decline in the last regions of the world, beginning the final phase of the demographic transition.[13] Of course, once fertility rates drop, there is a time lag before population-growth rates fall, as people who are now children come into their child-bearing years.

While the final phase of the transition seems to have begun everywhere, concern remains as to its pace and irreversibility. Organizations that earlier advocated population control programs to avert famine and environmental catastrophe, now say that precisely these programs have brought fertility down. They argue that population control efforts must be redoubled to assure that the gains are not reversed and that the subsequent declines in population-growth rates come quickly enough to avoid too many more people being born in the interim.[14] In order to address these concerns we must examine the specific mechanisms that make some countries move more quickly through the phases of transition than others. We will do that in a later section of this chapter on the causes of fertility decline.

As a conclusion to this section, however, we can say with confidence that there is abundant evidence that the human population-growth rate is slowing and will eventually stop. It is hardly out of control. Populations will continue to grow rapidly for several decades before leveling off in many third world countries, but that does not, in and of itself, mean that population density or growth causes hunger in our world, an issue we address in the following section.

Does "Overpopulation" Cause Hunger?

Our second question can now be restated as: Do too many people *already* cause hunger? If that were the case, then reducing population density might indeed alleviate hunger. But for one factor to cause another, the two must consistently occur together. Population density and hunger do not.

Hunger is not caused by too many people sharing the land. In the Central America and Caribbean region, for example, Trinidad and Tobago show the lowest percentage of stunted children under five and Guatemala the highest (almost twelve times greater); yet Trinidad and Tobago's cropland per person—a key indicator of human population density—is less than half that of Guatemala's.[15] Costa Rica, with only half of Honduras' cropped acres per person, boasts a life expectancy—one indicator of nutrition—eleven years longer than that of Honduras and close to that of northern countries.[16]

In Asia, South Korea has just under half the farmland per person found in Bangladesh, yet no one speaks of overcrowding causing hunger in South Korea.[17]

Surveying the globe, we in fact can find no direct correlation between population density and hunger. For every Bangladesh, a densely populated and hungry country, we find a Nigeria, Brazil, or Bolivia, where significant food resources per capita coexist with hunger.[18] Or we find a country like the Netherlands, where very little land per person has not prevented it from eliminating hunger and becoming a large net exporter of food.[19]

But what about population growth? Is there not an obvious correlation between rapid population growth and hunger? Without doubt, most hungry people live in Asia, Africa, and Latin America, where populations have grown fastest in recent decades. This association of hunger and rapid population growth certainly suggests a relationship between the two. But what we want to probe is the nature of that link. Does rapid population growth cause hunger, or do they occur together because they are both consequences of similar social realities?

In 1989 Cornell University sociologists Frederick Buttel and Laura Raynolds published a careful study of population growth, food consumption, and other variables in ninety-three third world countries.[20] Their statistical analysis found no evidence that rapid population growth causes hunger. What they did find was that the populations of poorer countries, and those countries where the poorest 20 percent of the population earned a smaller percentage of a nation's total income, had less to eat. In other words, poverty and inequality cause hunger.

Buttel and Raynolds did not explicitly look for the causes of high population-growth rates. However, University of Michigan ecologist John Vandermeer conducted a follow-up study using 1994 data that explicitly asked that question.[21] He found that inequality and poverty were the key factors driving rapid growth as well.

Poverty and Population Growth:
Lessons from Our Own Past

Let's try to understand why, by looking at our own demographic history. As recently as two or three generations ago, mortality rates in the United States were as high as they are now in most third world countries. Opportunities for our grandmothers to work outside the home were limited. And ours was largely an agrarian society in which every family member was needed to work on the farm. Coauthor Frances Lappé's own grandmother, for example, gave birth to nine children, raised them alone on a small farm, and saw only six survive to adulthood. Her story would not be unusual in a still fast-growing third world country today.

Faced with scarcity, poor families needed many children to help with work on the farm, and because of high infant-mortality rates, they needed many more pregnancies and births to achieve the necessary family size.

In the United States, the move to two-children families took place only after a society-wide transition that lowered infant death rates, opened opportunities to women outside the home, and transformed ours into an industrial rather than agrarian economy, so that families no longer relied on their children's labor. If we contrast Lappé's grandmother's story to a latter-day urban middle-class family, we can see that children who were once a source of needed labor are now a source of major costs, including tuition, an extra room in the house, the latest model basketball shoes, and forgone earnings for every year that a professional mom stays home with the kids.

The United States advanced through the falling-birth-rate phase of the demographic transition in response to these *societal* changes, well before the advent of sophisticated contraceptive technologies, even while the government remained actively hostile to birth control. (As late as 1965, selling contraceptives was still illegal in some states.)[22]

Using our own country's experience to understand rapid population growth in the third world, where poverty is more extreme and widespread, we can now extend our hypothesis concerning the link between hunger and high fertility rates: both persist where societies deny security and opportunity to the majority of their citizens—where infant-mortality rates are high and adequate land, jobs, education, health care, and old-age security are beyond the reach of most people, and where there are few opportunities for women to work outside the home.

Without resources to secure their future, people can rely only on their own families. Thus, when poor parents have lots of children, they are making a rational calculus for survival. High birth rates reflect people's defensive reaction against enforced poverty. For those living at the margin of survival, children provide labor to augment meager family income. In Bangladesh, one study showed that even by the age of six a boy provides labor and/or income for the family. By the age of twelve, at the latest, he contributes more than he consumes.[23]

Population investigators tell us that the benefit children provide to their parents in most third world countries cannot be measured just by hours of labor or extra income. The intangibles are just as important. Bigger families carry more weight in community affairs. With no reliable channels for advancement in sight, parents may hope that the next child will be the one clever or lucky enough to get an education and land a city job despite the odds. In many countries, income from one such job in the city can support a whole family in the countryside.

And impoverished parents know that without children to care for them in old age, they will have nothing.[24] They also realize that none of these possible benefits will be theirs unless they have many children, since hunger and lack of health care will kill many of their offspring before they reach adulthood. The World Health Organization has shown that both the actual death and the fear of death of a child will increase the fertility of a couple, regardless of income or family size.[25]

Finally, high birth rates may reflect not only the survival calculus of the poor, but the disproportionate powerlessness of women as well. Many women have little opportunity for pursuits outside the home, because of power relations internal to the family and/or in the larger society. Continued motherhood may then become their only "choice."

Perhaps the best proof that the powerlessness of women can undergird high fertility comes from extensive research on the effect of women's education. In one study after another, women's education turns out to be a powerful predictor of lower fertility. As women's schooling increases, fertility typically falls.[26]

Of course, we should guard against interpreting these findings literally—that what women learn is how to limit births. In fact, study after study has shown that people tend to have the number of children they want, regardless of whether more modern birth control methods are available or the government has a family planning program.[27] Rather, the fact that women are getting educated reflects a multitude of changes in society that empower women and provide them with opportunities in the workplace.[28]

Just as the powerlessness of women subordinated within the family and society may partially explain high birth rates, we must recognize that the men who hold power over women may themselves be part of subordinated groups in society. As long as poor men are denied sources of self-esteem and income through productive work, it is likely they will cling even more tenaciously to their superior status vis-à-vis women, and to a desire or need for more children.[29]

Good and Bad Fertility Decline

Rapid population growth, then, results from poverty and powerlessness, the need for family labor or the income children can bring home, high infant-mortality rates, and lack of education and opportunity for women. Our thesis for fertility *decline* is that, during the demographic transition, population growth *normally* slows only with far-reaching changes in society. Unfortunately, these changes can be of a positive or a negative nature.

On the positive side are economic and political changes that reduce infant mortality and convince the majority of people that social arrangements *beyond the family*—jobs, health care, old-age security, and education (especially for women)—offer security, or at least better

31

opportunities than does large family size. We can call that the positive way that fertility rates fall, or *because people are better off, they need fewer children.*

On the other hand, the nature of poverty and powerlessness can change in ways that transform children from a net benefit to the family into a net cost without empowering people or raising them out of poverty and hunger. That could also bring fertility rates down, but in a negative way. We might describe this as *things getting so bad that people can't even afford to have kids.*

Another negative scenario of lowered fertility might occur when the economic structures that make additional children necessary have been left intact, yet birth control has been enforced through coercion and/or indoctrination. Then people would have less children when for economic reasons they should be having more, deepening poverty still further. This might be described as *the tragedy of the sterilized, poor, older woman without children to support her.*

Positive Changes and Declining Fertility
Some of the earliest and most spectacular fertility declines occurred in the context of broad-based changes in living standards. Let's look at some of those examples.

Sri Lanka. From the postwar period to 1978, the Sri Lankan government supported the consumption of basic foods, notably rice, through a combination of free food, rationed food, and subsidized prices,[30] initiatiting a long-term decline in fertility and population-growth rates.[31]

Cuba. Rationing and setting price ceilings on staples kept basic food affordable and available to the Cuban people from the 1959 revolution to the economic crisis of 1989.[32] All citizens were guaranteed enough rice, pulses, oil, sugar, meat, and other food to provide them with nineteen hundred calories a day.[33] As universal health care and education were made available to all, Cuba's birth rate fell from 4.7 to 1.6.[34]

Kerala, India. In this Indian state eleven thousand government-run fair-price shops keep the cost of rice and other essentials like kerosene within the reach of the poor. This subsidy accounts for as much as one-half of the total income of Kerala's poorer families.[35] Its population density is three times the average for all India,[36] yet commonly used indicators of hunger and poverty—infant mortality, life expectancy,

32

and death rate—are all considerably more moderate in Kerala than in most low-income countries, as well as in India as a whole. Its infant mortality is half the all-India average.[37] Literacy and education levels are far superior to other states, particularly for women: the female literacy rate in Kerala is two and a half times the all-India average.[38] Not surprisingly then, Kerala rapidly reduced fertility and population growth in the postwar period. By 1991 Kerala had a birth rate that was one-third of the all-India average. That was about half the average for all low-income countries and only slightly higher than the United States.[39]

In most of these societies, income distribution is less skewed than in many other countries. The distribution of household income in Sri Lanka, for example, is more equitable than in Indonesia, India, or even the United States.[40]

In Thailand, the Philippines, and Costa Rica—other countries that experienced early fertility decline—health and other social indicators offer clues as to why. Infant death rates are relatively low, especially in Costa Rica, and life expectancy is high—for women, ranging between sixty-five and seventy-six years. Perhaps most important, in the Philippines and Costa Rica an unusually high proportion of women are educated, and in both the Philippines and Thailand, proportionately more women work outside the home than in most third world countries.[41]

Our careful reading of the scientific literature on fertility decline leads us to the conclusion that the bulk of it observed in the world so far has occurred for the "right" reasons. The Vandermeer study noted above indicates that reductions in poverty and inequality have been key factors. A 1994 Yale University study found that the education of women was the best predictor of reduced fertility rates among sixty-eight low-income countries.[42] While the researchers did not consider inequality and poverty in this study, it seems reasonable to assume that greater education of women goes hand in hand with reductions of both.

Negative Changes and Declining Fertility

Unfortunately, there are several cases of fertility decline that do not fit the pattern of improving conditions for the poor. In the late 1980s and early 1990s a very rapid decline in fertility rates began in Kenya and a number of other African countries. At first glance this fit with the notion of the demographic transition. Infant-mortality rates had dropped and women's enrollment in primary and secondary education had risen throughout the 1970s and early 1980s.[43] However, the actual declines, in the late 1980s and early 1990s, coincided with a severe economic crisis brought on by externally imposed "structural adjustment" policies, in which the poor were particularly hard hit (these policies are discussed in chapters 7 and 8).[44] According to one observer, "Parents suffered a decline in real incomes, a rise in the cost of children and lowered expectations of what children could do for them."[45] In response people either put off having more children or decided not to have them altogether.

Some observers have leapt to the frightening conclusion that economic crisis is the best contraceptive,[46] with all the policy measures that implies. Others have celebrated that we need no longer tackle the arduous task of poverty reduction in order to reduce population growth.[47] That makes no sense at all, on three levels. First, economic crisis may cause a temporary delay in childbearing, but once things get better, people will likely have the children they had put off. Second, economic crisis has unpredictable effects. Structural-adjustment–driven crisis in Costa Rica, unlike in Africa, led to an increase in fertility rates in the mid-1980s.[48] Third, and far more important, we must keep track of our principal focus: hunger. Even if economic crisis were a good way to lower fertility, it certainly would be no help at all in alleviating hunger!

Nevertheless, the evidence on fertility decline and crisis tend to support our earlier argument that by and large people have the number of children they want. That, however, does not mean that under exceptional circumstances people cannot be coerced, paid, or indoctrinated to have fewer children than would normally make sense for them.

But We Don't Have Time

In presenting the essence of our thesis—that the best way to lower fertility is to reduce poverty—to concerned audiences over the years, at least one questioner will invariably respond, "All well and good, but we don't have time! We can't wait for societywide change benefiting the poor. That takes too long. The population bomb is exploding now."[49]

While the bomb has been largely defused, the implication remains that to bring growth down more rapidly we should do the only thing we can do *now*: fund and promote family planning programs among fast-growing populations. The rest is pie in the sky.

Our response is twofold. First, demographers will tell you that even if average family size in a fast-growing society were cut by half tomorrow, its population would not stop growing until well into the next century. So every solution, including family planning programs, is a long-term one; there are no quick fixes. The second part of our answer is more surprising: simply providing birth control technology through family planning programs doesn't affect population growth all that much.

In 1984, D. J. Hernández, chief of the Marriage and Family Statistics Branch of the U.S. Bureau of the Census, reviewed all available research to determine the contribution of family planning programs to fertility decline. After examining the research on demographic change in eighty-three countries, he concluded that the best studies have found little net effect from family planning programs. Hernández observed that "perhaps as much as 10 percent but possibly as little as 3 percent of the cross-national variation in fertility change in the third world during the late 1960s and early 1970s was an independent effect of family planning programs."[50]

Naturally, Hernández was roundly attacked by family planning proponents. But even the study most cited by his critics, a 1978 overview of ninety-four third world countries, concluded that birth control programs alone accounted for only 15 to 20 percent of overall fertility decline, with largely social and economic factors accounting for the rest.[51] Follow-up studies published by different researchers in 1994 came to the same conclusion as the original Hernández study: the contribution of family planning to fertility decline is negligible compared to the contribution of socioeconomic change.[52]

Our highlighting of these findings—which reveal a relatively small impact of family planning programs on population—does not mean that we belittle their potential value. Making contraceptives widely available and helping to reduce inhibitions against their use are critical to the extension of human freedom, especially the freedom of women to control their reproduction. But these findings do confirm that what is truly pie in the sky is the notion that population-growth rates can be brought down to replacement levels through a narrow focus on the delivery of contraceptive technology.

Although the experiences of some countries suggest that birth rates can fall while great economic inequalities remain, an overwhelmingly clear pattern emerges from worldwide demographic change. At the very least, critical advances in health, social security, and education must change the lives of the poor—especially the lives of poor women—before they can choose to have fewer children. Once people are motivated to have smaller families, family planning programs can quicken a decline in fertility, but that is all; they cannot initiate the decision to have smaller families.[53]

Upping the Ante

Refusing to admit the implications of these findings, many governments and international agencies have responded to the marginal impact of family planning programs by upping the ante: designing ever tougher programs involving long-term injected or implanted contraceptives, sterilization, and financial incentives and penalties.

One example is the injectable contraceptive Depo-Provera. Although considered too hazardous for general use in the United States, it has been widely distributed in third world countries. Known short-term side effects include menstrual disorders, skin disorders, headaches, weight gain, depression, hair loss, abdominal discomfort, loss of libido, and delayed return to fertility. And while long-term side effects will not be known for some time, preliminary studies suggest that Depo-Provera is probably linked to an increased risk of cervical cancer.[54] The World Health Organization (WHO) and the International Planned Parenthood Federation (IPPF) approved Depo-Provera for use in the third world while it was banned in the United States, arguing that overpopulation requires an "entirely new set of medical standards for developing countries."[55] Another example is the hormonal implant Norplant, which is increasingly being used in the third world despite side effects being reported in 64.7 percent of users.[56]

The sterilization of women continues to be the preferred course of birth control in much of the third world, usually funded by Western donors. In many countries doctors, nurses, and paramedics have numerical sterilization targets they have to meet. Studies in India and Bangladesh show how in their urgency to meet their targets, nurses and doctors act hastily and hazardously, often disregarding their patients' needs and complaints. Furthermore, a variety of material incentives are used to induce patients to undergo sterilization or to use contraception.[57] Defenders of incentive programs stress that they are voluntary, but when you are hungry, how many choices are voluntary?

Sri Lankan scholar Dr. Asoka Bandarage reports that "not only do poor people lack all relevant information, but, in many cases, the desperation of poverty drives them to agree to accept contraception or sterilization in return for payments in cash or kind. In such cases, choice simply does not exist. Direct force has reportedly been used in some

36

countries . . . however, coercion does not pertain to simply the outright use of force. More subtle forms of coercion arise when individual reproductive decisions are tied to sources of survival like the availability of food, shelter, employment, education, health care and so on."[58] In Thailand, for example, roads, transportation, and latrines have been tied to the acceptance of contraception.[59]

The use of heavy-handed publicity campaigns, numerical targets, and subtle coercion had perhaps their saddest consequences in Puerto Rico. After the United States seized the island from Spain in 1898, U.S. sugar companies rapidly set up vast plantations while engaging in the wholesale eviction of small farmers. By 1925, less than 2 percent of the population owned 80 percent of the land, and 70 percent of the population was landless. With so many people out of work and livelihood, Puerto Rico suddenly had a problem that U.S. colonial officials labeled "overpopulation."[60]

In the 1940s light manufacturing industries began to move in from the U.S. mainland, attracted by cheap labor and low taxes. Young women were a key and "docile" part of that labor force, but subject to "loss" (from the employer's point of view) due to pregnancy. The result was a massive sterilization campaign carried out by the local government and the IPPF, with U.S. government funding. Women were cajoled and coerced into accepting sterilization, often not even being told that the process wasn't reversible. The result was that by 1968 one-third of the women of childbearing age had been sterilized.[61] The combination of mass sterilization and heavy out-migration due to a declining economy caused the population of Puerto Rico to actually drop—with no resultant improvement in living standards, or the environment.[62]

The television documentary *La Operación* vividly portrays the anguish of now middle-aged, childless women in depopulated Puerto Rican towns.[63] It is impossible to witness their tearful testimony of lives filled with loneliness and not sympathize with Asoka Bandarage and reproductive rights activist Betsy Hartmann when they characterize such programs as violations of the most basic of human rights.[64]

We may be witnessing a similar tragedy-in-the-making in Mexico, along the northern border with the United States. There many of the U.S.-owned *maquiladora* factories employing young women demand negative pregnancy tests as a condition of employment. Some even go so far as to require that female employees show their menstrual pads to a supervisor every month in order to keep their jobs.[65]

Here in the United States we face the specter of similar programs. Economic incentives for women on welfare to use Norplant inserts have been proposed by various state legislators including David Duke of Ku Klux Klan infamy. While such bills haven't yet passed, Norplant has been introduced into public school health clinics in several cities.[66] In fact, the attack on minority "teenage pregnancies" in the United States smacks of racism and misinformation in the same way as do many of the arguments about third world overpopulation.[67]

Can investment in birth control bring down fertility rates without broad socioeconomic change taking place? The case of *La Operación* suggests that it can, though no one should want to repeat that experience. Many family planning advocates today point to the experience of the Matlab region in Bangladesh as an example to be replicated.[68]

The most famous "social experiment" in family planning was carried out in Matlab by the International Center for Diarrheal Disease Research with funding from Western donors. The region was chosen because it was "uncontaminated" by any mother and child care system prior to the experiment's inception.[69] The project began in 1977 by providing half the villages in the region with intensive family planning services, including fortnightly home visits by a health and family planning promoter. The other half of the villages received no special services. By 1990 contraceptive use in the intensive villages was more than double that of the control villages, and fertility was a less impressive quarter lower.[70] This experiment does prove that intensive family planning alone, in the absence of any other change, can reduce fertility. But the financial costs were so high—$120 per "birth averted," or 120 percent of the per capita gross domestic product[71]—that the results are "not replicable at a national scale, let alone everywhere in the developing world."[72]

Such concerns led researchers to cost-cutting experiments, which showed that with a minimal package it is still possible to raise contraceptive use rates. They concluded, for example, that prenatal care and midwife training were superfluous, and that teaching about oral rehydration therapy for infants suffering from diarrhea actually interfered with contraceptive education and thus should be tossed as well.[73] The implications are grave. As Betsy Hartmann put it: "By holding up Bangladesh as a model, the population establishment is turning the whole concept of development on its head: it's all right if the poor stay as poor as ever, just as long as there are fewer of them born."[74] This is what we earlier called a "negative way that fertility can decline."

China's Solution?

Those who cling to family planning programs as the answer to population growth might do well to heed the current experience of China.[75]

Through a far-reaching redistribution of land and food, assurance of old-age security, and making health care and birth control devices available to all, China achieved an unprecedented birth rate decline. Since 1979, the country has taken a different tack. Believing that population growth was still hindering modernization, the Chinese government instituted the world's most restrictive family planning program. Material incentives and penalties are now offered to encourage all parents to bear only one child. According to John Ratcliffe of UC Berkeley's School of Public Health:

> Enormous pressure—social and official—is brought to bear on those who become "unofficially" pregnant; few are able to resist such constant, heavy pressure, and most accede to having an abortion. While coercion is not officially sanctioned, this approach results in essentially the same outcome.[76]

At the same time, Ratcliffe points out, some of China's post-1979 economic policies undercut both guaranteed employment and old-age security. This has thrown rural families back on their own labor resources, so that large families—especially boys—have once again become a family economic asset.

And what have been the consequences? Despite the world's most stringent population control program, China's birth rates have actually fallen more slowly since 1980 than before the one-child policy was introduced.[77] The message should be unmistakable: People will have children when their security and economic opportunity depend on it, no matter what the state says.

Advocates of more authoritarian measures seem to forget altogether the experience of the other poor societies that along with China have reduced their growth rates to below 2 percent. Recall that among them are Cuba, Kerala, and Sri Lanka. None relied significantly on social coercion or financial incentives. As health care was made available to all, Cuba's birth rates fell, for example, without even so much as a public education campaign on family planning, much less financial incentives.

No one should discount the consequences of high population density, including the difficulties it can add to the already great challenge of development. While in some African countries low population density has been an obstacle to sustainable agricultural development,[78] in many countries much higher population densities would make more difficult the tasks of social and economic restructuring necessary to eliminate hunger. But if it is eliminating hunger that we are after, then we should attack poverty, inequality, and powerlessness head on. That is especially true as they are the root causes of high fertility and rapid population growth. Improving living standards and lessening inequality, including providing education for women, have proven to be the best ways to lower fertility.

The Challenge Ahead

In this brief chapter, we've outlined what we believe are the critical points too often muddled in discussions of population:

- Fertility and population-growth rates are declining worldwide.
- Population density nowhere explains today's widespread hunger.
- Rapid population growth is not the root cause of hunger but is— like hunger—a consequence of social inequities that deprive the poor majority, especially poor women, of the security and economic opportunity necessary for them to choose fewer children.
- To bring the human population into balance with economic resources and the environment, societies must address the extreme maldistribution of access to resources—land, jobs, food, education, and health care. That is our real challenge.
- Family planning cannot by itself reduce population growth, though it can speed a decline. Family planning can best contribute to the transition when it is but one part of comprehensive changes in health care that expand human freedom and opportunity rather than control behavior.

We believe that precisely because population growth is such a critical problem, we cannot waste time with approaches that do not work. We must unflinchingly face the evidence telling us that the fate of the world hinges on the fate of today's poor majorities. Only as their well-being improves can we attack hunger and assure that fertility decline is sustainable.

To attack high birth rates without attacking the causes of poverty and the disproportionate powerlessness of people is fruitless. It is a tragic diversion our small planet can ill afford.

40

CHAPTER 4

Myth 4:
Food vs. Our Environment

MYTH: Pressure to feed the world's hungry is destroying the very resources needed to grow food. To feed the hungry, we are pushing crop and livestock production onto marginal, erosion-prone lands, clearing age-old rain forests, and poisoning the environment with pesticides. Clearly, we cannot both feed the hungry and protect our environment.

OUR RESPONSE: We *should* be alarmed. A many-pronged assault on the environment is damaging the resources on which food production depends. Environmental scientists alert us to these threats:

- Roughly 70 percent of the 5.2 billion hectares of dry lands used for agriculture around the world—almost 30 percent of the earth's total land area—is at risk of being turned into deserts. More than one billion people in 135 countries depend on this land.[1]
- If current rates of destruction continue, the world's surviving rain forests will have been leveled by the year 2031.[2]
- With global pesticide use increasing from virtually nothing only fifty years ago to 4.7 billion tons a year,[3] at least 6 people are poisoned by pesticides somewhere in the world every minute and an estimated 220,000 die annually.[4]

That an environmental crisis is undercutting our food-producing resources and threatening our health is no myth; but myths and half-truths confound our grasp of the root causes of the crisis and, there-fore, our ability to move toward solutions.

In many parts of the world, once productive lands are now deso-late. But claiming that population pressure and overgrazing cause spreading deserts is no more useful than saying that a person whose throat had been slit died from a lack of blood. That may describe what happened, but it hardly helps us understand why. Similar descrip-tive but not explanatory approaches confuse us as to the necessity of pesticides in feeding the hungry and to the reasons behind the fell-ing of rain forests. They block us from seeing that a trade-off between our environment and the world's need for food is not inevitable. Alternatives do exist, and no doubt many more are possible. Indeed, environmentally sound alternatives can be even more productive than environmentally destructive ones. In our next chapter, we ex-plore these possibilities.

Making a Desert

Over hundreds of years, many of the farmers and pastoralists in West Africa's Sahelian region and much of the continent's other semiarid areas fashioned an interactive mix of food crops, trees, and livestock. For the most part, the system maintained soil fertility and protected the land from wind and water erosion. Its diversity helped ensure some harvests even in years of poor rainfall, which were common.

In the late nineteenth century, by contrast, occupying colonial pow-ers viewed the land as a mine from which to extract wealth. In West Africa, colonial administrations imposed on local farmers monocul-tures of annual crops for export, notably peanuts for cooking oil and livestock feed and cotton for French and British textile mills.[5] But grow-ing the same crops year after year on the same land, without any mix-ing or rotation of crops, trees, and livestock, rapidly ruined the soils. Just two successive years of peanuts robbed the soil in Senegal of al-most a third of its organic matter.[6]

Rapidly depleting soils drove farmers to push export crops onto even more vulnerable lands. Geologically old sediments, well suited for grazing grasses or tree crops but too delicate to withstand hoeing, were torn up for continuous planting. Ever less land was left fallow.

Especially in East and Southern Africa, Europeans seized the fertile and well-watered lands for themselves—even the legendary Living-stone's trek through Africa was in part a search for the best land for cotton. By relocating and confining Africans to areas least suitable for farming, the Europeans made localized overpopulation inevitable.[7] Thus, even when the population living off the land was but a fraction of today's, food-producing resources in sub-Saharan Africa were rapidly being destroyed.

With formal independence (in the early 1960s for most European colonies), the pattern only intensified. To generate foreign exchange to finance "modern" lifestyles for a new urban elite and launch industrial investments, postcolonial African governments exerted pressure to produce more, not less.[8] Falling export prices in the late 1970s and early 1980s put pressure on governments to make up in volume what they were losing in value. And farmers themselves, receiving meager and falling prices for what they grew, had to produce even more just to meet their food and cash needs.

Due to the soil and climate characteristics of most of the continent, herd grazing is the most sustainable way to produce food in many regions of Africa.[9] But the spread of export crops, by crowding livestock herders into ever smaller areas, has contributed to overgrazing. Government restrictions on herders' traditional practice of migrating in response to rainfall patterns have often compounded the problem. The drive to intensify livestock production on ranches or replace herd grazing with row-crop agriculture, jeopardizes the traditional ecological balance in animal-herder-land relations.

Since early colonial times pastoralists have been steadily displaced to more fragile, arid lands, as good lands have been acquired by the wealthy for profit-making operations. By the early 1980s the arid regions of sub-Saharan Africa were home to 51 percent of the region's cattle, 57 percent of its sheep, and 65 percent of its goats.[10] According to two experts, "Explanations as to why pastoralism and poverty are now so highly correlated in Africa are that pastoralism has been more and more restricted to areas that otherwise could not support any human economy, much less a materially prosperous one."[11]

It is unclear to what extent deserts are still expanding in Africa today. Careful studies of the dynamics of grasslands used by African pastoralists over a number of years have found that the vegetation suffers during periodic droughts but recovers thereafter.[12] Thus, while lands previously brought into intensive crop or ranch-style production continue to degrade, there is little evidence that remaining pastoralists are desertifying new areas.

It is true that the desertification that occurred in Africa in the past— and the continued degradation of ranch and cropland—have human-made origins. Yet the underlying explanation hardly has to do with feeding increasing numbers of hungry African people.

Reclaiming a Desert

Machakos, Kenya, is a semiarid region that in the 1930s was seen as a classic example of desertification driven by a growing human population (although population density at the time was a paltry thirty-four persons per square kilometer).[13] In 1937 a colonial observer commented that Machakos was:

> ... an appalling example of a large area of land which has been subjected to uncoordinated and practically uncontrolled development by natives whose multiplication and the increase of whose stock have been permitted, free from the checks of war and largely from those of disease, under benevolent British rule.

> Every phase of misuse of land is vividly and poignantly displayed. ... The inhabitants are rapidly drifting into a state of hopeless and miserable poverty and their land to a parching desert of rocks, stones and sand.[14]

Yet time proved this diagnosis of the problem to be wrong. We can now say with some certainty that Machakos was severely *under*populated. Marginal soils can often be made productive through terracing, small-scale irrigation, intensive rotation of crops and livestock, and the incorporation of organic matter into the soil. But all of that requires labor, far more than is available in many areas of Africa (the population density of sub-Saharan Africa in 1995, for example, was 24 per square kilometer, compared to 108 in Asia).[15]

As the population of Machakos increased over time, so did the quality of the soil, as local people constructed terraces, planted trees and hedgerows, developed integrated crop-livestock systems, and constructed water catchment systems to capture scarce moisture and divert it to their crops.

Today Machakos is a green and relatively prosperous area with a population density of 110 people per square kilometer and a complex and beautiful terracing system reminiscent of small-farmer rice areas in East Asia. Soil erosion has been brought almost completely under control. Per capita production of corn, a key food crop, has risen from 350 kilos per person per year in 1950 to more than 1,200 kilos in 1990.[16]

In this case, population growth, environmental recovery, and increased food production went hand in hand.

Machakos shows vividly just how wrong the myth of food versus the environment can be. If it proves to be a good indication, history may eventually tell us that wider problems of land degradation and low productivity in African agriculture were largely a product of *low* population densities.

Soil Destruction at Home

Bringing our focus back to the United States should be enough to dispel the notion that population pressure is the root cause of soil erosion. In fact, North America is now the continent with the most severe desertification problem.[17] Since widespread farming began in the United States in the eighteenth century, an estimated 30 percent of total farmland has been abandoned because of erosion, salinization, and waterlogging.[18] Fully one-third of the topsoil in the United States has been lost.[19] Today about 90 percent of U.S. cropland is losing soil faster than it can rebuild, and over half of U.S. pastureland is overgrazed and subject to high rates of erosion.

Just as in the third world, the dramatic expansion of row crops for export in the early 1970s—primarily corn and soybeans—greatly accelerated soil losses. In the first three years of the export boom, soil erosion in the Corn Belt leapt 39 percent.[20]

As erosion continued unabated into the 1980s, national alarm mounted and conservation measures were incorporated into the 1985 Farm Bill legislation. This was a positive turn, without question. However, it was small compared to the bias of the U.S. agricultural system against resource-conserving production methods.[21] The 1996 Farm Bill, for example, continues to favor economic concerns over conservation. The emphasis is on "flexibility," leaving the enormous task of changing current trends in pesticide use and land degradation up to individual growers and the laws of the marketplace.[22]

Wholesale Destruction of Rain Forests

Rain forests cover but 7 percent of the planet yet contain 50 percent of the world's species of plants and animals. They are the lungs of the world, consuming the excess carbon dioxide produced by our industries; they are sources of foods and pharmaceuticals ranging from chocolate, cashews, bananas, and brazil nuts to cortisone and quinine; they are beautiful; and they are in great danger.[23]

During this century forests in the tropical third world have declined by nearly half.[24] Each year about half a million square kilometers are destroyed worldwide.[25] Many things can intervene in the process of deforestation, so predictions of future destruction are always tenuous; nevertheless, if current tendencies were to prevail, the outlook for remaining forests would be bleak indeed:

- ·Rain forest loss is most rapid in Asia, where total disappearance would take only ten years at current rates.[26]
- In the Americas, where the greatest reserves are found, it would take twenty-one years.[27]
- In Africa, with the most limited reserves yet the lowest rate of destruction, it would take thirty-six years.[28]

Rain forest destruction in Brazil has long been very severe. In the most developed state, São Paulo, only 3 percent of the former forests remain. In the *cerrado*, an open, savannalike forest formation, more than 60 million hectares have been cleared to make way for soybeans and pasture. Of Brazil's Atlantic rain forests, less than 10 percent remain. All of these speak to an extraordinary pulse of forest loss during the last two decades.[29]

Deforestation destroys the homes of and poses a genocidal threat to millions of indigenous forest peoples.[30] It also leads to massive soil erosion, exacerbating floods and silting rivers.

What lies behind such ominous devastation? Is it growing numbers of people in search of land to grow food? Evidence from around the world strongly suggests otherwise.

The Amazon River Basin

Every day during the 1980s, as many as thirty buses and flatbed trucks carrying poor Brazilian families arrived in the Rondônia region of the Amazon River basin. Like hundreds of thousands before them, these desperately impoverished farmworkers came in search of land. They cut down and burned areas of forest, planted crops, and then moved on after a few years when the soil was exhausted, only to start the cycle again.

Some commentators were quick to point at Brazil's large and rapidly growing population as the explanation for the influx of settlers. They failed to ask why settlers were forced into an area where eking

46

out a living from the land is so difficult. In fact, the colonists were driven into Rondônia by the expansion of soybeans in Paraná, Santa Catarina, and Mato Grosso. The soy boom in Brazil is largely for export and has been driven by European demand for animal feed. Only a small fraction is used to produce cooking oil for Brazilian consumption.[31]

Of the settlers in Rondônia, more than 60 percent failed to successfully start a new life, eventually moving to urban slums or tin and gold mines elsewhere in the region.[32] During the 1990s their former plots have been bought up by cattle ranchers. Increasingly, large-scale, mechanized soybean growers have also encroached on Rondônia's forest frontier.[33] In the late 1990s the dynamic of forest destruction has been driven by a combination of cattle ranching, increasing soybean acreage, and commercial logging.[34]

Certainly Brazil should have enough land for all, since its ratio of cropland to people is more generous than even that of most Latin American countries.[35] Landless Brazilians are forced to clear new areas not because of insufficient land elsewhere in Brazil but because relatively few own most of that rich resource. Since 1985 the number of small farms has sharply decreased from just over 3 million to under 1 million, as the expansion of ranches, soybeans, and other forces have driven small farmers off their land.[36] Brazil's largest farm units are growing in total area. The country's largest holdings, of 1,000 hectares or more, comprise only 1.6 percent of all farms but 53.2 percent of all agricultural land.[37] The largest seventy-five farms, with 100,000 hectares or more, control over five times the combined total area of all small farms.[38]

Further aggravating the problem is the pervasive use of prime agricultural lands for pasture and the high proportion of idle land among the country's largest land holdings. Overall, 42.6 percent of agricultural land is not cultivated, and among Brazil's largest land holdings (of 1,000 hectares or more) 88.7 percent of arable land is left permanently idle.[39]

For decades, wealthy land moguls have fiercely resisted pressures for more equitable distribution of land. From 1985 to 1996 there were 969 assassinations of peasants squatting on lands belonging to large landowners.[40] Yet during that time Brazilian courts convicted only five people of crimes associated with violence against the landless.[41]

In 1994 then minister of the economy and renowned sociologist Fernando Henrique Cardoso promised economic stabilization and land reform if Brazil would elect him president. Since taking office on January 1, 1995, President Cardoso's record has been greatly tarnished by the glacially slow pace of reform; the brutal assassinations of landless rural families at Corumbiara, Rondônia, and Eldorado dos Carajás; and the continued impunity of those responsible for the violence against those who struggle for land reform. During the first two years of Cardoso's term in office, at least eighty-six rural workers, family members, and landless activists were killed, most by the military police.[42]

The astounding concentration of land ownership in Brazil has left 4.8 million rural families completely landless,[43] not to mention millions of impoverished families who abandoned the countryside for the infamous urban *favelas* out of economic desperation. Moreover, as the mechanization of large soybean farms spreads through the country, farmworkers lose their jobs. So ever more landless workers must compete for ever fewer jobs.

While deforestation is frequently blamed on small farmers, in fact, large-scale forest conversion for ranching and increasingly for soybeans is far more widespread. In one of the few studies that actually compared large- vs. small-scale clearing (in the neighboring Bolivian Amazon), 80 percent of the clearing was carried out by large holders.[44] The forest is, by and large, *not* being cleared to feed the hungry.

Central America

Most of the tropical rain forest cover in Central America has been either entirely removed for different kinds of agriculture and cattle ranching, or subjected to unsustainable logging and similar practices.

In their book *Breakfast of Biodiversity*, ecologists John Vandermeer and Ivette Perfecto describe a complex "web of causality" that explains the loss of these forests.[45] Key elements in the web are transnational banana companies that are leading the drive to put more land into export plantations and logging companies, which, even when they do not clear-cut, still open roads into new areas. Added to that are small farmers displaced by export agriculture and banana workers laid off during dips in the boom-and-bust cycle of the global banana market who follow those roads in search of new lands to homestead. On their heels may come cattle ranchers turning forest and small farm plots into permanent pasture. Also part of the web are international financial institutions and the U.S. government, which pressure local governments to increase export earnings for debt service and Northern consumers with their insatiable appetites for bananas and tropical hardwoods.

Slashing and Burning the Tropics

In 1997 and 1998 newspapers were filled with stories of choking smoke throughout Southeast Asia, generated by forest fires raging out of control in Indonesia.[46] According to the *New York Times:* "The smoke from forest fires was everywhere, an unimaginable cloud that stings the eyes and tightens the chest, like the plume from a campfire—except that it has blotted out the sun across hundreds of thousands of square miles in Southeast Asia and left the region with the ambiance of an ashtray."[47]

During the same period weather satellites recorded an increase of more than 50 percent in the number of fires in the Brazilian Amazonia. A thick belt of smoke swathed the entire basin.[48]

In an analysis thick with racist overtones, the *New York Times* complained that "Asia's filth is becoming increasingly cosmopolitan . . . not only sullying their own countries but creating environmental catastrophes that cross international boundaries and create a burden for the entire planet."[49] Though the *Times* article mentioned loggers in passing, it strongly suggested that small farmers clearing plots for planting were the prime culprits. One photo caption read, "Purwadi, an Indonesian farmer, in the ruins of the forest he burned down to start his farm. 'There's no other way of clearing the land,' he said. 'I have got to plant my chilies.'" To drive home the point, the author then pointed out that "Asia's population is dense and growing rapidly."[50]

What were the real causes of these environmental catastrophes in Indonesia and Brazil? According to UCLA tropical forest expert Dr. Susanna Hecht, it was the combination of a harsh dry season caused by the El Niño climate phenomenon, together with clear-cut logging in Indonesia and selective logging in Brazil, which left an enormous quantity of "slash," highly flammable tinder, on the ground.[51]

So drought and logging created the basic conditions. What actually caused the Indonesian fires to start? According to Canada's *Globe and Mail,* "Forest and scrubland has been given to large industrial conglomerates wanting to invest in timber estates and oil-palm and rubber plantations. To clear their holdings . . . plantation companies are allowed to set 'controlled fires,' as long as other methods like bulldozing are not feasible. The government says this burning should be a last resort . . . but most companies use this as a first resort. It is the cheapest method."[52]

An investigation by *Mother Jones* magazine found that satellite data had pinpointed 176 logging and plantation concessions where fires were deliberately set to clear land. "Though the Indonesian government has historically blamed peasants for setting forest fires, officials have been forced to admit that corporations are the main culprits. In September [1997], Indonesia's minister of the environment, Sarwono Kusumaatmadja, released a long list of companies responsible for the fires," wrote the author.[53] According to the Center for Environment, Technology and Development in Malaysia, only 10–20 percent of the fires were caused by small farmers.[54] According to the Environmental Defense Fund, most of the fires in Brazil were started by cattle ranchers burning old pasture near forest edges.[55]

Growing more food for increased numbers of people in the tropics does not generate this demand for lumber and beef, or the plywood, rubber, and palm oil produced by forest plantations in Indonesia. It comes from Northern countries. The United States imports about $1.5 billion worth of beef and $200 billion worth of forestry products per year.[56] In 1996 the United States imported over $400 million worth of lumber, $900 million worth of rubber and latex, and $78 million worth of palm oil from Indonesia.[57] Japan and Europe are also to blame.

Logging, ranching, and tree plantations in the tropics represent the kind of development that redistributes wealth upward. The benefits provided by the forests—biological diversity, water catchments, soils, rivers, fertile land for gardening under forest-fallow systems, as well as energy sources for labor-intensive local industries—are available to all, including even the poorest with no market power. But commercial plantations, logging, and ranching liquidate such benefits in favor of those accruing mainly to existing elites and to affluent groups, largely foreign interests. Permanent, broadly distributed benefits are exchanged for temporary, highly concentrated ones. The whole process reflects the grossly unequal distribution of power, nationally and internationally.

These dynamics of destruction are extremely important, but in Brazil at least, the worst may be yet to come. Presently on the drawing boards are massive infrastructure construction programs to link up Brazil's center and west with shipping lanes on the Amazon, the development of a Pacific corridor to connect the western Amazon with Asian markets, and the expansion of the export corridor from Manaus to Caracas. These megaprojects presage a massive boom in oil and mineral mining, timber and fish exports, and continued soybean expansion. The investment is being carried out largely with private capital and thus is less vulnerable to political pressure for the compensation of those in the path of these projects. While indigenous populations are organizing to resist these threats to their homelands, governments, mining companies, and businessmen remain committed to mega-development in Amazonia.[58]

Pesticides and Our Food Security

Now let's turn to the third area of concern raised in this chapter: the threat to health and the environment from pesticides. We too once wondered whether people's legitimate food needs would not require using ever more pesticides. Already over 4 billion pounds of pesticides are used annually throughout the world.[59] In the United States alone, nearly 2 billion pounds of pesticides are injected each year into our environment—that's over 7 pounds for every American, and the amount is increasing.[60] In California, which consumes 25 percent of all U.S. pesticides, use rose 31 percent between 1991 and 1995.[61] Lest anyone think that less toxic products are being used, the use of known carcinogens increased by 129 percent during the same period.[62] Nation-wide the rate of increase in total pesticide use for agriculture shot up dramatically in the mid-1990s.[63]

Worldwide, pesticides now add $25.5 billion to farmers' costs annually,[64] while the human health toll is even more staggering. Estimates of pesticide poisonings in the third world are as high as 25 million people yearly.[65] In the United States some 300,000 farmworkers suffer pesticide-related illnesses each year,[66] and in California as many as one thousand pesticide poisonings have been registered per year.[67] A national survey by the U.S. Environmental Protection Agency (EPA) found that 10.4 percent of community water wells are contaminated with at least one of 127 different pesticides.[68]

The most harmful chemicals end up in the third world. Many of the pesticides that U.S. corporations export are banned, heavily restricted, or have never been registered for use here.[69] Most end up in fields where workers are not provided protective clothing and where safety precautions are the last concern of the farms' owners. On cotton and banana plantations in the Philippines, the Ivory Coast, and Central America, we found pesticides being indiscriminately sprayed from airplanes and from canisters strapped to the backs of unprotected workers. In a survey conducted in Central America we found that when they apply pesticides, 64 percent of farmers and farmworkers use no gloves, 62 percent use no boots, 72 percent no overalls, 60 percent no

51

hat, 55 percent no respirator, and 64 percent not even a long-sleeved shirt.[70]

A schoolteacher in Trinidad told us that each time the sugarcane plantations have been aerially sprayed, most of the children in her classes stay home sick the next day. They have fainting spells, vomit, and suffer bad skin rashes.

For the last fifty years, export plantations in Malaysia have depended on the cheap labor provided by women. More than thirty thousand women are temporarily employed today to spray pesticides. The great majority of them are badly paid and work unprotected. Exposure to paraquat and other highly toxic pesticides produces severe skin irritation and affects their reproductive health.[71]

Many Central American export crops such as melons, strawberries, and broccoli come originally from temperate climates; when brought to the tropics they suffer more severe pest problems than do native plants. In the tropics these imported crops also suffer greater pest attack than they do in the temperate zone, as the lack of winter makes for favorable pest conditions year-round. To make matters worse, crops that are exported fresh have to meet the cosmetic standards of Northern consumers, leading to more pesticide use to avoid blemishes. In a survey we found that from 28 to 56 percent of the melon farmers we interviewed had been poisoned by pesticides during the previous two years, depending on the country.[72]

Increasingly, transnational chemical companies have moved the manufacture of the most hazardous pesticides to the third world, where plant safety regulations are less stringent.[73] The lethal combination of deadly ingredients and deficient safety precautions was dramatically demonstrated by the 1984 leak at the Union Carbide pesticide plant in Bhopal, India, that killed more than 2,000 people and injured 200,000.[74]

While pesticides most endanger exposed factory workers and farmworkers, today everyone is at risk. "The weight of evidence is clear," says Dr. Charles Benbrook, former director of the National Academy of Sciences' agricultural board, "exposure to pesticides is a cause of cancer."[75]

Beyond causing cancer, new evidence suggests that pesticides may have many other dangerous effects. For example, many pesticides fall into a category of chemicals called "endocrine disrupters," some of which directly affect the reproductive system. The most frightening part is that this occurs at dosages much smaller than those at which we used to think pesticide residues were dangerous. It may soon be proven that pesticides have played a significant role in the alarming rates of increase in breast, testicular, and prostate cancer over the last fifty years, as well as in apparently declining human sperm counts and serious disruptions of ovarian function in women.[76]

Becoming aware of the mounting use of pesticides, involving both immediate harm and untold future hazards, we had to ask ourselves if pesticide use is really essential to the world's food security. In assessing this complex question, we had to struggle to fix the following facts in our minds—they run so counter to what is widely assumed about the necessity of and benefits from pesticides:

- About 25 percent of the pesticides in the United States are used not in agriculture at all but on golf courses, parks, and lawns and in homes, schools, and other buildings.[77]
- Despite a tenfold increase in the amounts and toxicity of pesticides since their commercial introduction in the late 1940s, crop losses to insects have nearly doubled.[78]
- Less than 0.1 percent of the pesticides applied to crops actually reaches target pests. The rest moves into ecosystems, contaminating the land, water, and air.[79]
- U.S. farmers could cut pesticide use by as much as 35 to 50 percent with no effect on crop yields, simply by using chemicals only when significant pest numbers are present.[80]
- For corn and wheat, together accounting for 30 percent of all pesticides used on U.S. cropland,[81] researchers estimate that crop losses from pests would increase only 1 or 2 percent if no pesticides at all were employed.[82]

Much of the problem with the use of pesticides is cultural: the cosmetic standards set by consumer preferences in industrial countries (especially in the United States) have driven producers all over the world into a never-ending search for the glossiest apple and most unblemished pear. In the United States it is estimated that from 60 to 80 percent of the pesticide applied to oranges and 40–60 percent of that applied to tomatoes is used only to improve appearance, with no improvement whatsoever of nutritional content.[83] The prevalence of form over content in our modern culture is something we will have to overturn if we are ever to become more ecological and less wasteful.

What these facts brought home to us is that much of the threat from pesticides is not related to food production at all and therefore a large portion of pesticides currently used on food crops could be eliminated without a significant drop in production.

And what about the third world? Do pesticides there help produce food for hungry people?

In much of the third world the bulk of pesticides are not used to grow the staple crops of the poor but are applied to export crops. In West Africa, in the mid-1980s the figure was over 90 percent.[84] In Latin America, "entrepreneurial farmers"—who grow most of the export crops—use 77 percent, while small farmers use only 11 percent.[85]

It is not surprising that pesticides are concentrated on export crops not staple foods. First, food producers are often the poorest farmers and simply cannot afford the cost. Second, monocultural export-crop operations are much more vulnerable to pests than smaller-scale, mixed-crop farms. Third, since pesticides must be imported in most third world countries, they are likely to be used on crops that earn the foreign exchange needed to pay for such imports.[86]

The Pesticide Treadmill

The striking increase in pesticide use worldwide—the dollar value of pesticides in world trade rose by 39 percent between 1990 and 1995[87] —results in part because pesticides lock farmers onto an accelerating treadmill.

The case of cotton in Central America is illustrative.[88] At the end of World War II the small countries of the region planted fewer than 20,000 hectares of cotton between them. But driven by growing demand in the United States and other Northern countries, the area grew exponentially over subsequent decades, peaking at almost 463,000 hectares in the late 1970s.[89] The cotton boom displaced tens of thousands of small-scale food producers from their land and ignited more than a decade of social unrest and violence in the region.[90]

This rapid expansion was facilitated early on by new synthetic pesticides used to control cotton pests. But those same chemicals soon became the downfall of an industry. Key pests like the boll weevil became resistant to the chemicals as a result of repeated exposure, forcing growers to continually increase dosages and frequency of spraying, as well as to buy ever more expensive products as they hit the market. Whereas growers only sprayed a few times in the early years, in the mid-1960s they were spraying ten times per season; by the end of the decade that had doubled.

Instead of fewer pests, they faced more: Insect species that had previously been under natural population control by other insects that preyed on them, were released from control as the chemicals wiped out their natural enemies. The number of sprays continued to grow, in some years reaching more than forty, and pesticide costs to farmers skyrocketed, eventually reaching more than 50 percent of the cost of production. That made cotton unprofitable, and the cotton boom was soon followed by the cotton bust, with the number of hectares planted in the region plunging to fewer than 100,000 in the 1990s. In trips to former cotton-growing regions during the 1990s, we have witnessed abandoned, wasted, and eroded soils depleted by decades of cotton monoculture, and once prosperous commercial centers reduced to ghost towns, the banks and stores boarded over and tumbleweed blowing down central thoroughfares.

The cotton boom-and-bust cycle, which was driven by pesticide use, fed nobody; in fact, the boom increased hunger by driving the poor off their lands, and the bust dragged down the entire economy of the region. In its wake, economic ruin and environmental devastation were left.

A Mounting Response to
Environmental Destruction

Since we began our work in the early 1970s, we have witnessed the rise worldwide of increasingly vocal and effective citizen organizations challenging the environmental destruction we have discussed in this chapter.

India. The Chipko ("hug the tree") Movement in the Uttarakhand region of the Indian Himalayas is perhaps the best example of a truly grassroots initiative to block forest destruction by outside interests. The movement started in 1973, when Mandal villagers came together to prevent the felling of a forest by a large company, as women placed their bodies in the way of loggers. The practice has spread successfully in a dozen other protests throughout the region, and the Chipkos have inspired other movements in India and abroad. Not only did they halt deforestation near their communities, but they also won reforestation programs from a reluctant government.[91] Dozens of other grassroots movements in India are actively fighting to stop deforestation, megadam projects with forced relocation of villages, and the establishment of polluting industries.

Brazil. The *seringueiros* or rubber-tappers movement in the state of Acre in the Brazilian Amazonia is another example of a grassroots challenge to environmental degradation and the social injustice that inevitably goes with it. From 1976 to 1988 they confronted rich cattle ranchers forty-five times, preventing the destruction of over 1 million hectares of forest. The assassination in 1988 of their leader, Francisco "Chico" Mendes, was condemned around the world, and the Brazilian government responded with the elaboration of the first national environmental policy, the creation of a Brazilian environmental protection agency, and the delimitation of several "extractive reserves," where forest protection will permit a sustainable livelihood for some rubber tappers. Today the movement continues to engage in struggle over much larger and more important areas of forest with great implications for the future of both rubber tappers and indigenous forest peoples.[92]

United States. The Californians for Pesticide Reform (CPR) coalition brings together more than sixty public interest organizations committed to protecting public health and the environment from the proliferation of pesticides. They are seeking a drastic reduction of pesticide use in California, which would set an example for many agriculturists around the world who assiduously follow developments in California agriculture.[93]

Hard Questions

Surely there are areas where population density exacerbates environmental destruction, yet most of the damage is not even caused by food production. A superficial diagnosis that blames the growing number of people (who often are victims themselves) leads us nowhere. Even where environmental destruction is severe, would cutting the population in half solve the problem?

We must dig for root causes, asking, Why are peasants denied productive agricultural land and forced onto lands that should not be farmed, or resettled in rain forests? Why are big operators allowed— and even publicly subsidized—to tear down tropical forests? If desertified areas are helped to regenerate, who will control the process, who will benefit, and who will lose? Why do most of the farmers who use chemical fertilizers and pesticides think they cannot afford the risk of shifting to less chemical-intensive methods? Why are environmentally sound alternatives for food production little known and even suppressed rather than fostered? And finally, can humanity afford to treat food and the resources to produce it just like any other commodity?

Hard questions like these must be confronted if we are serious about protecting and even enhancing for future generations our planet's finite food-producing resources, as well as an environment safe for all life. While we have a long way to go in developing our answers—and no one answer will fit every place and people—we hope this book helps clear our vision so that the right questions can be raised.

CHAPTER 5

Myth 5:
The Green Revolution Is the Answer

MYTH: The miracle seeds of the Green Revolution increase grain yields and therefore are a key to ending world hunger. Higher yields mean more income for poor farmers, helping them climb out of poverty, and more food means less hunger. While the Green Revolution may have missed poorer areas, with more marginal lands, we can learn valuable lessons from that experience to help launch a "Second" Green Revolution to defeat hunger once and for all.

OUR RESPONSE: People have been improving seeds through experimentation since the beginning of agriculture,[1] but the term Green Revolution was coined in the 1960s to highlight a particularly striking breakthrough. In test plots in northwest Mexico, improved varieties of wheat dramatically increased yields. Much of the reason these "modern varieties" produced more than traditional varieties was that they were more responsive to controlled irrigation and to petrochemical fertilizers, allowing for much more efficient conversion of industrial inputs into food. With a big boost from the International Agricultural Research Centers created by the Rockefeller and Ford Foundations,[2] the "miracle" seeds quickly spread to Asia, and soon new strains of rice and corn were developed as well.[3]

By the 1970s, the term *revolution* was well deserved, for the new seeds—accompanied by chemical fertilizers, pesticides, and, for the most part, irrigation—had replaced the traditional farming practices of millions of third world farmers. By the 1990s almost 75 percent of Asian rice areas were sown with these new varieties.[4] The same was true for almost half of the wheat planted in Africa and more than half of that in Latin America and Asia,[5] and about 70 percent of the world's corn as well.[6] Overall, it was estimated that 40 percent of all farmers in the third world were using Green Revolution seeds,[7] with the greatest use found in Asia, followed by Latin America. The Green Revolution, however, had made fewer inroads in Africa.[8]

Clearly, the production advances of the Green Revolution are no myth. Thanks to the new seeds, tens of millions of extra tons of grain a year are being harvested, Green Revolution promoters tell us. And we may be on the brink of a second Green Revolution based on further advances in biotechnology.[9]

But has the Green Revolution actually proven itself a successful strategy for ending hunger? Here the debate heats up. Let us capsulize two dominant sides in this debate.

Proponents claim that by increasing grain production, the Green Revolution has alleviated hunger, or at least has prevented it from becoming even worse as populations keep growing. Traditional agriculture just couldn't meet the demands of today's burgeoning populations. Moreover, they assert, dealing with the root causes of poverty that contribute to hunger takes a very long time and people are starving now. So we must do what we can—increase production. The Green Revolution buys the time desperately needed by third world countries to deal with the underlying social causes of poverty and to cut birth rates. In any case, outsiders—like the scientists and policy advisors behind the Green Revolution—can't tell a poor country to reform its economic and political systems, but they can contribute invaluable expertise in food production.

The above view was rarely questioned when we began our work over twenty-five years ago. It was the official wisdom. But in response to many independent analyses, including the work of our institute and the track record of the Green Revolution itself, this "wisdom" has been increasingly challenged.[10]

Those of us challenging the Green Revolution strategy know that production will have to increase if populations continue to grow. But we've also seen that focusing narrowly on increasing production—as the Green Revolution does—cannot alleviate hunger because it fails to alter the tightly concentrated distribution of economic power, especially access to land and purchasing power. If you don't have land on which to grow food or the money to buy it, you go hungry no matter how dramatically technology pushes up food production.

Introducing any new agricultural technology into a social system stacked in favor of the rich and against the poor—without addressing the social questions of access to the technology's benefits—will, over time, lead to an even greater concentration of the rewards from agriculture, as is happening in the United States.

Because the Green Revolution approach does nothing to address the insecurity that lies at the root of high birth rates—and can even heighten that insecurity—it cannot buy time while population growth slows. Finally, a narrow focus on production ultimately defeats itself, as it destroys the very resource base on which agriculture depends.

We've come to see that without a strategy for change that addresses the powerlessness of the poor, the tragic result will be more food and yet more hunger.

This debate is no esoteric squabble among development experts—it cuts to the core of our understanding of development and therefore deserves careful probing. So first we will explore why a narrow production strategy like the Green Revolution is bound to fail to end hunger, drawing on the experience of the past four decades. Then, recognizing that this debate itself overlooks critical considerations, we will step outside its confines to ask what approach could offer genuine food security.

More Food and Yet More Hunger?

In 1985, the head of the international body overseeing Green Revolution research, S. Shahid Husain, declared that the poor are the beneficiaries of the new seeds' output. He even went so far as to claim that "added emphasis on poverty alleviation is not necessary" because increasing production itself has a major impact on the poor.[11] Husain's statement must have embarrassed many promoters of the Green Revolution, because by the 1980s few of even its avid defenders would make such a sweeping claim.

In fact, some within the World Bank—which finances the research network Husain chaired—concluded in a major 1986 study of world hunger that a rapid increase in food production does not necessarily result in food security, that is, less hunger. Current hunger can be alleviated only by "redistributing purchasing power and resources toward those who are undernourished," the study said.[12] In a nutshell—if the poor don't have the money to buy food, increased production is not going to help them. At last! was our response—for this fundamental insight was a starting point of our institute's analysis of hunger more than two decades ago.[13]

Despite three decades of rapidly expanding global food supplies, there are still an estimated 786 million hungry people in the world in the 1990s.[14] And where are these 786 million hungry people?

Since the early 1980s, media representations of famines in Africa have awakened Westerners to hunger there, but Africa represents less than one-quarter of the hunger in the world today. We are made blind to the day-in-day-out hunger suffered by hundreds of millions more.

By the mid-1980s, newspaper headlines were applauding the Asian success stories—India and Indonesia, we were told, had become "self-sufficient in food" or even "food exporters."[15] But Asia, precisely where Green Revolution seeds have contributed to the greatest production success,[16] is the home of roughly two-thirds of the undernourished in the entire world.[17]

Serious questions are raised when we look at the number of hungry people in the world in 1970 and in 1990, spanning the two decades of major Green Revolution advances. At first glance it looks as though great progress was made, with food production up and hunger down. The total food available per person in the world rose by 11 percent over those two decades,[18] while the estimated number of hungry people fell from 942 million to 786 million,[19] a 16 percent drop. This was apparent progress, for which those behind the Green Revolution were understandably happy to take the credit.[20]

But these figures merit a closer look. If you eliminate China from the analysis, the number of hungry people in the rest of the world actually *increased* by more than 11 percent, from 536 to 597 million.[21] In South America, for example, while per capita food supplies rose almost 8 percent, the number of hungry people also went up, by 19 percent. It is essential to be clear on one point: It is not increased population that made for more hungry people—total food available per person actually increased—but rather the failure to address unequal access to food and food-producing resources.

In South Asia there was 9 percent more food per person by 1990, but there were also 9 percent more hungry people.[22] The remarkable difference in China, where the number of hungry *dropped* from 406 million to 189 million,[23] almost begs the question: which has been more effective at reducing hunger, the Green Revolution or the Chinese Revolution?

61

The volume of output alone tells us little about hunger. Whether the Green Revolution or any other strategy to boost food production will alleviate hunger depends on the economic, political, and cultural rules that people make. Those rules determine who benefits as a *supplier* of the increased production (whose land and crops prosper and for whose profit) and who benefits as a *consumer* of the increased production (who gets the food and at what price).

According to *Business Week* magazine, "Even though Indian granaries are overflowing now," thanks to the success of the Green Revolution in raising wheat and rice yields, "5,000 children die each day of malnutrition. One-third of India's 900 million people are poverty-stricken." Since the poor can't afford to buy what is produced, "the government is left trying to store millions of tons of food. Some is rotting, and there is concern that rotten grain will find its way to public markets." The article concludes that the Green Revolution may have reduced India's grain imports substantially, but it did not have a similar impact on hunger.[24]

Early Criticisms of the Green Revolution

The impact of the Green Revolution on the rural poor has been controversial, with persuasive supporters and strong critics of this development strategy. While the two sides still disagree with each other on the fundamental issues, each has, over the years, accepted some points made by the other.[25] Yet the balance of evidence weighs in against the Green Revolution approach as a tool to alleviate hunger and poverty.

Early supporters of the Green Revolution varieties claimed that boosting production would raise the incomes of farmers, thus raising them out of poverty. Yet in the early decades of the Green Revolution a disturbing trend was revealed, which fueled criticisms: Larger farmers were much quicker to adopt the new varieties than poorer ones, and the landless could, of course, do nothing with new seeds, lacking the land in which to plant them. The larger, wealthier farmers were producing more than ever, and the increased production brought grain prices down, putting the squeeze on smaller, poorer farmers. The poor were thus often left in a weaker competitive position than before the new seeds had arrived. Critics of the Green Revolution argued that technologies that required purchased inputs—improved seeds, fertilizers, and pesticides—would inherently favor those with money over the poor, who would eventually lose their land and be forced to migrate to burgeoning urban shantytowns.[26]

Other early criticisms leveled at the Green Revolution were that it focused on just two or three crops, ignoring the rich diversity of foods grown by small farmers such as pulses and legumes, which are nutritionally key for lower-income families; that the technologies worked only on good-quality farmland with irrigation and were inappropriate to the diverse and marginal lands farmed by the poor;[27] and that agrochemicals were dangerous to the health of farmers and to the environment.[28]

Green Revolution Supporters Respond

Yet as the years passed, many poor farmers did eventually adopt modern varieties and begin to use chemical fertilizers and pesticides as well, sometimes even earning higher incomes as a result of yield increases.[29] As to why it took longer for small farmers to adopt new technologies, research by Green Revolution supporters revealed that the institutions that give credit, technical assistance, and marketing support to farmers are biased against the poor. This, rather than anything intrinsic about seeds, fertilizer, or pesticides, the supporters now say, explains the slower adoption by the poor. They argue that seeds, pesticides, and fertilizers do not discriminate between richer and poorer farmers because they are "divisible" into tiny amounts—you can buy just a few ounces if that is all you can afford—unlike a tractor, for example, which is totally out of reach for a very small farmer.[30]

In the late 1980s and early 1990s the supporters tried to take back the initiative from the critics of the Green Revolution,[31] arguing for a redoubling of efforts to address the anti-poor biases of institutions, so that the benefits of the new technologies could be better shared by the poor.[32] In the past, they conceded, government institutions—ministries of agriculture and extension services—failed to effectively deliver Green Revolution technological packages to small farmers in marginal areas, while nongovernmental organizations (NGOs, called nonprofits here in the United States) showed a greater capacity to reach and work with the poor.

Thus, the principal supporters of the Green Revolution now argue that foreign aid monies be partially redirected from government institutions toward NGOs to assure that the second Green Revolution reaches those left out by the first.[33] The idea is a sort of affirmative action for improved seeds, chemical fertilizers, and pesticides. Supporters further point out that research has now been initiated on a whole range of food crops grown by poor farmers and on how to adapt the basic technological packages for use on marginal lands.[34]

What Critics Have Said All Along

Prominent Green Revolution critic Keith Griffin finds it odd that blame has now been placed on societal structures. He argues that "the purpose of the Green Revolution was precisely to circumvent the need for institutional change. Technical progress was to be regarded as an alternative to land reforms and institutional transformation—the Green Revolution was to substitute for the red—and it is misleading twenty years later to claim that the fault lies entirely with inappropriate institutions and policies."[35]

The critics of the Green Revolution have argued all along that institutions that are biased against the poor are a significant part of the problem. They might also agree that NGOs should be part of an alternative. But critics stop short of absolving the technology and blaming only the institutions. One cannot separate a technological package made up of expensive inputs—agrochemicals—that farmers must purchase with their limited money, which are manufactured by global corporations with vested interests in increasing sales, from the institutions that promote and perpetuate those technologies. It is well documented that, from the beginning, chemical companies and development institutions collaborated in the promotion of Green Revolution technologies.[36]

Today, two leading pesticide companies figure among the funders of the "2020 Vision" program of the International Food Policy Research Institute (IFPRI), which serves as the ideological leader in the push for the second Green Revolution.[37] The International Fertilizer Industry Association—representing manufacturers—works closely with IFPRI, the World Bank, and the Food and Agriculture Organization of the UN (FAO), to promote increased fertilizer use as part of the package.[38]

Furthermore, while Green Revolution proponents argue for change from above—mandated by international lenders and aid agencies—critics argue that real change, truly benefiting the poor, is possible only if it is driven from below, i.e., by the demands of the poor themselves.[39]

The critics of the Green Revolution are very concerned about the repetition and intensification of mistaken policies. Several kinds of evidence underlie this concern.

It is only in areas that had relatively low levels of inequality before the Green Revolution arrived that inequity has not totally derailed potentially poverty-alleviating effects of the new technologies. The least disruptive impacts have come in those areas of Asia with centuries-long traditions of irrigated rice. In those areas a long history of communally managed traditional irrigation systems has left a legacy of relative equality in land holdings, and it is there that we see the most uniform adoption of the new seeds.[40]

By comparison, other crops and other areas, like corn in Latin America, are highly inequitable, and the entry of relatively costly Green Revolution practices into communities has often sharpened the differences, leading to increased poverty and even conflict. The 1994 Zapatista rebellion in Chiapas, Mexico, was partially driven by a growing gap between rich and poor farmers, produced by the introduction of Green Revolution technologies, principally herbicide and chemical fertilizer.[41]

In a 1995 study reviewing every research report published on the Green Revolution over a thirty-year period—more than three hundred in all—the author showed that 80 percent of those with conclusions on equity found that inequality increased, including even 70 percent of the studies that focused on India and the Philippines.[42]

This is not a minor problem. If hunger and poverty existed principally because the poor didn't know how to grow corn, or rice, then one might be willing to accept greater inequality as the cost of teaching them how to do so with "modern" technology. This argument is further bolstered if the "rising tide" of higher yields "raises all ships," that is, if the poor obtain higher yields too, even if they didn't benefit as much as the wealthy, precisely what a few pro–Green Revolution studies show.[43]

But in fact people are *not* hungry and poor because they do not know how to grow corn. They are not even hungry because not enough corn or rice is grown in the world; there is plenty for all, today, as we showed in chapter 1. Rather, as we argue throughout this book, they are hungry and poor because of *inequalities*—inequalities in access to land, to jobs, to income and other resources, and to political power. We cannot strike at the roots of hunger and poverty with approaches that accentuate their very basis in inequality.

The Green Revolution and the Landless

In theory, the Green Revolution was to alleviate hunger by helping poor farmers produce more food for themselves and generate more income from their land. But the new seeds' potential to relieve poverty and hunger by making farmers more prosperous depends—to start with—on what portion of the poor are farmers. This seems pretty elementary, but it is often overlooked—despite the fact that more than half a billion rural people in the third world are either landless or have too little land to feed their households.[44] Very often the landless are the most hungry, and in many countries they make up the majority of the poorest in rural areas.

Given a choice between redistributing land and boosting crop yields, those with little or no land clearly would gain the most from redistribution. Yet proponents of the Green Revolution correctly argue that the landless may also gain if production increases generate more off-farm jobs or lead to greater demand for farmworkers and therefore higher wages. Investigators dispute to what extent either has in fact happened. While the findings are mixed, a number of studies have reported improvements in both employment and wages in some Green Revolution areas.[45] But research also shows that employment and wage gains are frequently offset by the tendency for successful farmers to use herbicides and/or to mechanize, thus reducing demands for hand weeding and labor-intensive land preparation techniques. Furthermore, the Green Revolution has by and large bypassed those marginal areas where rural poverty—and the landless—are most concentrated.

British economist Michael Lipton, in the most comprehensive and even-handed treatment of the Green Revolution to date, concluded: "We have learned that employment gains per hectare, created by modern varieties, fall off as better off farmers seek labour saving ways to weed and thresh. . . . More important, poverty—and modern varieties' impact on it—is not a problem mainly for farm households in [Green Revolution] lead areas, but for farm households outside them."[46]

Within Green Revolution areas, whether the landless benefit hinges in large part on how those profiting from the new seeds use their new wealth. Do they replace workers with machines, thereby reducing the number of jobs? Even the staunchest supporters of the Green Revolution admit this is a problem,[47] though they rightly point out that the massive import of tractors by third world countries often preceded the introduction of new varieties.[48]

Subsidies to large, better-off farmers and overvalued exchange rates have long encouraged the adoption of labor-saving technologies, ironically, in parts of the world where labor is most abundant and capital most scarce. Lipton calls this mechanization a "socially-inefficient response, made privately profitable for big farmers only by their success in lobbying for subsidies on fuel, credit and tractors to displace labor."[49] Of course, large growers want to mechanize not for higher yields but to dispense with "labor" problems like unions, demands for minimum wages, and uppity tenant farmers.[50]

Much depends on the political organization of the landless. In the Indian state of Kerala, where agricultural workers are well organized, real wages of farmworkers rose, in contrast with many other parts of India.[51] In fact, Kerala is the state with the largest drop over the last thirty years in the percentage of the population living in poverty, far outstripping Green Revolution lead areas like Punjab and Uttar Pradesh.[52]

The Intertwined Fates of Rich and Poor

In most of the Indian subcontinent, it is "generally true" that "the poor benefit from the Green Revolution but not equally or proportionately because of the several advantages enjoyed by the rich and the handicaps suffered by the poor," argues one of the architects of India's Green Revolution, D. P. Singh. The gulf between the two, he concludes, "widens in absolute as well as relative terms."[53]

What are those handicaps suffered by the poor? Most of all, the poor lack clout. They can't command the subsidies and other government favors accruing to the rich. Neither can the poor count on police or legal protection when wealthier landowners abuse their rights to resources.

The poor also pay more and get less. Poor farmers can't afford to buy fertilizer and other inputs in volume; big growers can get discounts for large purchases. Poor farmers can't hold out for the best price for their crops, as can larger farmers whose circumstances are far less desperate.[54]

In much of the world, water is the limiting factor in farming success, and irrigation is often out of the reach of the poor. Canal irrigation favors those near the top of the flow. Tubewells, often promoted by development agencies, favor the bigger operators, who can better afford the initial investment and have lower costs per unit.[55]

Credit is also critical. It is common for small farmers to depend on local moneylenders and pay interest rates several times as high as wealthier farmers. Government subsidized credit overwhelmingly benefits the big farmers.[56]

So what? some will say. If the poor are using the improved seeds, haven't they gained, even if not as much as the better off?

But poor and rich participate in a single social dynamic—their fates are inevitably intertwined. A study of two rice-growing villages in the Philippines dramatizes this reality. In both villages, large and small farmers alike adopted the new seeds. In the village where landholdings were relatively equal and a tradition of community solidarity existed, the new technology did not polarize the community by disproportionately benefiting the better off. But in the village dominated by a few large landowners, their greater returns from the Green Revolution allowed them to advance at the expense of the small farmers. After ten years, the large farms in the village had grown in size by over 50 percent.[57] Land absorbed by the rich meant less for the poor.

Where a critic might want to blame the Green Revolution for the greater misery of poor farmers, the real fault, as some proponents have argued, lies in a social order permitting a tight grip on resources by only a few families. But contrary to what these proponents might like, that social order is a reality, one that the Green Revolution, as a technology-based, production-oriented approach, fails to, and in fact cannot, address.

Who Survives the Farm Squeeze?

With the Green Revolution, farming becomes petro-dependent. Some of the more recently developed seeds may produce higher yields without manufactured inputs,[58] but the best results require the right amounts of chemical fertilizer, pesticides, and water.[59]

So as the new seeds spread, petrochemicals become part of farming. In India, adoption of the new seeds has been accompanied by a sixfold rise in fertilizer use per acre. Yet the quantity of agricultural production per ton of fertilizer used in India dropped by two-thirds during the Green Revolution years.[60] In fact, over the past thirty years the annual growth of fertilizer use on Asian rice has been from three to forty times faster than the growth of rice yields.[61]

Because farming methods that depend heavily on chemical fertilizers do not maintain the soil's natural fertility, and because pesticides generate resistant pests, farmers need ever more fertilizers and pesticides just to achieve the same results.[62] At the same time, machines—though not *required* by the new seeds—enter the fields, as those profiting fear labor organizing and use their new wealth to buy tractors and other machines.

This incremental shift we call the industrialization of farming. What are its consequences?

Once on the path of industrial agriculture, farming costs more. It can be more profitable, of course, but only if the prices farmers get for their crops stay ahead of the costs of petrochemicals and machinery. Green Revolution proponents claim increases in net incomes from farms of all sizes once farmers adopt the more responsive seeds. But recent studies also show another trend: Outlays for fertilizers and pesticides may be going up faster than yields, suggesting that Green Revolution farmers are now facing what U.S. farmers have experienced for decades—a cost-price squeeze.[63]

In Central Luzon, Philippines, rice yield increased 13 percent during the 1980s but at the cost of a 21 percent increase in fertilizer use. In the Central Plains yields went up only 6.5 percent, while fertilizer use rose 24 percent and pesticides jumped by 53 percent. In West Java a 23 percent yield increase was virtually canceled by 65 and 69 percent increases in fertilizers and pesticides, respectively.[64]

To anyone following farm news here at home, these reports have a painfully familiar ring—and why wouldn't they? After all, the United States—not Mexico—is the true birthplace of the Green Revolution. Improved seeds combined with chemical fertilizers and pesticides have pushed corn yields up nearly threefold since 1950, with smaller but still significant gains for wheat, rice, and soybeans.[65] As larger harvests have pushed down the prices farmers get for their crops while the costs of farming have shot up, farmers' profit margins have been drastically narrowed since World War II. By the early 1990s, production costs had risen from about half of gross farm income to over 80 percent.[66]

So who survives today? Two very different groups: those few farmers who chose not to buy into industrialized agriculture, and those able to keep expanding their acreage to make up for their lower per-acre profit.

Among this second select group are the top 1.2 percent of farms by income, those with $500,000 or more in yearly sales, dubbed superfarms by the U.S. Department of Agriculture. In 1969, the superfarms earned

16 percent of net farm income, and by the late 1980s they garnered nearly 40 percent.[67]

Superfarms triumph, not because they are more efficient food producers,[68] or because the Green Revolution technology itself favored them, but because of advantages that accrue to wealth and size.[69] They have the capital to invest and the volume necessary to stay afloat even if profits per unit shrink. They have the political clout to shape tax policies in their favor. Over time, why should we expect the result of the cost-price squeeze to be any different in the third world?

In the United States, we've seen the number of farms drop by two-thirds since World War II,[70] and average farm size has more than doubled.[71] The gutting of rural communities, the creation of inner-city slums, and the exacerbation of unemployment all followed in the wake of this vast migration from the land. Think what the equivalent rural exodus means in the third world, where the proportion of jobless people is already double or triple our own.

Not Ecologically Sustainable

There is growing evidence that Green Revolution–style farming is not ecologically sustainable, even for large farmers.[72] Furthermore, dependence on expensive purchased inputs can increase indebtedness and the precarious nature of small-farmer life.[73]

In the 1990s Green Revolution researchers themselves sounded the alarm about a disturbing trend that had only just come to light. After dramatic increases in the early stages of the technological transformation, yields began falling in a number of Green Revolution areas. In Central Luzon, Philippines, rice yields grew steadily during the 1970s, peaked in the early 1980s, and have been dropping gradually ever since.[74] Long-term experiments conducted by the International Rice Research Institute (IRRI) in both Central Luzon and Laguna province confirm these results.[75] Similar patterns have now been observed for rice-wheat systems in India and Nepal.[76] The causes of this phenomenon have to do with forms of long-term soil degradation that are still poorly understood by scientists.[77]

An Indian farmer told *Business Week* his story: "Dyal Singh knows that the soil on his 3.3-hectare [8-acre] farm in Punjab is becoming less fertile. So far, it hasn't hurt his harvest of wheat and corn. 'There will be a great problem after 5 or 10 years,' says the 63-year-old Sikh farmer. Years of using high-yield seeds that require heavy irrigation and chemical fertilizers have taken their toll on much of India's farmland. . . . So far, 6 percent of agricultural land has been rendered useless."[78]

Where yields are not actually declining, the rate of growth is slowing rapidly or leveling off, as has now been documented in China, North Korea, Indonesia, Myanmar, the Philippines, Thailand, Pakistan, and Sri Lanka.[79]

Pests and pesticides have been another source of problems for the Green Revolution. IRRI released the first Green Revolution rice variety, called IR8, in 1966. With irrigation, chemical fertilizers, and pesticides, IR8 produced more than twice as much per acre as older varieties in traditional cropping systems. But with hindsight we can see that IR8, and other new varieties, had serious ecological drawbacks. Because of their high degree of genetic uniformity, they had a narrower base of resistance to insect pests than did the more diverse traditional varieties. And their shorter stature—an attribute deliberately bred for in order to support more grain per plant—made them poor competitors against weeds, increasing the need for labor for weeding or for herbicides.[80]

Within a few years of releasing IR8, reports started trickling in of major insect, crop disease, and weed problems. Relatively minor pests exploded to epidemic proportions. Tungro virus, transmitted by an insect called the green leafhopper, destroyed tens of thousands of acres of rice in the Philippines in 1971 and 1972. The brown planthopper, a minor pest in the 1960s, devastated rice across Southeast Asia in the 1970s. Massive spraying of insecticides proved useless in fighting the outbreak.[81]

In late 1973 IRRI released IR26, a rice variety containing a resistance gene for brown planthopper. Shortly thereafter, the institute released IR28, IR29, and IR30, other varieties with the same gene—all in the Laguna region of the Philippines. For two years it appeared that the solution had been found. But in 1975 a new strain of the brown planthopper, labeled biotype 2, broke out in the Laguna area. It could successfully attack all of the supposedly resistant varieties because they carried the identical gene against planthoppers. Biotype 2 soon spread to other parts of the Philippines and to Indonesia, where it wiped out 600,000 acres in one fell swoop.[82]

In 1975 IRRI released IR32, with a resistance gene for biotype 2. Once again it appeared that the solution had been found. But three years later biotype 3 appeared and attacked IR32. Farmers stepped up insecticide spraying, with very serious health effects for themselves,[83] but utterly failed to control the planthopper, which was resistant to the chemicals.

71

Experiments at IRRI showed that early application of insecticides actually led to thirty- to fortyfold increases in planthopper numbers thereafter—a phenomenon dubbed the "pesticide treadmill," as it led farmers to spray over and over again. Dr. Peter Kenmore, then in the Philippines working on his doctoral dissertation for the University of California at Berkeley, discovered that the pesticides eliminated other insects that normally preyed on the planthopper, thus releasing it from natural population controls.[84]

This story has a relatively happy ending, however. Thanks in large part to Dr. Kenmore's later work at the Food and Agriculture Organization of the UN, and to an anthropologist named Dr. Grace Goodell, a new approach to pest management was pioneered in the Philippines. Recognizing that the top-down approach, by which international scientists developed technology packages at research stations, just wasn't producing the desired results, Dr. Kenmore turned to the farmers themselves. Over the next few years, farmers were organized into "field schools," where they learned pest biology and acquired the skills needed to manage pests based on observation and minimal pesticide use.[85]

Pest management based on farmer field schools has now spread from the Philippines to Indonesia, Malaysia, Thailand, Sri Lanka, Bangladesh, India, China, and Vietnam. By 1993 some 18,000 extension agents and 500,000 farmers participated in field schools, achieving an average 50 percent reduction in insecticide use, equivalent to $325 million per year.[86]

While this is a very positive step, questions remain. The scale of farmer field school success is enormous yet pales when measured against the estimated 120 million rice farmers in Asia. "Are the benefits of extending the model worth the cost?" asks Green Revolution advocate Dr. Prabhu Pingali. He questions whether a couple of simple rules suitable for dissemination via mass media, like "Don't spray in the first forty days," might not be more cost effective than the field schools.[87]

This approach raises a fundamental question about the directions of technological change in agriculture. Green Revolution critics see the pesticide treadmill in rice as symptomatic of the top-down research and extension process that characterizes the international research centers, and they see the farmer field schools as proof that empowering farmers is far more important in the larger scheme of things.[88] A couple of simple rules may resolve today's problem, but they can leave farmers dependent on outside experts when the next problem arises.

On the other hand, empowering farmers with the self-confidence to analyze and solve their own problems, while seeking outside advice only on an as-needed basis, creates the basis for long-term sustainability and self-reliance. Furthermore, the cost of organizing farmer field schools is only high as long as the job is done by international centers with staff earning international salaries. The very successful farmer-to-farmer program in Central America has been run largely by farmer organizations with minimal outside funding.[89]

The larger question is what the farmer field school experience tells us about the Green Revolution itself. Economist Pingali argues that it proves the "system works," that it is able to innovate new methodologies when faced with crisis.[90] Critics feel that it is more evidence that the top-down, capital-intensive approach is fundamentally wrong.

A partially successful solution to one problem does little to avoid further problems. The newest crisis to emerge in Asian rice production is that of weeds—even as insecticide use drops, herbicide use is skyrocketing.[91] As research centers release higher-yielding varieties that are weaker competitors against other plants, weed problems grow. Wealthier farmers use herbicides, fine tuning of irrigation water, and mechanization to deal with these problems, while poorer farmers are increasingly at a disadvantage.[92]

Thus, critics argue for alternative, more ecologically sound methods of food production. Farmers' organizations must be empowered and supported in their efforts to develop alternatives tailored to the needs of the rural poor in diverse circumstances.[93] NGOs can and should assist in this task.

Big Winners off the Farm

We've tried to clarify which farmers come out ahead in the Green Revolution, but the biggest winners may not be farmers at all. "Neither the farmer nor the landlord reaped the benefits of the Green Revolution," writes researcher Hiromitsu Umehara about the Philippines. "The real beneficiaries were the suppliers of farm inputs, farm work contractors, private moneylenders and banks." In his village study in Central Luzon, their share of the value of the rice harvest rose from one-fifth to more than one-half in only nine years.[94]

In the United States, the same pattern holds. Not only has the share of the consumer food dollar going to the farmer dropped from 38 to

17 percent since 1940, but of that 17 percent the farmer must pay out an ever bigger share to banks and corporate suppliers.[95]

The pressure toward the industrialization of agriculture—leading to ever bigger and fewer farms—may be no more inherent in the new seeds themselves than in any farm technology that costs money. But any strategy to increase production that does not directly address this underlying dynamic will ultimately contribute to the displacement of rural people, and thus, especially in the third world, to greater poverty and hunger.

The Green Revolution:
The Price of Dependency

The more dire consequences of displacing people from the land is one obvious difference between the industrialization process now under way in the third world and that well advanced in U.S. agriculture. But there's a less visible difference. Here the manufacturers of farm inputs are largely based in this economy. So as corporations selling inputs to farmers capture a bigger share of the national food dollar, at least it ends up in part creating jobs and returning profits here.

But in countries in the third world that must import most of their fertilizers, pesticides, irrigation equipment, and machines, benefits leave the country altogether. In India, the cost of importing fertilizer rose 600 percent between the late 1960s and 1980.[96] And India has exceptional industrial capacity and is unusually well endowed with its own fertilizer-making resources. Even where multinational firms set up plants in third world countries to produce, for example, fertilizers and pesticides, profits are controlled by the parent company.[97]

With the agriculture of third world countries increasingly dependent on imports that must be purchased with scarce foreign exchange, rural poverty becomes vulnerable to fluctuations in exchange rates, dollar reserves, and inflation. In the late 1980s and early 1990s India implemented free-market economic reforms including cuts in subsidized agricultural inputs and currency devaluations, which caused inflation. The result was a dramatic upsurge in rural poverty.[98]

The future breakthroughs of the Green Revolution promise to make farmers and entire nations even more dependent on a handful of corporate suppliers. The first stage relied on improving seeds by breeding for desired qualities. These seeds were for the most part developed within the public domain in research institutes funded by governments and international lending agencies.[99]

The next stage of the revolution is biotechnology, especially gene splicing from one species to another to create "transgenic" varieties. Its techniques can be applied to virtually any crop and even to livestock. These products are being patented by major chemical and pharmaceutical companies, which have already acquired a major share of the seed industry.[100]

Among the consequences may be even greater dependency of third world farmers on imported inputs. For example, new seeds from Monsanto and AgrEvo are genetically engineered to work only with certain herbicides, and a farmer must purchase the whole package. What will farmers' cost savings be if they buy the genetically engineered seed—and then have to buy still another product?[101]

Even those who see great potential benefits for third world agriculture in biotechnology breakthroughs, such as the Agricultural and Rural Development Department of the World Bank, are concerned about what one might call research dependency.[102] The widespread patenting of biotechnology processes and products will make it more difficult—and prohibitively expensive—for third world scientists to adapt biotechnologies to the needs of their countries. Moreover, poor farmers just don't make an attractive market for the private sector.[103]

There are considerable ecological and environmental risks associated with transgenic crops. Among these is the possible "escape" of herbicide tolerance genes to wild relatives of crops, perhaps creating "super weeds" that are resistant to control.[104] Many concerns have been raised about the transfer of a gene from the bacteria *Bacillus thuringiensis*, known as Bt, to crop plants. Bt is currently widely used as a safe alternative for controlling insect pests by organic farmers and others who want to reduce their reliance on chemical pesticides. Its recent release by Monsanto in commercial crop varieties means that insects will be exposed to it much more regularly, probably leading to accelerated resistance and the loss of Bt as a useful tool in alternative or organic pest management.[105] Finally, the patenting of crop genes means that farmers in the future may be obliged to pay royalties to foreign companies on varieties bred by their ancestors.[106]

The Green Revolution: Some Lessons

Having seen food production advance while hunger widens, we are now prepared to ask, under what conditions are greater harvests doomed to failure in eliminating hunger?

First, where farmland is bought and sold like any other commodity and society allows the unlimited accumulation of farmland by a few, superfarms replace family farms and all society suffers.

Second, where the main producers of food—small farmers and farmworkers—lack bargaining power relative to suppliers of farm inputs and food marketers, producers get a shrinking share of the rewards from farming.

Third, where dominant technology destroys the very basis for future production by degrading the soil and generating pest and weed problems, it becomes increasingly difficult and costly to sustain yields.

Under these conditions, mountains of additional food could not eliminate hunger, as hunger in America should never let us forget. Fortunately, there are alternatives and substantial evidence that they work.

Toward an Agriculture We Can Live With

The post–World War II Green Revolution represents not just the breeding of more responsive seeds and a (flawed) strategy for ending hunger; it is a way of viewing agriculture. In the Green Revolution-*cum*-industrial agriculture framework, farming means extracting maximum output from the land in the shortest possible time. It is a "mining" operation. In this process, humanity seeks to defeat its competition—nonfood plants, insects, and disease. So agriculture becomes a battlefield, in a war we believe we're winning as long as growth in food production stays ahead of population.[107]

In this war, weapons are chosen through a cost-calculus derived from the marketplace, from the apparently extrahuman economic laws of supply and demand. If the market tells farmers that more pesticides and chemical fertilizers will produce enough to cover their costs, then, of course, they use them.

But there's one big problem: Intent on winning the war, we fail to perceive how the food-producing resources on which our very security rests are being diminished and destroyed. In this chapter, we have

76

noted how the potential of food resources is diminished as prime land gets degraded. In the previous chapter we touched upon some of the modes of destruction—desertification, soil erosion, and pesticide contamination. But the list goes on:

- Groundwater is being rapidly depleted.
- Overuse and poor drainage are causing the salinization of water used in agriculture.
- Prime farmland is being gobbled up by urban sprawl.
- The world's plant genetic resources, essential for developing new seed varieties, are shrinking. In India, which had thirty thousand wild varieties of rice only half a century ago, no more than fifty will likely remain in fifteen years.[108] (The industrial countries are heavily dependent on the third world's genetic diversity. According to one analysis, genes from local and wild varieties have contributed an estimated $66 billion to the U.S. economy, more than the combined debts of Mexico and the Philippines. Most of this material once belonged to sovereign states and local peoples in the third world, the vast majority of whom have never been compensated.)[109]
- Fossil fuels, on which the industrial model of agriculture rests, are being depleted, and they are nonrenewable resources.

This is only a partial list. Yet none of these threats is addressed within the Green Revolution framework. We therefore have to ask if there are alternative approaches up to the challenge of feeding today's growing populations.

Over thousands of years, in many areas of the world, agricultural systems have evolved along principles that are fundamentally different from those of industrial agriculture. Productivity is an important goal, but not above stability and sustainability. Today, the emerging field of agroecology[110]—built on the ecological principles of diversity, interdependence, and synergy—is applying modern science to improve rather than displace traditional farming wisdom.[111]

Industrial agriculture is simple; its tools are powerful. Agroecology is complex; its tools are subtle. Industrial agriculture is costly in both money and energy. Agroecology is cheap in dollars and fossil fuel energy, but in knowledge, labor, and diversity of plant and animal life it is rich.[112]

Traditional rice farming in Asia, for example, produced ten times more energy in food than was expended to grow it, but today's Green Revolution rice production cuts that net output in half, according to

77

Cambridge University geographer Tim Bayliss-Smith. The gain drops to zero, he reports, in a fully industrialized system, such as that of the United States.[113]

Why such a difference? Instead of continuous production of one crop, agroecology relies on intercropping, crop rotations, and the mixing of plant and animal production—all time-honored practices of farmers throughout the world. With intercropping, several crops grow simultaneously in the same field. Rotating cereals with legumes (fixing nitrogen in the soil for use by other plants) and interplanting low-growing legumes with a cereal or in stubble help to maintain soil fertility without costly purchased fertilizers. Mixing annual and perennial crops better uses the soil's lower strata and helps prevent the downward leaching of nutrients.[114]

Ecologist John Vandermeer of the University of Michigan at Ann Arbor explains the scientific basis of intercropping.[115] Because different plants have different needs and different timings of those needs, intercropping takes better advantage of available light, water, and nutrients so more total growth takes place. Instead of depleting the soil, as does monocropping of row crops (with soil between the rows exposed to rain and wind erosion), intercropping increases the organic matter content of soils, thereby promoting better tillage and higher yields. It also insures against disaster, since the more plant varieties, the less chance of all failing simultaneously.

Integrating crops and animals on the same farm allows the return of organic matter to the fields. Using some animals—ducks or geese in rice farming, for example—can reduce weeds without herbicides. Animals also provide emergency income and food, adding overall stability to the farmstead. Limiting pest damage by crop rotation and intentional diversity, along with careful timing of planting and harvesting, can maximize yields without the heavy doses of pesticides that threaten farm families' and consumers' health.

Miguel Altieri of the University of California at Berkeley highlights three types of traditional agriculture from which much can be learned:

- paddy rice culture, which can produce edible aquatic weeds and fish as well as rice
- shifting cultivation, involving complex combinations of annual crops, perennial tree crops, and natural forest regrowth
- raised-bed agriculture, the ancient Aztec method of constructing islands of rich soil scraped from swamps and shallow lakes

Striking biodiversity and a relatively closed nutrient cycle typifies each of these farming systems. Throughout the tropics, farming systems involving both crops and trees commonly contain over one hundred plant species used as construction materials, firewood, tools, medicinal plants, and livestock feed, as well as human food.[116]

Agroecology does not mean going backward—it means applying modern biological science to improve rather than displace traditional agriculture. This can be done only by empowering farmers themselves to take the lead, using scientists trained in agroecology as consultants.[117]

But why, then, has traditional agriculture been perceived simply as an obstacle to development?

If It Could Have Worked, It Would Have

In a heated response to our criticisms of the Green Revolution, one of its most distinguished defenders once told us that the notion of an alternative drawn from traditional agriculture is hopelessly naive. Obviously, if traditional agriculture could have fed the third world's growing populations, it would have; today's terrible hunger is proof of its failure.

Did traditional agriculture really fail, or was it destroyed by the Green Revolution and by the forces we touch upon in chapter four?[118] Such disdain for traditional farming practices clearly bolsters the role of corporate suppliers of manufactured inputs. Calgene is one such supplier, a U.S.-based biotechnology firm proud of its seeds with "built-in management," such as resistance to herbicides. Norman Goldfarb, Calgene's chief executive, suggested that such seeds would be particularly relevant in Africa. "In Africa, there are a lot of unsophisticated farmers," he said. "You can't even expect them to drive a tractor straight; you might ask them to put the seed on the field evenly."[119]

Goldfarb's arrogance reflects more than simple ignorance. It typifies a widespread blindness to traditional agriculture's potential. Because its principles profoundly contradict the rules that guide industrial agriculture—particularly, allowing market values almost exclusively to dictate use of resources—traditional agriculture has been undervalued. Criteria derived from industrial agriculture are simply inadequate for assessing traditional approaches.

In measuring success, industrial agriculture asks, How much of the main commercial crop is produced this year per acre and per labor hour? But in traditional agriculture, where intercropping of several crops is more common, such a single measure grossly underestimates production. And judging productivity by how few people can produce a given quantity of food—the industrial yardstick—is hardly appropriate in societies where many people are out of work. Finally, traditional agriculture asks how much can be harvested not just this year but indefinitely into the future.

To move beyond industrial agriculture thus involves rethinking how we judge performance. What happens when we evaluate an entire farming system—including its year-to-year stability, its sustainability, and the productivity of its diverse elements—instead of just this year's output of the top cash crop?

In agroecological farming, two or more crops in the same field produce a total output that would require as much as three times more land if the crops were cultivated separately.[120] As many as twenty-two crops in the same field is not unknown in traditional systems.

Such systems hold special importance for Africa, where fragile soils have been seriously abused for many decades but considerable knowledge of alternatives remains.[121] In West Africa's Senegal, for example, where soils have been depleted by cash crops, one study suggests that the traditional mix of millet, cattle raising, and a parklike cover of acacia trees could support a population almost double the present density, already considered high. Acacia trees yield nitrogen the soil so badly needs and high-protein pods for animal feed. The tree's drought-tolerant tap root goes down almost one hundred feet, and, conveniently, the leaves fall just before the short crop-growing season, so the trees do not compete with millet for sunlight, moisture, and nutrients.[122]

Ironically, Africa is now seen as the main target for the second Green Revolution.[123] A "Washington Consensus" of the World Bank, the U.S. Agency for International Development, IFPRI, FAO, and others has coalesced around the idea that what Africa needs is more new seeds, agrochemicals, biotechnology, and free trade.[124] For the reasons outlined in this chapter and in chapter 8, we think that would be a disaster for the poor and the hungry in Africa.

The alternative exists, not just for Africa, but for everywhere. It is to create a viable and productive small-farm agriculture based on land reform, as described in the next chapter, and using the principles of agroecology.[125] That is the only model with the potential to end rural poverty, feed everyone, and protect the environment and the productivity of the land for future generations.[126]

Successful Examples

That sounds good, but has it ever worked? From the United States to India, alternative agriculture is proving itself viable. In the United States, a landmark study by the prestigious National Research Council found that "alternative farmers often produce high per acre yields with significant reductions in costs per unit of crop harvested," despite the fact that "many federal policies discourage adoption of alternative practices." The Council concluded that: "Federal commodity programs must be restructured to help farmers realize the full benefits of the productivity gains possible through alternative practices."[127]

In South India, a 1993 study was carried out to compare "ecological farms" with matched "conventional," or chemical-instensive farms. The study's author found that the ecological farms were just as productive and profitable as the chemical ones. He concluded that if extrapolated nationally, ecological farming would have "no negative impact on food security" and would reduce soil erosion and the depletion of soil fertility while greatly lessening dependence on external inputs.[128]

But Cuba is where alternative agriculture has been put to its greatest test.[129] Changes underway in that island nation since the collapse of trade with the former socialist bloc provide evidence that the alternative approach can work on a large scale. Before 1989 Cuba was a model Green Revolution–style farm economy, based on enormous production units, using vast quantities of imported chemicals and machinery to produce export crops, while over half of the island's food was imported.[130] Although the government's commitment to equity, as well as favorable terms of trade offered by Eastern Europe, meant that Cubans were not undernourished, the underlying vulnerability of this style of farming was exposed when the collapse of the socialist bloc was added to the already existing and soon to be tightened U.S. trade embargo.

Cuba was plunged into the worst food crisis in its history, with consumption of calories and protein dropping by perhaps as much as 30 percent. Nevertheless, by 1997 Cubans were eating almost as well as they did before 1989, yet comparatively little food and agrochemicals were being imported.[131] What happened?

Faced with the impossibility of importing either food or agrochemical inputs, Cuba turned inward to create a more self-reliant agriculture based on higher crop prices to farmers, agroecological technology, smaller production units, and urban agriculture.

The combination of a trade embargo, food shortages, and the opening of farmers' markets meant that farmers began to receive much better prices for their products.[132] Given this incentive to produce, they did so, even in the absence of Green Revolution–style inputs. They were given a huge boost by the reorientation of government education and research and extension toward alternative methods, as well as the rediscovery of traditional farming techniques.

As small farmers and cooperatives responded by increasing production, while large-scale state farms stagnated and faced plunging yields, the government initiated the newest phase of revolutionary land reform, parceling out the state farms to their former employees as smaller-scale production units. Finally, the government mobilized support for a growing urban agriculture movement—small-scale organic farming on vacant lots—which, together with the other changes, transformed Cuban cities and urban diets in just a few years.[133]

The Cuban experience tells us that we *can* feed a nation's people with a small-farm model based on agroecological technology, and in so doing we can become more self-reliant in food production. A key lesson is that when farmers receive fairer prices, they produce—with or without Green Revolution inputs. If these expensive and noxious inputs are unnecessary, then we can dispense with them.

A Metaphor

This chapter opened with a sketch of one of the arguments used by proponents of the Green Revolution. Outsiders, we are told, are not the ones to instigate the political and economic reforms essential to ending hunger. All that concerned foreigners can really offer is expert technical help—like the Green Revolution—to boost production.

In chapter 10, we document the many ways U.S. citizens—whether we like it or not—mightily affect the lives of people within the third world, often blocking the very changes needed to alleviate hunger. As outsiders, we can help reverse the nature of our influence. But from this chapter another response emerges: Should not the many negative consequences of our "expert" advice render us more humble in assuming that our development model is superior to the values and knowledge that have been developed in many third world societies over hundreds, even thousands, of years?

The Green Revolution–*cum*–industrial model single-mindedly asks, How can we get more out of the land? And to anyone raising questions, the response is, How heartless you are—without the Green Revolution many more people would be dying of hunger!

Perhaps a metaphor will clarify our answer. Imagine for a moment our global food resources as a large house gradually burning to the ground. The fire destroying the house represents all the ways in which our present food-producing resources are being degraded and diminished. How does the Green Revolution respond to the catastrophe? It rushes into the burning dwelling to rescue as many people as possible. Its defenders then declare, "Look, the Green Revolution works—it saves lives."

There's only one problem. The house is still burning! The fire is consuming all who remain inside and making the house uninhabitable for those who will need its protection in the future. And much evidence suggests that the rescue team itself—the Green Revolution—inadvertently adds oxygen to the flames as it smashes down the doors to save as many victims as possible. The "oxygen" is its single-minded pursuit of production, which contributes to the soil degradation, erosion, pesticide abuse, and so on that helped start the fire in the first place.

Clearly, congratulating the rescue team for saving lives is beside the point. We must rebuild the dwelling and make it fireproof.

As we put out the flames and begin to rebuild, we must never forget that, as we have shown in this chapter, increased production can go hand in hand with greater hunger. So even if the house were made sound, keeping its doors open for all depends on social forces, not technical ones. By social forces we mean the rules people make through custom, laws, and—too often—brute force that govern the life-and-death question of who eats and who doesn't. The new, fireproof dwelling can offer genuine security only as people change those rules, as they make the claim to food, the right to life itself, effectively universal.

The model of industrial agriculture that the Green Revolution carries with it is constructed by the rules of the market and the unlimited accumulation of productive resources. In later chapters, we stress that ending hunger does not necessitate throwing out the market or property ownership. It will require, however, transforming such rules from dogma into mere economic devices serving the entire community, no longer a privileged few. Here are some questions that can free us from dogma and allow us to begin addressing the underlying forces generating hunger:

- How can claims to land and other food-producing resources and claims to income to buy food be made equitable?

- How can poor farmers—the majority of the world's food producers—augment production and maintain and improve soil fertility without increasing their dependency on costly technologies?
- How can decisions leading to the destruction of food-producing resources be brought under democratic direction so that the destruction can be reversed?

Only by facing such questions squarely can we assume our rightful responsibility—no longer abdicating our morality to supposedly automatic laws of the marketplace. Once we are moving in this direction, farming practices could be based on a more sophisticated calculation of cost effectiveness. Melding traditional wisdom and growing scientific appreciation of our complex biological interdependence with plant and animal life, we could then finally achieve food security for everyone and responsibly safeguard resources needed by future generations.

After more than three decades of the Green Revolution we stand at a crossroads. Do we stake the food security of the poor on a second, "new and improved" Green Revolution; or do we change directions, opting for a more agroecological path, in which grassroots movements supported by NGOs and enlightened governments play a role in helping empower the poor to develop their own alternatives?

CHAPTER 6

Myth 6:
Justice vs. Production

MYTH: No matter how much we believe in the goal of greater fairness, we face a dilemma. Since only the big growers have the know-how to make the land produce, redistributing control over resources would undercut production. Reforms that take land away from the big producers will lower food output and therefore hurt the hungry people they are supposed to help.

OUR RESPONSE: Fortunately, justice and production turn out not to be competing goals; instead, they are complementary. The discouraging notion of an inevitable trade-off between the two is still widely held, in part because so many people do not perceive the ways in which unjust food production systems—those dominated by a few—are *inefficient*. They both underuse and misuse food resources. People will understandably fear change in the direction of greater fairness until it becomes clear precisely how injustice blocks development.

Wealthy landowners hardly need to use every acre. And by all indications they don't. In Brazil, large landowners cultivate on average only 11.3 percent of their land.[1] While Brazil may be an extreme example, it is widely recognized that throughout Latin America large landowners leave a disproportionate share of their land idle.[2]

With so much land left unused by the big operators, it is no surprise that small farms are almost always more productive. A study of fifteen countries (primarily in Asia and Africa) found that per-acre output on small farms can be four to five times higher than that on large estates.[3] Even comparing output only on actually cultivated land, small farms are still significantly more productive.[4] That this is a fact is now widely recognized by agricultural economists, who call it the "inverse relationship between farm size and productivity" and debate at length as to its underlying causes.[5]

Small farmers achieve higher output per acre in part because they work their land more intensively than do big farmers. In Colombia, small farms use labor twenty times as intensively as large ones. In Kenya, farms under five acres use ten to twenty times more labor per acre than do farms with one hundred acres or more—resulting in ten times more value of output per acre than the bigger farmers achieve.[6] Not only do they apply more labor, but small farmers also make more efficient use of space. The smaller the farm, the more likely that it is an integrated production system, with diverse crops cultivated together and/or staggered over time, and livestock or even fish to feed on crop residues and provide manure as fertilizer. Such systems are far more productive per unit of area than are the monocultural systems employed by large farmers.[7]

Combine the superior performance of small farms with the fact that large landholders, those least productive, control more[8]—and better—land than small farmers. Only then is it possible to begin to appreciate how profoundly *counter*productive are present, elite-controlled farm economies.[9]

The Illusion of Efficiency

Even in the United States, where mechanization favors larger farms, the same "inverse relationship" holds. Small farms have almost double the total output and profit margin per acre of large farms.[10] Unfortunately, that does not mean that small farms are economically viable. U.S. government policies and the monopolization of commerce in farm products by large corporations artificially depress the prices that farmers receive (without lowering what consumers must pay). The result is that profits per acre are so low—for any farm size—that many, many acres must be added together, thus favoring average farm sizes much larger than efficient food production would argue for.[11]

Studies also place large, capital-intensive farms at the low end of the efficiency scale in terms of energy. Growing food uses many forms of energy, some renewable and some not, including sunlight, human and animal labor, petroleum, and electricity. It also produces energy: the calories contained in the food we eat. Traditional farming systems produce from five to fifty calories of food for each calorie expended in production, whereas capital-intensive farming as in the United States yields a single calorie for every 10 expended.[12] Not only that, but traditional systems use more renewable forms of energy (humans, draft animals, manure), while capital-intensive agriculture depends largely on fossil fuels.

With so much evidence to the contrary, why do so many people believe that bigger is better—that large-scale operations are most efficient?

At first glance, it is easy to confuse the very size of a large-scale operation with proof of superior know-how. The real reasons for the success of the big producers—advantages resulting from wealth and political clout—are all but invisible. They include preferential access to credit, irrigation, chemical fertilizers, pesticides, technical assistance, and marketing services. Policies of governments and aid institutions are also biased in their favor, as we document in chapters 5 and 10. With this understanding, small producers' ability to out perform the big growers becomes all the more impressive.

Motivation for Good Farming Undermined

Where a few large landowners control most of the land, rental and sharecrop arrangements are common, and wage laborers do much of the farmwork. All of these arrangements undermine the best, most careful use of the land, compared to farming systems in which those who work the land have a direct stake in its long-term productivity. Without secure rights to their land, how could one expect the millions of poor tenant farmers in the third world to invest in land improvements, judiciously rotate crops, or leave land fallow for the sake of long-term soil fertility?

Consider the disincentive built into the sharecropping system in Bangladesh.[13] Landlords often prefer to evict tenants regularly because they fear that long-term tenants might someday assert legal rights to the land. Suppose a poor farmer goes 200 taka into debt to buy improved seeds and fertilizer. He realizes a 400 taka increase in output but then has to hand over half his crop and 200 taka plus interest to repay the landlord. He ends up with no gain at all. It's not hard to understand why much of Bangladesh's excellent food-producing resources are so underdeveloped—it reflects not peasants' "backwardness" but their economic common sense.[14]

In the United States, a similar pattern exists. Tenant-operated farms have higher rates of topsoil loss than owner-operated farms. In the early 1950s, a report of a major research group concluded that tenure problems in the Corn Belt were one of the major stumbling blocks to the adoption of conservation practices.[15] A more recent study found that in Iowa, tenant farms lost a third more topsoil than owner-operated farms.[16]

Hired labor also characterizes big-scale farming. Most farmwork in the United States is now performed by people who don't themselves live on a farm.[17] In the third world, laborers also do much of the work on big estates. They have still less stake in the operation than tenants, and they naturally worry about their wages, not the landowner's or the agribusiness corporation's yields. State farms—another form of large-scale operation in which workers often do not have a direct stake in output—have faced similar motivation problems. In Cuba the productivity of small farmers consistently surpassed that of huge state farms. As a result, in 1993 the Cuban government began the massive conversion of state farms into small semiprivate farms belonging to former farmworkers.[18]

Cooperation Thwarted

Monopoly control over food-producing resources also thwarts their full use by undermining the motivation for community cooperation needed to develop them. Historically, cooperation has played a crucial role in agricultural development. A study by the UN Food and Agriculture Organization notes that "repair and maintenance of rural water courses, reservoirs, tanks, etc. . . . have always been the responsibility of the community."[19] In Bangladesh, for example, cooperation in digging and maintaining ponds for irrigation and fish cultivation was common before 1793, the year the British instituted individual land ownership. Today when 10 percent of rural households have come to control over half the land while almost half of the families have virtually none, village cooperation is a thing of the past. Traveling in rural Bangladesh, we were struck by the many ponds, once a village asset, now silted up and useless.[20] Why should the land-poor majority pitch in if the benefits go mainly to the village's few better-off landowners? For their part, the landowners find that thanks to aid programs they can irrigate with a pump, dispensing altogether with the need for a pond.

The Misuse of Food Resources

Thus far we have asked how antidemocratic farming systems controlled by a few thwart the fullest and most careful use of resources. But we can go further, approaching the problem from the perspective of the big landowner or absentee investor. Seeking the greatest profits in the shortest time, big growers are willing to overuse the soil, water, and chemical inputs without thought to eroding the soil, depleting the groundwater, and poisoning the environment. Since they are likely to have other income-generating investments and can take over additional land if need be, why should they concern themselves about the long-term viability of a particular piece of land, to say nothing of the health of workers and the larger community exposed to toxic chemicals?

In Nicaragua under the Somozas, wealthy cotton growers increased output by 80 percent in only eight years and at the same time succeeded in turning their country into the pesticide capital of the world.[21] Mother's milk in Nicaragua contained forty-five times the amount of DDT considered tolerable by health authorities. Wealthy cotton growers had vastly expanded production by escalating applications of DDT.[22]

In the United States, with more and more farmland in the agricultural heartland owned by nonfarmer investors with no attachment to the land beyond annual profit statements, we can expect abuse of the land to increase. For example, when John Hancock Mutual Life Insurance bought up the Hauck family farm in Wabasha County, Minnesota, it proceeded to undo conservation practices that the Haucks had built up over decades. The farm's annual soil loss had soon increased tenfold.[23] Absentee ownership of this type is on the rise; farm management companies already control a quarter of American farmland.[24]

The Wealth Produced Leaves Town

Surely more bushels of grain is not the only goal of farm production; farm resources must also generate wealth for the overall improvement of rural life—including better housing, education, health services, transportation, local business diversification, and more recreational and cultural opportunities.

But when a few control most of the land, what happens to the wealth produced? It leaves town! We remember visiting northwest Mexico, an area with some of the country's most lucrative farm production. But stopping in neighboring towns, we saw only squalor. Wealth from the rich farmland, pocketed by a few, had gone into savings accounts in foreign banks, fancy cars, and private planes for hopping over the border on shopping sprees. Virtually none of that wealth stayed around to enrich the community. And our firsthand observations are confirmed by rural economists. A UN study mission to rural Sri Lanka concluded that the rural areas were in a "chronic and worsening condition of underdevelopment" because the "rural surplus is extracted by the banking process mainly for use outside the rural sector."[25]

In Costa Rica, where much of the agricultural production is intended for export to the United States and Europe, three transnational corporations control vast regions in banana plantations. These transnationals sit in a position of power and influence second to none. Wealth is drained from both ends of the market—from producers as well as consumers—by these three corporations, which have a virtual monopoly of the banana industry, controlling 67 percent of Costa Rican exports.[26]

Of the price U.S. consumers pay for bananas, only 14 percent actually returns to Central America in the form of wages and taxes levied by the governments. A startling 86 percent ends up in the hands of corporations that control production, shipping, ripening, distributing, and retailing. Shipping companies—which are mostly subsidiaries of the same corporations—receive more of the consumers' money than all the producers in Central America combined.[27]

A similar pattern holds in the United States. In corporate farming communities the wealth produced goes elsewhere, notes the author of a now classic study contrasting two California communities in the rich San Joaquin Valley. "In towns surrounded by family farms, the income earned in agriculture circulates among local business establishments," while in corporate-farm towns "the income is immediately drained off into larger cities to support distant, often foreign enterprises." Where family farms still predominate, there are more local businesses, paved streets and sidewalks, schools, parks, churches, clubs, and newspapers, better services, higher employment, and more civic participation.[28]

Unfortunately, we are moving in the wrong direction. Over the past thirty years the high costs of industrial agriculture combined with low

90

crop prices have led to innumerable farm bankruptcies and liquidations, decimating rural America. From 1975 to 1990 the U.S. farm population dropped by 30 percent, from 9.3 million to 6.5 million.[29] With fewer farmers, the remaining farms—many of them corporate—have grown in size.[30] The average farm grew from 175 acres in the 1940s to well over 500 acres in the 1990s, while the total number of farms is at its lowest point since before the Civil War.[31] Just 4 percent of the landowners now own 47 percent of U.S. farmland, amounting to over half a billion acres.[32]

The Fruits of Reform

As we came to grasp the many ways in which agrarian systems controlled by narrow elites both underuse and misuse resources, we found ourselves asking if virtually any alternative could be worse. Wouldn't greater production—certainly more sustainable production—have to follow where access to land, credit, and knowledge is more fairly shared?

A landmark study by the World Bank and the International Labour Organization in six countries—India, Malaysia, Brazil, Colombia, Pakistan, and the Philippines—reinforced our sense that the answer to that question must be yes. The study considered the likely productivity impact of a more equitable distribution of land and concluded that land reform could bring significant production gains not only in land-abundant countries in Latin America but even in the land-scarce, intensively farmed countries of Asia.[33] Everything being equal, transforming the countryside into small, family-owned and -worked farms would boost agricultural output by amounts ranging from 10 percent in Pakistan to 28 percent in Malaysia and Colombia.[34] In northeast Brazil, the study argued that redistribution of farmland into small holdings could raise output an astounding 79.5 percent.[35]

Unfortunately, testing such predictions as to the benefits of fairer access to land isn't easy. Big landowners use all of their considerable power to resist. In the mid-1980s, large landowners in Brazil were so frightened of land reform that they invested $5 million to buy arms and hire gunmen to protect their land against peasant occupations.[36] In every genuine effort to redistribute land, entrenched interests feel threatened. Fearing that land and power will be taken from them, landowning elites have been known to sabotage production. Either they liquidate what they can of their resources—slaughtering livestock, for instance—in order to take their wealth out of the country; or they try to disrupt the economy in hopes of stirring popular discontent against the government carrying out the reform. If support from foreign sources gives the privileged oligarchy hope that it can successfully resist the changes, it is all the more likely to attempt such sabotage.[37]

Genuine Land Reform

Modern history offers relatively few examples of genuine agrarian reform. Nevertheless, in this century several far-reaching reforms have been carried out. Examining their impact can tell us a great deal about the concerns raised in this chapter.

Japan. Fearing social unrest in the aftermath of World War II, a conservative government carried out a major land reform with prodding and support from U.S. occupation forces. Transforming tenant-farmers into owner-cultivators, the reform not only resulted in greater equity but may also have removed constraints on the growth of Japanese agriculture.[38] Today, Japanese cereal yield per acre is one of the highest in the world; in Asia it is second only to that of South Korea, another of our examples here.[39]

South Korea. Whereas more than half of South Korea's agricultural households had been landless, only 3 percent remained without land after a sweeping land reform in the early 1950s. More than a quarter of the cropland was redistributed, all beneficiaries ending up with roughly the same amount of land. Within a decade, yields far surpassed pre-reform levels,[40] and today cereal yields are the highest in Asia.[41]

Taiwan. In the years 1949 to 1953, mainland Chinese forces—driven out of China by the peasant-based Red Army demanding land reform—themselves imposed reforms on the Taiwanese landed aristocracy. They increased the proportion of farm families owning their land from 33 to 59 percent, reduced the share of farmland worked by tenants from 41 to 16 percent, and reduced rents and insecurity on the remaining tenancies.[42] As a result, agricultural productivity rose, income distribution became more even, and rural and social stability were enhanced.[43]

China. In the early 1950s, the Chinese undertook perhaps the most far-reaching land reform ever attempted. Half a billion rural people were affected. Looking back over almost fifty years of agrarian change in China, we can say that when authority over the use of the land was wrested from wealthy landlords and eventually passed into the hands of large administrative units, production increases were not exceptional. But when responsibility for land was further devolved to individual families and rewards were made more commensurate with effort (bringing rural incomes more in line with urban ones), production advanced well ahead of population growth,[44] even though the drop in fertility rates had slowed. In just six years, from 1978 through 1984, agricultural output per capita grew a phenomenal 39 percent,[45] and has continued growing steadily ever since.[46]

Zimbabwe. Agrarian reform also involves redistributing credit, which is almost as important as land itself. In 1985, the Zimbabwe government allocated substantially more credit to small peasant producers. It had already granted women the formal right to own property, and women then gained access to credit and training as well.[47] These changes help to explain how Zimbabwe achieved a million-ton surplus of corn in 1985, despite seven years of the worst drought in decades. Its small farmers increased their corn output tenfold over any pre-independence year. However, land reform is yet incomplete in Zimbabwe, and its full potential remains to be seen.[48]

Kerala, India. The 1969 land reform in Kerala, India, abolished tenancy, allowing for a massive redistribution of land rights. In effect, absentee landowning, a system characterized by high levels of exploitation and oppression, was abolished and the foundations for participatory democracy and protection of human rights were laid.[49] Over 2 million acres have since been redistributed, with 1.5 million tenants becoming small owners.[50] For the vast majority of people in the countryside, subsistence and the general quality of life improved greatly.

In addition to these specific examples, we have examined the results of several overview studies of the impact of agrarian reform. Those studies that focus on *genuine* land redistribution uniformly show net benefits in productivity, efficiency, and alleviation of poverty, as well as positive ripple effects through the larger economy.[51] Where even limited, localized, yet genuine, reforms have occurred, whether in China, Latin America, South Asia, or Africa, the results have been positive. Nevertheless, the policy analysts at dominant institutions belittle this most effective of reforms. According to Michael Lipton, a highly respected British economist:

> Many otherwise well-informed people believe that, since the post-war reforms in Japan, Korea and Taiwan, there are few if any success stories of land reform. They believe that it has been legislated with so many loopholes that very little has happened; or that it has been evaded, or has failed to get land to the poor, or has been reversed; that it runs against modern farming, with (alleged) economies of scale and complex techniques and marketing; that, even where desirable, it is politically infeasible; in short, that the golden age of land reform, if it existed at all, was over by the mid-1960s. *All these statements are false, and are generally agreed to be so by subject specialists, whatever their analytical or political preference.* There is almost no area of anti-poverty policy where popular, even professional, opinion is so far removed from expert analysis and evidence as land reform.[52]

The naysayers typically confuse, intentionally or not, genuine and egalitarian efforts to redistribute quality land with inegalitarian colonization projects that send the landless to remote areas with poor soils, or window-dressing reforms that touch on some aspect of land tenure without addressing underlying inequities.[53]

People are understandably confused when governments speak of land reform but use policies that protect, not alter, the status quo. When the potential of reform is measured by the consequences of these fake land reforms, the conclusions can be pretty discouraging.

Giving Reform a Bad Name

Mexico. In the 1930s, the government of Lázaro Cárdenas enacted a sweeping land reform that raised the hopes of millions of peasants. But subsequent governments never came through with the other ingredients essential to genuine redistribution of productive resources—credit, improved seeds, irrigation, and so on—which have remained the province of wealthy, politically powerful growers. In the early 1980s, after more than four decades of land reform, 2 percent of landowners controlled three-quarters of the land, and more than half of all rural adult workers remained landless.[54] Today, landlessness and poverty are growing in the Mexican countryside as a result of the counterreform effected by the

94

government in order to pave the way for the North American Free Trade Agreement (NAFTA). In 1992, Article 27 of the Mexican Constitution was amended to terminate land reform. Many feel that decision contributed directly to the Zapatista uprising on January 1, 1994.

El Salvador. During the 1980s the U.S. government forced the reluctant ruling party in El Salvador to engage in a halfhearted land reform. The measure left untouched the backbone of the rural oligarchy, the coffee estates, and ignored the needs of the landless majority in the countryside. Haciendas turned into cooperatives by the reform were starved for credit, technical assistance, and timely provision of seeds by government agencies controlled by a political party opposed to reform. To "demonstrate" the economic costs of reform, the cooperatives were sabotaged.[55]

Examples of such fake reforms abound—in the Philippines, Honduras, Pakistan, India, and other countries. Carried out by governments beholden to the rural oligarchy, they inevitably leave the rural power balance intact.[56] Such "reforms" can therefore contribute neither to greater production nor to the alleviation of poverty at the root of hunger. Unfortunately, they contribute to the false notion that land reform can't work.

Land Reform from Below

While policy makers say that land reform isn't politically feasible anymore, the poor are taking matters into their own hands. After the Zapatista uprising in Chiapas, Mexico, landless peasants seized more than 200,000 acres belonging to wealthy landlords.[57] One year after the start of the rebellion, thirty rebel municipalities, independent of the Mexican government, were created in Zapatista territory. There local people have organized "production societies" that produce food, cattle, coffee, and artisanry in an attempt to build a more vibrant local economy.[58]

In Brazil the Landless Movement (MST), frustrated by government foot-dragging on promises of land reform, seized more than 50 million acres between 1990 and 1995 alone. While some MST squatters are struggling to get their new farms up and running, others have been relatively successful. Some MST land occupations have been transformed into productive farm cooperatives providing ample food, cash income, and basic services for thousands of families. Small industries have even been created on the most advanced co-ops, including a clothing factory in Rio Grande do Sul, a tea-processing plant in Paraná, and a creamery in Santa Catarina.[59]

Not Just Size but
Structure of Decision Making

Shifting the power balance to favor the poor majority is the heart of genuine land reform. But we should not let the size question confuse us on this point. What we are evaluating here are the consequences of different structures of power and accountability. Size is often a handy stand-in for these concepts. To refer to big landowners is actually to refer to a particular authoritarian structure of power, in which a few make all the decisions over the use of a vital resource, farmland.

Just because an agricultural system is dominated by small farms, we should not assume it is necessarily equitable. If small farmers are at the mercy of those who control distribution of farm inputs and marketing of farm commodities, they are powerless even if large operators do not monopolize the land. When we surveyed small farmers in Central America who grow cantaloupe melons for export to the United States, we found that they must pay 2 percent higher interest rates for farm loans and receive a 65 percent lower price for their melons than do large growers who have good connections at the bank and own the packing sheds.[60] Thus, more than land tenure must be addressed. In the more effective, genuine land reforms, small farmers have been provided with marketing mechanisms, infrastructure, credit, and technical assistance.[61]

Production for What?

While common sense and historical experience convince us that fairer control over agricultural resources can bring greater, not lower output, a more fundamental consideration ought never to be forgotten:

Even if one could prove that an elite-dominated agricultural system were more productive, we would still ask, So what? Is not food production of value only if it fulfills human needs? If a society's agricultural system is strikingly productive but its citizens go hungry, of what use is it?

The problem of production must therefore never be posed in isolation. The question must not be what system can produce the most food but under what system—elite-controlled or democratically controlled—is hunger most likely to be alleviated.

If as a result of a redistribution of assets the poor gained more buying power, the composition of crops would likely respond to their needs and the production of luxury crops might slump. Families with more land might for the first time consume all they need, thus failing to increase marketed production. Indeed, the market value of production might fall—yet hunger could be falling too. Our point is simply a reminder that we should never focus so narrowly on production that we forget why we care in the first place, forget that our real concern is how to end needless hunger.

Many people have been made to believe that we must choose between a fairer economic system and efficient production. This tradeoff is an illusion. In fact, the most inefficient and destructive food systems are those controlled by a few in the interests of a few. Greater fairness can not only release untapped productive potential and make long-term sustainability possible, it is the *only* way that production will contribute to ending hunger.

CHAPTER 7

Myth 7:
The Free Market Can End Hunger

MYTH: If governments just got out of the way, the free market could solve the hunger problem.

OUR RESPONSE: Unfortunately, such a market-is-good, government-is-bad formula can never help address the causes of hunger. Such thinking misleads us into believing that a society can opt for one or the other, when in fact every economy on earth combines market and government in allocating resources and distributing wealth.

Take the example of the very capitalist and market-oriented United States, where annual government spending as a proportion of GNP is about half of that in the more "socialist," or social democratic, Netherlands, Norway, and Belgium.[1] Yet slightly more than a third of annual U.S. government spending, an estimated $448 billion, consists of direct and indirect subsidies for corporations and wealthy individuals, in direct violation of free-market principles.[2]

South Korea and Taiwan, until recently the favorites of free-market purists, owe much of their striking growth records during the postwar period to numerous government interventions, not the least of which have been government-imposed land reforms and support for key industries.[3]

Worst of all, such black and white thinking blocks us from identifying the truly critical questions we must ask to learn how *either* the market and/*or* government can alleviate hunger.

Defenders of the market have a lot of evidence on their side—certainly, any society that has tried to do away with the market has faced serious headaches.[4] The problem comes when a useful device gets raised to the level of dogma. We lose sight of what it can and cannot do. For all the market's virtues, three of its shortcomings contribute directly to the causes of hunger.

The Market Responds to Money

Several years ago we had the opportunity of publicly responding to perhaps the market's greatest advocate, Nobel laureate Milton Friedman. Friedman insisted that the most salient virtue of the free market is that it responds to individual preferences. In our response we said we thought that the preference of most individuals was to eat when they're hungry—yet more than 800 hundred million people in the world (30 million of them in the United States alone) are *not* able to do so.

The lesson is unmistakable: The first shortcoming of the market is that it does not respond to individual preferences—or even needs. It responds to money.

Let's look at the hunger consequences of this simple lesson. From the beginning of our book, we've described the increasing concentration of decision-making power over all that it takes to grow and distribute food—fewer and fewer people owning more and more land and controlling credit, water, marketing channels, and so forth. As the rural poor in ever greater numbers are pushed from the land, they are less and less able to make their demands for food register in the market.

Paralleling this in urban areas, a small elite often controls banking, industry, and commercial institutions. In Chile nearly twenty years of extreme free-market policies under the military government of former president Pinochet led to an unprecedented concentration of wealth and ownership in the hands of a small number of domestic and foreign investors.[5] In Mexico during the 1988–94 reign of free-market advocate President Carlos Salinas, the number of Mexican billionaires appearing in the *Forbes* magazine annual list of the world's richest people rose from two in 1991 to thirteen in 1993 and twenty-four by the time Salinas left office. The connections between some of these nouveau billionaires and the ex-president's immediate family caused national scandals.[6]

With such concentrated power, the wealthy are free to indulge in investments that employ relatively few workers and to resist workers' demands for a living wage. Under those conditions, what does the market do? The only thing it can: It responds to the tastes of those who can pay, the privileged minority. They alone have the income to make what economists call "effective demand." Production inevitably shifts to items desired by the better off, such as meat, fresh fruit and vegetables, imported laser discs and CD players, and Chivas Regal. This is an invisible food revolution, in which basic foods for the majority are increasingly displaced by luxury crops for the minority. In international commerce, food flows from the hungry to the well fed, as we document in the next chapter.

Here in the United States, we witness the same affront to logic and our sensibilities. New York City, for example, now has a greater income disparity between rich and poor than does Guatemala.[7] Window displays offer a feast for the wealthy: organic food, gourmet coffee, expensive diet foods, and imported wines and cheeses, even as the number of the hungry and homeless rises.

Left to its own devices, the market simply mirrors inequalities in wealth and income and should be seen for what it is: a useful tool for distribution and nothing else. We must not delude ourselves into thinking that it registers the needs and wishes of all people.

The Market Is Blind

A second drawback of the market is that it is blind—blind to the social and resource costs of the production engine it is supposed to drive. An example from the United States will make this clear. U.S. agricultural exports have boomed, totaling $62 billion in 1995. What a bonanza, the market tells us. All of those exports could help pay for imported oil.[8]

But the market failed to tell us that the prevailing system of mechanized agriculture in the United States is highly wasteful of energy: About three kilocalories of fossil-fuel energy are required to produce just one kilocalorie of human food.[9] In economic terms, this amounts to at least a third of the money generated.[10]

The market also failed to tell us that our soil is being eroded and our aquifers depleted at higher rates than they can be replenished.[11] The total costs to society of soil erosion in the United States have been calculated at $17 billion per year.[12]

Nor does the market tell us about the social costs of farmers being made more vulnerable to the vagaries of the international market. Hundreds of thousands of livelihoods wiped out, increased rural landlessness, the decline of whole rural communities, and the shocking sight of farmers on food stamps—to all this destruction the market is blind.[13]

The Market Leads to Concentration

Finally, left to its own devices, the market has another drawback that undermines some of our most deeply held values. It leads to the concentration of economic power. Those with greater economic power undercut and gobble up those with less.

Concentration of economic power directly contributes to hunger and seriously compromises political democracy. This is relatively easy to see when we look at the third world. The connection between hunger in Guatemala and the extremely concentrated pattern of land ownership is obvious.[14] Can we see such a connection between the accelerating concentration of economic power and needless human suffering here at home?

Let us take the example of U.S. agriculture again. The export boom that began in the 1970s produced enormous profits, but they were not evenly distributed. By the early 1980s, a mere 1 percent of farm operators—many of them corporate—captured 60 percent of net farm income. In the 1990s giant corporations have continued to expand their control over the production, distribution, and marketing of an increasing number of farm products. Today 20 percent of all farms are responsible for more than 80 percent of total production. Less than 4 percent of the largest farms (with $1 million or more in sales) produce 66 percent of vegetables, sweet corn, and melons.[15] Whereas in 1973 the top four beef-packing companies in the United States slaughtered 29 percent of the total steers and heifers, today the proportion has risen to over 80 percent, and the U.S. beef industry is dominated by just three transnational corporations. Similar patterns now prevail in the pork and poultry industries.[16]

Market theory alone doesn't explain such a dramatic transformation. In theory, the market rewards hard work; in reality, it *requires* hard work and production but *rewards* only those who have considerable equity in their land or in processing facilities—those who have wealth. They have easier access to credit and can therefore better withstand the market's inevitable swings, and only the wealthy can expand to make up in volume what all are losing in profits per acre, as a production push leads inevitably to price-depressing gluts.

Food Flight and Supermarket Redlining

On the distribution side of the food system, the market has failed to provide food where it is most needed. In the 1980s a binge of mergers and leveraged buyouts affecting sixteen of the top twenty national supermarket chains led to across-the-board downsizing.[17] As the new mega-chains entered into intense competition with one another, with "efficiency" as the criterion of success, they started lopping off their weaker limbs, specifically lower-profit-margin stores in poor inner-city neighborhoods. In a pattern repeated across the United States, Boston lost 34 of its 50 supermarkets over little more than a decade; Los Angeles lost 374; and Chicago lost more than 500.[18]

Because the closures have been targeted at minority neighborhoods, we call this process "supermarket redlining" or "food flight," echoing the terms used to describe the practice of banks refusing home mortgages to people of color and the flight of the middle class from the inner city to the suburbs.[19] The closed-down supermarket boarded up with graffiti-decorated plywood should be familiar to anyone who has driven through the inner city in recent years.

As supermarkets close, inner-city residents are left without a local source of fresh produce and meat, or indeed, any affordable food items. The liquor stores and mini-marts that remain offer a limited array of canned and dry goods at prices that average up to 49 percent higher than the same products in suburban supermarkets. Low-income families must travel long distances to find affordable food, often taking several buses, as many do not own cars.[20]

Imagine for a moment that you are a single mother in a minimum-wage job. You come home exhausted to kids desperate for food and attention, yet you must travel forty minutes to buy food and struggle with bursting shopping bags on several crowded buses. Or imagine that you are an elderly person living alone and must make a similarly daunting trip or pay 49 percent more from your meager social security check. The bottom line is that the market does not bring food or services to those who need them most.

"Adjusting" the Market

During the 1980s and 1990s international agencies such as the International Monetary Fund (IMF) and the World Bank forced structural changes on third world economies. Loans desperately needed to restructure foreign debts were conditioned on the performance of "structural adjustment" programs, technocratic plans whose declared aim was to make economies more "efficient," "competitive," and capable of growth. In fact, a principal effect and perhaps even aim of these programs has been to pry open third world economies for foreign corporations, providing new markets and investment opportunities. This has been accomplished by imposing diverse free-market policies, including privatization of state enterprises, deregulation (removal of restrictions on investment, both domestic and foreign), slashing of government budgets for health, education, and social services, and removal of import barriers.[21]

In country after country the impact of these adjustments on the living conditions of the majority has been disastrous. Carried out on a large scale and in a very short time span, privatization transferred the benefits of institutions and resources from the general public to private businesses. In most countries the gap between rich and poor widened as economic power became more sharply concentrated in increasingly fewer hands. As a result, poverty and hunger escalated in the third world during the 1980s and early 1990s, especially in Latin America and Africa, where "adjustment" was more assiduously implemented by local elites. In Latin America, violence, unrest, and deterioration of the social fabric was accompanied by a return of tuberculosis and cholera throughout the continent. In sub-Saharan Africa, cholera is spreading and the AIDS epidemic has reached a devastating magnitude in the wake of public health cutbacks.[22]

The new free market in imports has allowed a deluge of foreign-manufactured luxury goods to inundate third world economies, exacerbating trade deficits. After a decade of adjustment Costa Rica's trade deficit rose almost 100 percent, from $350 to $532 million. Leading the way, the yearly tab for imported consumer goods, which included thirty-two shades of Max Factor lipstick, Barbie town houses, and Aladdin dolls, rose from $134 to $657 million. Mercedes Benzes, Porches, Toyotas, and Hondas were among the 76,800 cars that entered tiny Costa Rica in just three years.[23] At the same time, a flood of cheap, imported grain drove local farmers out of business as the number growing corn, beans, and rice, the staples of the local diet, fell from 70,000 to 27,700.[24] That is a loss of 42,300 livelihoods, or about one farmer for every 1.8 cars imported. Such were the benefits of the market for Costa Ricans.

Once made aware of the market's drawbacks, it might be tempting to throw out the market altogether in favor of government control. But to get at the root of hunger, we must take a more thoughtful, studied look at these issues.

How Can the Market Work to End Hunger?

For those who believe in the usefulness of the market and who also want to end world hunger, the urgent question is, Under what conditions can the market respond to human needs and preferences? Since, by definition, the market responds to economic power and not to need, the answer in our view is fairly straightforward. *The more widely dispersed purchasing power is, the more the market will respond to actual human preferences and needs and the more power the market will have to end hunger.*

In other words, what must be promoted is not the market but the consumers. For where there are customers, there is money to ask for services, and thus there are entrepreneurs—and *voilà*! The market booms. In Cuba, to the extent that the greater use of the market worked to overcome a food crisis, it is because purchasing power is relatively widely distributed,[25] the fruit of making access to work and productive resources more equitable.[26]

For those who believe in the utility of the market, the challenge is to promote policies that counter the concentration of buying power and ensure its wide dispersion. But this perspective raises a final question. Focused on the market, we have yet to take up the equally challenging issue of under what conditions can government serve genuine development?

Ending Hunger:
Is There a Role for Government?

Those who see government, by definition, as the obstacle to development fail to appreciate the role that government has played in our own society's development. Without public support for infrastructure, including not only roads, bridges, railroads, and the like but also public education and public health, where would our nation be?

Government is clearly essential to development. But having acknowledged that, the temptation is to debate *how much* government versus *how much* market will best contribute to development. This simple tradeoff helps us little. It fails to probe the nature of government's contribution. For example:

- Is a government's public health budget spent largely on big hospitals in urban centers using expensive imported technology, as in the Philippines? Or is that same amount of money spread throughout the countryside, as in the Indian state of Kerala, to support primary health clinics serving the majority?[27]
- Is the government's agricultural budget going to support large-scale farms while ignoring the needs of the majority of rural producers, as in Mexico or the United States?[28] Or is priority given to small farmers through cheaper credit and appropriate technical assistance?
- Is the government allowing scarce foreign exchange to drain out of the country for luxury imports consumed by the wealthy, as in the case of Costa Rica? Or are limited resources being directed to reducing poverty and ending hunger?

These and many similar questions are the really meaningful ones to ask about the nature of a government's role in development. They will be answered according to which group a government sees itself as accountable to. A government beholden to a wealthy elite will use its resources for that group's disproportionate gain. A government that knows its survival depends on the support of the majority will work to respond to that majority's needs.

Government as Monitor of the Market

In addition to vital human and material infrastructure, many societies recognize two other critical roles for government: to prevent undue concentration of economic power and to guarantee basic rights. We feel they are just as important in determining whether it can help alleviate hunger.

As we emphasized above, the market left to its own devices will concentrate wealth and purchasing power and therefore undermine its usefulness in meeting human needs. But a government responsible

105

to majority interests can make rules and allocate resources to counter-act the tendency toward concentration. Here's where the government can *help* the market.

Specifically related to hunger, such a mandate requires genuine land reform—including enforcing rules to keep ownership from becoming reconcentrated. It means tax and credit policies that benefit poor farm-ers. And it requires that all public policies—credit, tax, land, social welfare, or workplace reforms—actively disperse buying power. Per-haps most critical to such wide dispersion is making sure that anyone who wants a job can get one.

This isn't interference with the market. Policies that disperse pur-chasing power actually help the market do what it is supposed to do: respond to human needs and preferences.

Do We Have a Right to Eat?

Finally, government's role is to protect rights. Indeed, government uniquely has the power to do so, for nothing is an effective right until government protects citizens' enjoyment of it. We have a meaningful right to free speech, for example, only to the degree that the courts will stop anyone who tries to prevent us from speaking.

A few societies have decided that among basic human rights should be the right to food itself—that indeed this right should be of primary concern. For how can we enjoy any other right without it?

Not all democratic societies protect the right to eat. Many in fact protect human lives only when they are threatened by physical assault not physical deprivation. Some, like our own, assume that while gov-ernment should organize fire departments and police forces for the physical safety of its citizens, those citizens should fend for themselves when it comes to getting a decent job, enough to eat, and affordable medical care.

Only when the concept of basic rights is enlarged to include economic and social rights is government obligated to ensure that each citizen has access to employment, a healthy diet, and adequate health ser-vices. In fact Article 25 of the Universal Declaration of Human Rights, adopted by the UN General Assembly on December 10, 1948, states:

> Everyone has the right to a standard of living adequate for the health
> and well-being of himself and of his family, including food, clothing,
> housing and medical care and necessary social services, and the right

to security in the event of unemployment, sickness, disability, widow-hood, old age or other lack of livelihood in circumstances beyond his control.[29]

This does not mean that the government itself has to provide these goods; it means only that the government ensures that no one goes without them. A variety of approaches can be discovered in a wide spectrum of societies.

Consider the Indian state of Kerala, which we highlighted in our discussion of population in chapter 3. Within India, Kerala has considerably less hunger than the rest of the country, as suggested by an infant death rate that is half the all-India average and a much longer life expectancy. Kerala still tolerates concentration of land ownership but has mitigated the extreme effects by turning poor renters of farmland into owners. And it no longer treats food as a commodity to be sold to the highest bidder. Fair-price shops keep food prices low.[30]

Among Northern countries, those of Scandinavia illustrate a positive role for government in protecting family-farm agriculture. Take Sweden, for example. Although wealth is still tightly concentrated in Swedish society, Swedes some time ago decided that farming and food were too important to be left to the market alone. So in Sweden, only working farmers can own farmland, and sales of farmland are closely monitored by county boards to ensure that prices paid are not so high as to eliminate family farmers from the competition.[31] Moreover, wholesale food prices are not allowed to fluctuate with the market, wreaking havoc on the family farm. Instead, they are periodically set when farm representatives, government, agribusiness, and consumer food cooperatives sit down at the negotiating table.[32]

These far-flung illustrations suggest a willingness to acknowledge the failure of the market alone to alleviate hunger. Even World Bank analysts acknowledge that growth alone could not alleviate chronic hunger in an acceptable period of time—direct intervention in the market is necessary to enhance the ability of the hungry to acquire food.[33]

In such a brief book, we cannot hope to provide answers to the critical controversy over the proper roles of the market and government as instruments of development and promoters of human freedom. More modestly, we hope to show that hunger will never be eliminated if our vision is blocked by rigid dogma, detached from real life experience. The government-or-market tradeoff fails to help us grasp the truly urgent questions we must address in order to end hunger.

Under what conditions can both the market and government serve to alleviate hunger? Clearly the answer to such a question cannot be found in economic theory alone but rests on the relationship of citizens to decision-making power. For neither the market nor government can end hunger as long as control over economic resources is in the hands of a few and political authority responds largely to the booming voice of wealth.

CHAPTER 8

Myth 8:
Free Trade Is the Answer

MYTH: Without protectionist barriers, world trade could reflect the "comparative advantage" of each country—each exporting what it can produce most cheaply and importing what it cannot. Third world countries could increase exports of those commodities favored by their geography, and their greater foreign exchange earnings could be used to import what they need to alleviate hunger and poverty.

OUR RESPONSE: The theory of comparative advantage sounds perfectly sensible. Growth in exports generates increased foreign exchange to fuel a nation's development. Didn't all of us learn in junior high school how "natural" it is that Juan Valdez in South America grows coffee for us while we in turn export industrial goods his country needs, and that in a world of unhampered free trade we all win?

Such an appealing theory! It falls apart only when we apply it to the real world.

If increased exports contributed to the alleviation of poverty and hunger, how can we explain that in so many third world countries exports have boomed while hunger has continued unabated or actually even worsened? Basically, because those who profit from the exports—large growers, processors, exporters, shippers, and others—are not the poor and do not use their profits on behalf of the poor, and because all too often export agriculture displaces food crops and the small farmers who grow them. The following examples illustrate how little the poor benefit from booming exports.

Brazil. During the 1970s, Brazil achieved phenomenal success in boosting its agricultural exports. Soybeans, virtually unplanted in Brazil twenty years earlier, had, by the end of the 1970s, become that country's number one export,[1] almost all of it going to feed Japanese and European livestock. During the same period the hunger of Brazilians markedly worsened, spreading from a third of the population in the 1960s to two-thirds by the early 1980s.[2] By the mid-1990s, Brazil ranked as the world's third largest agricultural exporter (trailing only the United States and China), the area planted to soybeans having grown 37 percent from 1980 to 1995, when it reached more than 11.6 million hectares, gobbling up forests and displacing poor farmers along the way. Over the same period the per capita production of rice, a basic staple of the Brazilian diet, fell by 18 percent.[3]

Thailand. Between 1985 and 1995 agricultural exports from Thailand grew an astounding 65 percent.[4] By the early 1990s Thailand was the only net food exporter in Asia, accounting for 35 percent of world rice exports (almost twice the volume of U.S. exports).[5] But the bulk of the small-farmer population has not benefited from those accomplishments. In the early 1990s an estimated 43 percent of the rural population lived below the poverty line,[6] and nationally, 21.5 percent of preschool children suffered from stunted growth.[7]

Bolivia. In 1990 more than three-quarters of Bolivia's population lived below the poverty line, including fully 95 percent of people in rural areas, who earned less than a dollar per day on average.[8] Yet that followed half a decade of the most spectacular agricultural export growth in Bolivian history, with a dollar-value increase of more than 600 percent in just five years.[9]

Chile. By the early 1990s, Chile had become the world's number one exporter of table grapes, its sales (mainly to the United States) accounting for 90 percent of total world trade in that commodity.[10] The grim and often overlooked side of this economic "miracle" was that poverty widened dramatically.[11] While in 1970 the poor were 20 percent of the population, by 1990 the figure had risen to 41 percent, the number living in extreme poverty doubling as well.[12] Despite their free-trade economic miracle, the people of Chile ate less than they had in the 1970s, with significant drops in caloric intake and consumption of animal protein.[13]

These far-flung examples tell a story. Where the majority of people have been made too poor to buy the food grown on their own country's soil, those who remain in control of productive resources will, not surprisingly, orient their production to more lucrative markets abroad. Fruits, vegetables, coffee, feed grain, sugar, meat, and so on are shipped out of the third world, and thus we have the global supermarket, part of the invisible food revolution we described in chapter 7.

In the global supermarket, even Fido and Felix can outbid the third world's hungry. Vast quantities of fish caught in the third world, although regarded as a desirable, protein-rich food by the poor, ends up feeding pets in Europe and North America.[14]

Comparative Advantage Reconsidered

Exports increase while the well-being of the majority of people deteriorates because reality does not fit the logic of comparative advantage. While it is popularly assumed that a nation's comparative advantage lies in its geographic endowment, the relative qualities of soils and climates turn out to have virtually nothing to do with who produces what. Low wages are the real advantage of third world nations.

When the Ministry of Trade of the Philippines placed an ad in U.S. business magazines headlined "WE WANT YOU TO TAKE (COMPARATIVE) ADVANTAGE OF US," its message was right on target.[15] Low wages reflect business and landowner power to block workers from collective bargaining and circumvent whatever meager minimum-wage law may be on the books. Mexico exports tomatoes, for example, not because its climate is better than Florida's or California's (except for a couple of weeks in late winter), but because the Mexican farmworkers make less in a day than their Californian counterparts do in an hour.[16]

Global corporations are also key in determining to what ends third world nations put their land and other resources. In the 1970s, after organized field workers in Hawaii had achieved livable wages for farmwork and land costs skyrocketed, Del Monte and Dole shifted production of virtually all canned pineapple to the Philippines, where labor organizing was, in effect, prohibited under the Marcos regime and land was obtained by taking it from poor farmers.[17]

111

When the Marcos dictatorship finally fell, President Corazón Aquino's nominal land reform program in 1988 excluded the land of commercial agricultural enterprises. Still, eight thousand hectares of government land that Del Monte had been leasing since 1938 were theoretically to be returned for redistribution. But Del Monte retained the land through the transparent ruse of forming a "cooperative" of its own employees, who "agreed" to lease it back immediately to Del Monte.[18]

Del Monte has since discovered that "free-market" practices are even better, and has changed its strategy from direct control over land to control over the production process via "independent" farmers under exclusive, or "tied-up," contracts. The company provides seeds, credit, and detailed technical instructions to the farmers (for which they are later billed), on the condition that they sell only to Del Monte, at a price unilaterally imposed by the company. This makes abundant sense, as in the process of turning petroleum and industrial products (fertilizer, tractors, etc.) into canned pineapples sold in U.S. supermarkets, the least profitable step, the one where all the risks of bad weather and pests are concentrated, is actual farming. Thus, the small farmers assume all the risks of crop losses, while Del Monte keeps the profits from farm chemical sales, shipping, processing, and wholesale distribution.[19]

Dole has done the same. In 1998 two thousand former employees of Dole's Philippine banana subsidiaries—now "independent" farmers under exclusive contract—went on strike. Since becoming the owners of the land, their daily earnings had fallen from an average of $3 per day to about $2, and they lost their benefits. Falling incomes have forced many families to take their children out of school and put them to work in the fields, where eleven to seventeen year olds earn about $1 a day.[20]

"The company reduced its labor costs by no longer employing us directly," one farmer told the *San Francisco Chronicle*. "They told us we would make big profits," he continued. "We really didn't understand how to compute our costs, and the company said they wouldn't negotiate with us if we brought in experts from the union."[21]

When Dole turned over the land, it was complying with the land reform law. But a loophole allowed the company to retain control over the network of cables needed to transport the bananas, the packing sheds, and the roads on the plantation. When the farmers tried to sell their bananas to other companies, Dole said it would refuse to let them use the infrastructure. "It's true the government is allowing land reform to take place, but it also allows so many loopholes that the former owners benefit from it more than the workers," said one expert, who concluded that the government's actions are part of an overall plan to make the country more attractive to foreign investors.[22]

What's the Advantage?

In desperate bids for foreign investment, third world governments are ready to grant foreign corporations everything from direct subsidies to tax exemptions to freedom from cumbersome labor or environmental regulations. Del Monte has been able to rent government land in the Philippines at the ridiculous rate of 1 peso per hectare per year;[23] Shell Oil may well have had environmental critics hanged in Nigeria;[24] and General Electric, Sanyo, and General Motors have been free to conduct pregnancy screenings at job interviews in Mexico, in order to avoid having to pay for pregnancy leave later on.[25] In each of these cases and in many others, the comparative *advantage* accrues not to the people or the environment of a third world country, but rather to foreign interests.

In today's world economy, comparative advantage has less to do with geographic endowments than with the power of a minority to suppress wages, obtain access to resources, and capture big subsidies from the government, or the power of big transnationals to capture and manipulate government support across countries.

Globalization

Since the previous edition of this book was published, the entire world has taken a sharp turn right, toward what is euphemistically called "trade liberalization." Free trade and comparative advantage have made their biggest comeback since the "free hand" of Adam Smith and have been prescribed like snake oil as the cure for everything from underdevelopment, bureaucracy, and government corruption, to hunger, dictatorship, and general lack of freedom and democracy.[26]

"Globalization" is the buzzword on the tip of every tongue, as technological advances in transportation and electronic communications have allowed global corporations to even further disperse industrial and agricultural production around the world, always seeking the lowest wages, the most lenient regulations, and the cheapest resources. This has intensified what many have called the global "race to the bottom," as working people and governments compete for jobs with other workers and other countries; and the basis of that competition is: Who will work for less? Who will accept part-time employment? Who will forgo health insurance and occupational safety regulations? Who will allow toxic dumping in their backyard?[27]

Thus, the Ford Motor Company can produce a "world car," for which each component—steering wheel, speedometer, right front door—is produced in several countries. If union organizing raises production costs in one country through a successful strike, production quotas are just shifted to a plant somewhere else, the successful strikers are laid off, and the union is busted.[28] The same thing is happening in agriculture, where it would not be inappropriate to refer to a "world pineapple," "world banana," or "world apple":

> Imagine a farm so vast that in the course of a full 24-hour day the sun always illuminates at least one of its many fields; a farm that spans both hemispheres to evade the limitations of seasonal climatic variation on its ability to produce. When it is winter in the United States this farm's Northern Hemisphere fruit trees are dormant, but its Southern Hemisphere trees are lush and productive because it is summer there.[29]

This quotation comes from an article about Dole—which at last count contracted for almost one hundred fresh fruit and vegetable products in fifteen countries—but it could just as well refer to Chiquita Brands, Del Monte, Polly Peck International, Grand Metropolitan, or any of a number of other rapidly growing agricultural conglomerates.[30]

Companies like these take advantage of free-trade opportunities to play a game similar to musical chairs, which some call "slash-and-burn capitalism."[31] Melon exporters in southern Mexico, for example, plan for no more than seven years of business in any given location, after which they expect to relocate, as pest problems, the resistance of pests to pesticides—associated with the overuse of chemicals, rising wages, and the discontent of contract farmers—make further production untenable in that area.[32]

An export spokesman in Choluteca, Honduras, told us they were ready to "move like the Mexicans" as pesticide resistance and pest problems built up in that southern region.[33] When a company pulls up and leaves a given location, land prices decline, unemployment rises, and wages drop, inviting a new cycle of investment to take advantage of the crisis conditions left by the last one. The rise of export melons in Honduras, for example, was predicated on the previous crises of

114

cotton, cattle, and sugar, which left farmers bankrupt and workers unemployed, pushing down land values and wages—creating the "perfect" investment opportunity.

Together, these factors constituted Choluteca's comparative advantage when the melon boom hit. Ironically then, the crises that multinationals leave behind them when they pull up stakes and move production create ideal conditions for another company, or perhaps even another division of the original one, to move in. This dynamic, however, leaves the permanent residents of these regions more deeply impoverished, living amid ecologically deteriorated landscapes, while the transnational operators blithely move on.[34]

NAFTA: The Dangers of Freer Trade

When the North American Free Trade Agreement (NAFTA) went into effect on January 1, 1994, opinion in the United States was split as to whether it would boost our economy by creating jobs producing goods for export to Mexico, or hurt our economy as jobs would be "sucked south" by the lure of low wages and lax environmental standards. Most expected that Mexico would gain jobs, as foreign investors would rush to take advantage of the opportunities created by NAFTA. By 1997 it was clear that the reality was more complex. In a sense both positions were correct, as some jobs were created in the United States, and others moved to Mexico; but in neither case was the number of new jobs nearly enough to compensate for jobs lost. On the U.S. side, net loss had amounted to 250,000 jobs, while Mexico had it even worse with 2 million jobs lost.[35]

In the United States the jobs created to produce exports to Mexico were simply insufficient to cover the jobs that were exported to Mexico in search of lower wages. Meanwhile, Mexico suffered from integration into a larger economy.

What happens when you integrate two economies (or three, in the case of NAFTA, which also includes Canada) is that a larger economy is created. A larger economy automatically leads to economies of scale that favor those companies able to use mass-production techniques to produce more goods at lower prices. Those companies can flood the larger economy with goods at prices so low that smaller firms, which can't afford high-tech, labor-saving technology, cannot compete and go bankrupt instead. The problem is that a mass-produced good—a shoe, for example—requires much less labor than one produced in a

115

medium- or small-scale factory—a shoemaker's shop, for example. That is one reason so many Mexican jobs were lost: Domestic industry was largely medium and small scale and could not compete with a flood of mass-produced goods (another reason is that a decade of free-market reforms to the Mexican economy had so destabilized it that the peso suffered a full-scale collapse).[36]

The result has been fewer jobs and downward pressure on wages on both sides of the U.S.-Mexico border. The freedom that U.S. companies now enjoy to relocate their production sites southward has undermined the bargaining power of workers in the United States,[37] while in Mexico average salaries fell by 40 percent as 28,000 local companies were driven out of business.[38] Between 1993 and 1996 the number of unemployed Mexican workers doubled, and under-employment rose substantially, with an estimated 10 million children having been put to work in informal jobs such as shoe shiners or street vendors to support the newly destitute families.[39] Before NAFTA 32 percent of Mexicans lived at or below the poverty line; that figure is now 51 percent.[40]

Adjusting for Trade

In the last chapter we described some of the consequences of the "structural adjustment" programs that third world governments were forced to accept during the 1980s and 1990s. A central tenet of those programs, imposed by the World Bank and the International Monetary Fund at the behest of Northern countries, was trade liberalization.[41] On the one hand, that meant removing barriers to imports, leading to the flooding of local markets with imports, the hemorrhaging of scarce foreign exchange for luxuries, and many local producers being driven out of business, as we showed in the case of Costa Rica.

On the other hand, it meant reorienting domestic production in each country away from national consumers and toward the export market. This was accomplished by an array of measures under the guise of cutting deficits and stopping government interference with "market forces"—measures such as elimination of subsidies, removal of tariff protection, reduction of credit—designed to make production of food or manufactures for the local market less profitable. At the same time, a series of subsidies, special credits, and free services were created to promote production for export, which often had even more

116

negative impacts on budget deficits than had earlier subsidies of production for the local economy.[42]

In Costa Rica the government created special tax credit certificates called *Certificados de Abono Tributario,* or "CATS," that gave producers of new export products a bonus equal to 15 to 20 percent of the value of those exports. Over the course of the 1980s the cost of the CATS rose from around $8 million to more than $60 million per year, accounting for 8 percent of all government expenditures and 22 percent of the Costa Rican federal deficit.[43] The total cost of the program over its lifetime approached $40 billion,[44] in a country with total yearly exports of less than $1.5 billion.[45] In a classic case of corporate welfare, less than 5 percent of the companies that earned CATS in 1989 received more than 50 percent of the total value, and one, PINDECO, a subsidiary of Del Monte, earned nearly 10 percent of the total, more than three times the amount awarded to the next largest recipient, as this one transnational came to control more than 95 percent of Costa Rican pineapple exports.[46]

Far from the new free-trade policies benefiting Costa Ricans, by the end of the 1980s foreigners owned more than 50 percent of the country's agricultural businesses and heavily dominated exports of macadamia, citrus, flowers, ferns, house plants, papaya, mangoes, and melons.[47] Each export crop came to be controlled by a small elite of large companies, as the percent of total exports accounted for by the top three companies varied from a low of 33 percent for cassava to a high of 99 percent for papaya.[48]

This pattern has been repeated in country after country forced to undergo similar policy prescriptions. In Honduras, for example, the top three companies came to control from 47 percent of plantain exports to 98 percent of pineapple exports; in the case of pineapples, Dole alone accounted for 96 percent.[49] Across Central America, as new exports were promoted and the growing of staple foods for local consumption was undercut, regionwide per capita production of corn, beans, and rice dropped 13, 33, and 6 percent, respectively.[50]

Only a fraction of the revenue generated by the exports remains in the country of origin, in the form of farmworker wages, farmer profit, and local transport and port fees. For every dollar that a U.S. consumer pays for a Honduran melon, some nine cents are spent in Honduras, less than two of which are earned by the farmer.[51] If it's a melon from El Salvador, the farmer earns less than one penny of that dollar.[52] In each case, the big winners are U.S.-based shippers, brokers, wholesalers, and retailers (in many cases the first three are in the hands of a single fruit conglomerate).

GATT and WTO: Locking in the Changes

As the world economy is globalized, what is produced and consumed must increasingly cross international borders. Goods crossing borders have historically provided governments with opportunities to levy taxes: import duties, export taxes, customs fees, etc. These fiscal tools have allowed governments to both generate revenues and exert influence on the directions of national economic development—what will be produced locally versus what will be imported—by regulating trade.

While we might find those to be worthwhile aims, corporations see them as infringing on their freedom to make profits in any way they see fit. They would rather be the ones to determine the directions of economic development in ways that facilitate profit taking, and they would rather not lose part of those potential profits to taxes. Structural adjustment programs forced third world governments to unilaterally reduce or drop taxes on trade and dramatically weakened their ability to influence their own economies, by progressively stripping them of the tools to do so.

Among the mechanisms that governments once used to regulate their own economies that have been eliminated or substantially weakened are tariffs and other trade restrictions, the ability to set exchange rates for national currencies, government spending as a tool to stimulate economies, regulations on foreign investment, and many others.[53] As governments lose those abilities, their economies are increasingly vulnerable to the dictates of economic forces and actors beyond their borders.

Yet structural adjustment policies have not been enough to satisfy the Northern nations, which house so many powerful corporate players. Because these programs were negotiated and imposed in a piecemeal, country-by-country fashion, they offer little guarantee of long-term permanency or irreversibility. In this context, the Uruguay Round of negotiations concerning the General Agreement on Tariffs and Trade (GATT)—an evolving international treaty regulating international trade—was used by the Northern nations to set these changes into much more permanent treaty law via the creation of the World Trade Organization (WTO) on January 1, 1995.

Under structural adjustment third world governments "agreed" to reduce or eliminate tariffs, but with the Uruguay Round accord, third world countries have through treaty law been locked into further reductions and have lost their right to use nontariff barriers—including

subsidies or other favorable treatment for locally produced goods—
to protect their domestic food markets.[54] While Northern countries
made some concessions in terms of reducing some of their tariffs and
cutting some subsidies for their own farmers, those have been trivial
compared to what the third world has had to yield.[55]

The net effect has been to create a distinctly uneven playing field with
clear advantages for both Northern countries and transnational corporations, where the net losers continue to be smaller-scale, more local,
and poorer producers and consumers. The WTO itself is to function as
a "court of ultimate resort," a court *for corporations* that feel that their
rights to trade freely have been hampered by governments.[56]

The Tragedy of the Path Not Taken

Neither NAFTA, nor structural adjustment, nor GATT, nor the WTO
has created the inequitable structures of world trade that allow some
to get richer at the expense of others. The basic structures have been
with us since colonialism or even earlier. What these recent impositions
by Northern countries have done is to reinforce, deepen, and perpetuate those structures. Perhaps the greatest tragedy is that of the path
not taken, for the postwar period has offered us relatively successful
examples of countries that have climbed out of poverty. *But they have
not done so through free trade.* They have done it through inward-oriented
development.

The remarkable post–World War II growth and improvement in living standards in Japan, Taiwan, and Korea were made possible by a
set of policies that included the prohibition of food imports and direct
foreign investment, as well as true land redistribution, massive government subsidies, and tariff protection for domestic manufacturers. The
key was to increase the incomes and purchasing power of the poor—
peasants and workers—who became a strong domestic market that
supported local industries by buying their products. We might call this
"bubble-up" economics, by which the benefits of improved living standards at the base percolate upward through the economy, making true
development possible. This is in contrast to conventional theories,
which argue that net gains for the wealthy will eventually "trickle
down" to the poor, for which reality offers scant evidence. Only after
those first Asian "Tiger" economies became strong did they begin large-
scale exporting,[57] and only recently, under heavy U.S. pressure, have
they begun to relax other parts of the basic policy package.[58]

Sadly, as today's third world countries increasingly find themselves in straitjackets of structural adjustment, free-trade agreements, GATT, and WTO—with their elites as willing collaborators—the possibility of following these positive models becomes more difficult. That is the tragedy of the late twentieth century, though we hope not a permanent one: we have yet to see the treaty that cannot be broken or the policy that cannot be reversed.

Reflections on the Pitfalls and Promises

Because of the title of our earlier book, *Food First*,[59] some have been led mistakenly to believe that we are against all trade—that we advocate autarky, with all people eating from their own backyards. But "food first" does not mean food *only*, or that export crop production is in itself the enemy of the hungry.

In fact, we believe that trade can contribute to development. But in this chapter we want to warn against the uncritical notion that trade in itself represents progress, that exports in themselves generate resources for alleviating hunger and poverty.

To summarize our warning: In most third world societies today free trade and export-oriented agriculture hurt the poor because:

- They allow local economic elites to be unperturbed by the poverty all around them that limits the buying power of local people. By exporting to buyers in higher-paying markets abroad, they can profit anyway.
- They provide incentives to both local and foreign elites to increase their dominion over third world economies and fuel their determination to resist economic and social reforms that might shift production away from exports.
- They necessitate subsistence wages and miserable working conditions. Third world countries "compete" effectively in global free markets only by crushing labor organization and exploiting workers, especially women and children.
- They throw poor farmers in third world countries into competition with foreign producers who dump cheap food into the local economy, driving local producers out of business and increasing the vulnerability of newly food-dependent nations to the capricious swings of global commodity markets.

But recognizing the positive *potential* of trade, we then must ask the same question we asked of the free market in our preceding chapter: Under what conditions can trade contribute to development?

Where third world citizens achieve more equitable claims over the use of resources, including the use of foreign exchange; where agricultural workers are free to organize and bargain collectively, and can build solidarity with their counterparts across national borders; where third world governments cooperate to limit their self-defeating competition and challenge the power of transnational trading corporations' control over markets—under these conditions foreign exchange generated by agricultural exports can contribute to genuine, broad-based development.

Genuinely rewarding trade also requires self-reliance in at least the basics for survival. How else can a nation avoid selling its products at rock-bottom prices, as it desperately seeks foreign exchange to stave off famine? Consider how in recent years China's greater food self-reliance has put it in a position to use the world market, instead of being used by it, as are most third world countries. For decades, China has exported rice and imported wheat, coming out ahead. In this case, no one's survival has depended upon the imported wheat or been threatened by the export of rice. This is true only because Chinese policy has placed a high priority on producing basic foods as well as ensuring adequate purchasing power for most citizens. Furthermore, by "opening" less to the world economy and protecting domestic manufacturers, the Chinese economy has managed to avoid the kind of economic disaster that afflicted Latin American countries in the 1980s and the Asian "Tigers" in the late 1990s.[60]

Free traders might call our preconditions for nonharmful trade utopian, and dismiss them out of hand. But what is more utopian than clinging to a textbook model of comparative advantage, stubbornly refusing to peek out at the real world? Of course, free trade and export agriculture are not themselves the enemy of the hungry; but in this real world of extreme power differentials, both reflect and fuel the forces generating needless hunger.

CHAPTER 9

Myth 9:
Too Hungry to Revolt

MYTH: If initiative for change must come from the poor, then the situation truly is hopeless. Beaten down and ignorant of the real forces oppressing them, poor people are conditioned into a state of passivity. They can hardly be expected to bring about change.

OUR RESPONSE: Bombarded with images of poor people as weak, hungry, and helpless, we lose sight of the obvious: For those with few resources, mere survival requires tremendous effort. The poor often travel great distances just to find work, labor long hours, and see possibilities where most of us would see none. Survival demands resourcefulness and learning the value of joint effort. If the poor were truly passive, few of them could even survive!

But this myth centers on the question of initiative. Can those at the bottom of the social hierarchy, often treated worse than animals, come to realize their innate dignity, grasp their potential for creative action, and then work effectively for change? We know the answer is yes, but how can we be so confident? Because our work has helped us perceive the many examples all around us.

We'll never forget our first research trip together. We drove into northwest Mexico in the fall of 1976. There we talked to poor peasants who only days before had seized land promised to them for decades by the Mexican government. Standing in the middle of the barren fields, we saw no tools, no houses, nothing. We tried not to reveal our skepticism, while wondering to ourselves how they would ever make it.

Almost a decade later, when Institute colleague Medea Benjamin visited the same area, she discovered that we had greatly underestimated the courage and ingenuity of the peasants. In nine years, not only had they achieved yields comparable to those of the neighboring big landowners, but they had developed their own credit, marketing, and insurance systems—so that they were no longer dependent on a government that had proven itself unresponsive to their needs.[1]

A few years later, visiting the Philippines, we met banana plantation workers who labored twelve to fourteen hours a day but still found energy to try to start a union. Holding clandestine meetings, they were risking their jobs and even their lives. The evident courage of the Filipinos we met on that trip, made us, perhaps, less surprised than most Americans when in 1986 millions of Filipinos stood firm and toppled the Marcos dictatorship.

In Nicaragua, we met peasants who inspired our book *Now We Can Speak*. Under the Somoza dictatorship, many had worked for decades to get land of their own. One told us how he and his entire family had finally saved enough money to buy some land, but the big landowner in the area—threatened by their success—had their crop burned. Unable to repay a bank loan, the peasant's family lost their land. But he did not give up. Concluding that his family's only hope was to overthrow Somoza, he chose to fight. Not long after the victory over Somoza, his family received land under the government's reform program. When we visited, they were working the land as a cooperative with other families. While listening to their story, we sat on sacks of newly harvested beans, tangible proof that their suffering had not been in vain.[2]

It turns out that not only are the poor not passive and helpless, but they in fact lead critical movements for change, in the process extending a hand to and mobilizing others less poor than themselves yet also suffering under unjust and undemocratic economic policies.

Mexico. On January 1, 1994, the date NAFTA took effect, the beautiful colonial city of San Cristóbal de las Casas and several other important towns in the southeastern Mexican state of Chiapas were taken militarily by the Zapatista National Liberation Army (EZLN), a ragtag but highly organized guerrilla army consisting mostly of Mexico's poorest people, the long forgotten Mayan Indians.

Inspired by the ideals of Emiliano Zapata, the legendary peasant leader of the Mexican Revolution, these indigenous peasants did not call for ethnic warfare against mestizo (people of mixed Spanish and Indian descent) oppressors, but rather reached out to larger Mexican society. Who, after all, could argue with the essential rightness of their ten basic demands: work, land, a roof, food, health, education, independence, liberty, democracy, justice, and peace?[3] Almost immediately their message found echo and support across the length and breadth of Mexico, even striking a chord internationally. It was the outpouring of international protest in the first few days of the rebellion that forced a reluctant Mexican government to accept a cease-fire and enter into protracted negotiations, which have brought the very nature of Mexican society and politics into question.

The Zapatistas opened a Pandora's box of long-suppressed discontent in the Mexican people, discontent fueled by living standards dragged down during the 1980s and 1990s by the Mexican government's increasing acquiescence to and embracing of free-trade policies. Since January 1, 1994, the Mexican polity has been turned upside down, and powerful popular movements have sprung up among the urban poor, small farmers, schoolteachers, and even credit card and home mortgage holders, in a flowering of grassroots political power. In 1997 the opposition candidate won an overwhelming victory in the first-ever elections for mayor of the capital city, and it seems but a matter of time before the Mexican nation sees yet greater changes. Meanwhile, the Zapatista uprising—and its growing global support movement via the Internet and international activist "summits"—has been viewed by policy makers as a sign of the social costs of free-trade and structural adjustment policies, forcing serious internal discussion if not overt changes.[4]

Brazil. Frustrated by decades of hollow promises by Brazilian politicians to redistribute land, in 1985 landless peasants founded the Movimento dos Trabahaldores Rurais Sem Terra (MST), or Landless Movement. Over the next ten years more than 150,000 landless families occupied more than 21 million hectares of farmland left idle by wealthy landlords. They braved the fury of local elites who hired paramilitary gunmen and pressured the police and army to evict them, which led to several hideous massacres, managing to build many successful cooperatives on the lands they seized. By reaching out to broader Brazilian society—buffeted across social classes by structural adjustment policies and economic crises—they have helped form broad

124

front movements for change. As a result polls show that the majority of Brazilians support their struggle for land and an alternative development strategy that would put people before the profits of the wealthy and giant corporations.[5]

Africa. The "new economic order" of free trade and corporate domination requires struggle at the level of international politics. In the late 1980s, just a few years after the imposition of structural adjustment programs by the World Bank and the IMF, women in many African movements and organizations began to challenge those policies that work against the poor and middle classes. The link was provided by the All African Council of Churches, through a Women's Programme that included an "economic literacy" program. In 1994 women from countries as diverse and distant from one another as Zimbabwe, Kenya, Ghana, Cameroon, and Uganda formed the African Women's Economic Policy Network (AWEPON), constituted to facilitate communication and action among women struggling for a voice in economic policy in Africa.[6]

To date AWEPON consists of seventeen nongovernmental member organizations from twelve African countries, and five international supporters, including the Development Group for Alternative Policies and Oxfam America. One key role of AWEPON has been to articulate the underrepresented viewpoints of African women and the poor in international forums like the United Nations, where policies are created that directly impact their lives. AWEPON is also a forum to share experiences at the local, national, and international levels and promotes training and popular education to strengthen the capacity of African women to influence policy.[7]

India. Small farmers have been at the forefront of struggles against the growing domination of the Indian economy by transnational corporations. Cargill, a giant grain trading corporation and the world's fourth largest seed company, entered the Indian seed business in 1992 with sunflower seeds that failed to produce more than a third of normal yields, driving many farmers close to bankruptcy. Cargill reputedly began buying up seeds locally and reselling them elsewhere in India at up to twenty times the price. Invoking the Gandhian tradition of autonomy, self-reliance, and resistance to colonialism, the Karnataka State Farmers' Association—which has more than 10 million members—burned the seeds, records, computer disks, and other office materials of Cargill Seeds India in a huge bonfire. The farmers said they were campaigning against "free trade, which everyone in India, on the ground, sees as freedom for the corporate world and the ultimate denial of freedom for the citizens of the world."[8]

In July of the following year the farmers sacked and destroyed Cargill India's seed-processing factory.[9] Then on January 30, 1996, they smashed the Kentucky Fried Chicken outlet in Bangalore, in protest over KFC attempts to introduce U.S.-style factory farming of poultry to India.[10] While Cargill and KFC felt they were victims of violent and indefensible vandalism, it is important to understand the farmers' side of the story. According to Institute staff member Anuradha Mittal, who is from India, they were "engaging in non-violent direct action—not aggressive to life—against institutions that pose a threat to their way of life and environment."[11]

The Spark of Change

Many Americans believe that when the poor rise up or otherwise take matters into their own hands, it is because they have been stirred up by outside ideologues taking advantage of their desperation. This view fails to appreciate the varied sources of initiatives for change and how often the poor themselves understand only too well the mechanisms of their oppression.

The poor "have an understanding of the working of the economic system and can describe in detail the processes (wage exploitation, money lending, bribery, and price discrimination) through which exploitation takes place," write four Asian development specialists with years of experience in organizational work with the rural poor.[12] And this view confirms our own experiences in many different parts of the world.

And where the poor aren't rising up against their exploiters, we shouldn't presume that their fatalistic attitudes stand in the way. More likely they have realistically assessed the forces poised against them. Lasse and Lisa Berg, writing of their experiences in India in their book *Face to Face,* observed that while middle-class Indians often explain their daily actions as based on religious beliefs, the poor almost never do. "If asked why they do not revolt," note the Bergs, "they do not answer that they want to be reborn to a better position; they answer that they are afraid of the landowner or the government or the police."[13]

But the poor's perception of the possibility for change can change. It is changing, in fact, as we see in many countries where there are growing movements involving poor people.

The example of others can show that change is possible. In the village of Shivalaya in southern Bangladesh, Karima's small son died because her husband, a landless laborer, did not have enough money for medicine. Despite her poverty, her illiteracy, and women's customary dependency on men and isolation from one another, Karima was determined to prevent such a tragedy from happening again.

Over a period of weeks, she brought together other landless women from the village. Together they decided to save money, taka by taka, so that any member could borrow to buy medicine in an emergency. They also persuaded the village teacher to help them learn to read and keep basic accounts. Two years later, during which time they had often talked over their common problems and their numbers grew, they decided to pool all their money. With the sum they rented a small plot to grow potatoes and sugarcane. Their profits went to buy better tools and a calf, which they fattened and sold at a nice profit. They then planted vegetables for local markets and raised a few chickens. Part of their profits helped launch a basic nutrition education program.

As word of the accomplishments of these women from poor, landless families spread, poor women from nearby villages came to see for themselves. In less than two years, some thirty cooperatives started by over a thousand landless women had sprung up. As the movement continued to spread from village to village, a number of the women's cooperatives initiated programs such as small schools to teach themselves and their children better farming techniques.[14]

The belief that one's sacrifice has meaning, even if the rewards are not in one's own lifetime, can be a force for change. History has shown the willingness of human beings to face indignities and suffer brutality for goals realizable only beyond their own lifetimes. Why? Each of us would probably answer that question differently. Many people will unhesitatingly do what they would never do for themselves if they believe it has even a chance of bettering the lives of their children. On our many visits into rebel territory in Chiapas, we have been struck by the oft-repeated slogan of the Zapatista militias, words that speak to personal sacrifice for a better world: *"Para Todos, Todo; Para Nosotros, Nada,"* ("For Everyone, Everything; For Ourselves, Nothing").

For many, religious faith—instead of instilling a fatalistic acceptance of their misery—inspires the decision to act. Many Nicaraguans who participated in the overthrow of Somoza told us that their religious convictions ultimately left them no choice but to act. "The priest in my community helped me to understand that we all are made in God's image, and so we too have rights, above all the right to live," one peasant told us. "And that means we have the right to land to feed our families."

Religious faith motivated many in the Philippines who worked for years to free their country from the Marcoses. Who will forget the televised images of nuns blocking the way of army tanks on the streets of Manila? In Haiti, in the final years of the Duvalier tyranny, the key resistance movement grew out of over two thousand grassroots Christian communities and the Catholic radio station's broadcasts in Creole about the injustices and horrors of the regime.[15]

Sometimes a disaster "helps" by shaking up old patterns and perceptions. In Kuala Juru, a tiny fishing village in Malaysia, fishermen banded together to confront the destruction of their river by chemical pollutants. While they did not stop the pollution, the experience of joining together in protest led to a common strategy to rebuild their shattered economy. They switched from individual fishing to cooperative farming of cockle, a fish more resistant to the pollutants. All members share the harvests and profits, and the collective savings of the cooperative have allowed it to set up a coffee shop and sundries store.[16]

Getting Onboard

Many of us see the poor as passive victims because of the selective way news of the world comes to us. How many poor people have you seen interviewed on the evening news or in your newspaper? The newsmakers appear to be only government officials and business leaders, never poor people. We must regularly bring alternative sources of news into our lives; otherwise, the real struggles for change will remain invisible. The search for news that reveals more of the real world is a goal of Food First. That's why in the final section of this book, we suggest some of the news sources we have found useful.

Thinking of the third world's poor as passive also confuses us about the nature of our responsibility. Visualizing hungry people as so oppressed as to be ignorant and immobilized makes us think our responsibility is to go in and set things straight. In our next chapter, we challenge this assumption.

Wherever people are suffering needlessly, "the train is already moving"—that is, movements for change are already underway. Appreciating this truth, we understand our responsibility differently. It is not to start the train, but to remove the obstacles in its path and to get onboard ourselves!

CHAPTER 10

Myth 10:
More U.S. Aid Will Help the Hungry

MYTH: In helping to end world hunger, our primary responsibility as U.S. citizens is to increase and improve our government's foreign aid.

OUR RESPONSE: Once we learned that hunger results from antidemocratic political and economic structures that trap people in poverty, we realized that we couldn't end hunger for other people. Genuine freedom can only be won by people for themselves.

This realization doesn't lessen our responsibility, but it does profoundly redefine its nature. Our job isn't to intervene in other countries and set things right. Our government is *already* intervening in countries where the majority of people are forced to go hungry. Our primary responsibility as U.S. citizens is to make certain our government's policies are not making it harder for people to end hunger for themselves.

In light of the demonstrated generosity of many Americans, most of us would probably be chagrined to learn that U.S. foreign aid is only 0.15 percent of our nation's gross national product—that's less than half the percentage of GNP Germany provides, for example, and less than one-fifth of that provided by the Netherlands.[1] Total U.S. bilateral assistance dropped greatly during the first half of the 1990s, as it has for most other wealthy nations.[2] From a high of $20.2 billion in 1985, it fell to $12.3 billion by 1994 and has remained low.[3]

For the world's hungry, however, the problem isn't the stinginess of our aid. When our levels of assistance last boomed, under Ronald Reagan in the mid-1980s, the emphasis was hardly on eliminating hunger. In 1985, Secretary of State George Shultz stated flatly that "our foreign assistance programs are vital to the achievement of our foreign policy goals."[4] But Shultz's statement shouldn't surprise us. Every country's foreign aid is a tool of foreign policy. Whether that aid benefits the hungry is determined by the motives and goals of that policy— by how a government defines the national interest.

During the postwar decades of the Cold War, U.S. foreign assistance was largely defined by a view of the world as divided into two opposing camps. That often meant arming and propping up undemocratic and repressive governments—in Iran, the Philippines, El Salvador, Indonesia, and many other countries—only because they were loyal U.S. allies.

The U.S. government acted as if our vital interests were threatened by any experiment that didn't mimic the U.S. economic model—the free market and unlimited private accumulation of productive assets. Any nation seeking to alter its economic ground rules—Nicaragua, for example—was immediately perceived as having "gone over to the other camp" and thus an enemy. Punishment was swift—usually including the suspension of aid and the arming of opponents of the offending government.[5]

In the rather negative panorama of the Cold War, U.S. foreign assistance did nevertheless have poverty alleviation as a goal, albeit not for the best of motives. Driven by the fear that "communism" would defeat capitalism in the battle for the "hearts and minds" of poor third world populations—by offering them the possibility of greater improvements in material well-being—the United States followed an on-again-off-again policy of funding "basic needs."

In Central America, while propping up corrupt dictatorships with Economic Support Funds (ESF)—basically cash disbursements—and keeping them in power with generous military aid and training, the United States also pressed for and financed basic poverty alleviation policies. The latter included very limited land reforms, marketing boards to help small farmers sell their grain, basic infrastructure development, etc. These reforms were seen as necessary complements to military aid to mollify the populace and keep our friendly strongmen from being overthrown by the disgruntled masses.[6]

During the entire Cold War it often seemed as though the real goal of foreign aid was making the world safe for U.S.-based corporations.

Nevertheless, this goal was often mixed up with Cold War strategic aims, making such a black-and-white analysis difficult. Since the end of the Cold War, however, the more blatant economic aims of foreign assistance have come to the forefront.

From defending freedom in the face of the "communist threat," the goals of foreign aid have more clearly emerged as the promotion of the free market and free trade—of the sort we described in chapters 7 and 8. A 1997 newsletter of the U.S. Agency for International Development (USAID), the government agency in charge of U.S. foreign assistance, put it this way: "The principal beneficiary of America's foreign assistance has always been the United States. .... Foreign assistance programs have helped the United States by creating major markets for agricultural goods, new markets for industrial exports and hundreds of thousands of jobs for Americans."[7] The same report argued forcefully that the amount of money spent on aid be upped significantly in order to maintain U.S. "leadership in the global arena."[8]

Defining our national interest as opening markets for free trade lines up our nation's might—with our tax dollars and our country's good name—against the interests of the hungry. As we have seen, a different kind of change—profound, society-wide change in control over food-producing resources—is a *sine qua non* for ending hunger. It is impossible to be both against this kind of change and for the hungry.

Poverty Is Not the Focus of Aid

Looking at our foreign aid, we want to highlight seven of the consequences of the current definition of the national interest.

First, U.S. economic assistance is highly concentrated on a few governments. Its focus has nothing to do with poverty. Out of the 130–odd governments receiving U.S. bilateral economic assistance in the mid-1990s,[9] just 15 countries got over half of the total (see table). Israel and Egypt—representing U.S. geopolitical interests—together got almost one-third. The world's 10 poorest countries—most of them in Africa— received less than 5 percent of all U.S. bilateral economic assistance in fiscal year 1994.[10] Despite widespread poverty in sub-Saharan Africa, for example, only two of the top ten recipients, South Africa and Ethiopia, are in that region, and the former is its most economically developed nation.

Top 15 Recipients of U.S. Economic Assistance*
in 1996 ($ millions)

1. Israel	1,200.0
2. Egypt	815.0
3. Russia	263.0
4. Ukraine	161.4
5. India	156.3
6. South Africa	131.9
7. Peru	123.9
8. Bolivia	121.0
9. Haiti	116.0
10. Ethiopia	108.0
11. Turkey	105.8
12. Bosnia-Hercegovina	80.6
13. Bangladesh	77.8
14. West Bank/Gaza	76.0
15. Philippines	74.9

*Economic assistance includes development assistance, Economic Support Fund, Food Aid, Peace Corps, International Narcotics Control.

Source: U.S. Agency for International Development, Congressional Presentation, Fiscal Year 1996 Request.

Lured by the opportunities of virgin markets, U.S. foreign policy and assistance have found a new target: Eastern Europe and the former Soviet Union, which now compete for aid with the much poorer third world countries (see table).

Second, aid is used as a lever to impose structural adjustment packages on the third world. Since the 1980s U.S. foreign assistance worldwide has been conditioned on the adoption of structural adjustment packages designed by the World Bank and the International Monetary Fund,[11] policies that we described in chapters 7 and 8.

Making a grant or loan conditional on some action being taken by the recipient is called "conditionality." Conditionality works by "tranching" economic assistance packages—that is, dividing the total sum to be donated or loaned to a recipient country into a series of smaller disbursements to be made over time, called tranches. Before each disbursement is made, the recipient must make policy changes spelled out in the "covenants" of the aid agreement that they must sign with USAID.[12]

132

Between 1982 and 1990 nine U.S. economic assistance packages provided to the Costa Rican government contained a total of 357 "covenants" that made disbursement conditional on more than twenty structural changes in the domestic economy. These included eliminating a grain marketing board that assisted small farmers; slashing support prices for locally grown corn, beans, and rice; allowing more imports from the United States; easing regulations on foreign investment and capital flows; and complying with specific clauses in similar agreements signed with the World Bank and the IMF.[13]

Such conditionality works in a carrot-and-stick fashion. When the Costa Rican congress balked at approving an outrageous new law demanded by the United States that would allow aid to bypass the government and go directly to the private sector, USAID suspended a $23 million disbursement.[14] Ironically, this came at the very moment at which the Costa Rican Central Bank had exhausted the foreign exchange reserves needed for the daily operation of the economy. An internal USAID memo written several months before the incident occurred—which we obtained access to years later—showed just how cynical the United States can be. A top USAID administrator predicted the month in which the reserves would run dry and recommended timing a key disbursement to take advantage of that moment as leverage to guarantee that the desired law would be passed.[15]

It was precisely the replication of changes like this—and of structural adjustment—throughout the third world that produced rising inequalities in the 1980s and 1990s. For most of the third world the 1980s were a lost decade, during which living standards of impoverished majorities fell to pre-1960s levels. Not surprisingly, this became a period of widespread economic, social, and ecological crisis. Millions of the rural and urban poor were cut out from opportunities for progress. Credit, extension, subsidies, and technical education all fell by the wayside as budgets were slashed, and the lifting of tariffs flooded local economies with imported foodstuffs often placed on the world market at prices below local costs of production. As a consequence, poor farmers were caught in a squeeze between the high price of chemicals and other farm inputs and low crop prices, often losing their lands and moving to cities.[16]

Third, food aid often does not target the hungry. When they hear about foreign aid, many people automatically think of ships loaded with food, but such aid constitutes only a fraction of total U.S. bilateral foreign aid, hovering around 9 percent during the 1990s.[17] Moreover, only about 5 percent of total aid is for emergency relief.[18]

Of the nearly 3 million tons of food aid provided by the United States in 1996, almost one-quarter was in the form of PL 480 Title I sales,[19] in which food is sold to third world governments on easy credit terms for resale to local livestock industries as feed, and to local food-processing companies who make pasta, bread, cooking oil, and other products for urban consumers.[20] While the proceeds from these sales must generally be used for "development" purposes, which are specified by USAID, Title I has long been used as a primary tool to create new markets for U.S. grain exports. In practice, it functions as corporate welfare. According to a study published by the University of Nebraska Press:

> The food-aid program represents a free government service designed to help grain-trading companies expand both their current and future sales. Title I sales generate the same profits for the big U.S. grain companies as does any other commercial export. The only difference is that the U.S. government immediately pays the bill. From the point of view of the grain corporations, then, Title I creates immediate markets by having the U.S. government finance purchases that otherwise might not have been made. The recipient countries, meanwhile, come to depend on these foreign food supplies. . . . By encouraging the growth of poultry farms, wheat mills, and soap and vegetable-oil factories, PL 480 helps create a structural dependence on continued imports. When the food aid stops, these industries, needing the supplies to continue their level of operations, will pressure their governments to keep importing the commodities on commercial terms.[21]

USAID bragged in a 1996 report on food aid that "nine out of ten countries importing U.S. agricultural products are former recipients of food assistance."[22] Far from feeding the hungry, Title I food aid first of all puts money in the pockets of giant grain corporations like Cargill, who provide and ship the products;[23] second, supports factory-style poultry producers and food processors; and finally, helps shift consumer tastes in recipient countries away from locally grown crops toward wheat products like bread and pasta.[24]

Much aid to Africa, for example, has been in the form of wheat, even though wheat grows well in very few parts of the tropics. For many countries, such a shifting of tastes is no small concern—it makes long-term self-reliance even more difficult. South Korea became the largest third world importer of U.S. agricultural goods after years of food aid coupled with intensive marketing of wheat products by AID. This marketing campaign changed the South Korean diet drastically by creating a growing demand for wheat.[25]

Even the funds earned from food sales that are earmarked for "development" frequently end up working against the hungry. These often go for so-called "self-help" measures, like the promotion of further trade with the United States, and market-development activities like trade fairs and port construction.[26]

A second kind of food aid, Title III, works just like Title I but is for poorer countries, allowing the United States to forgive the loans for the purchased food. In 1996 it accounted for about one-eighth of total food shipped.

The Food for Progress program, another type of food aid, was created in 1985 to reward governments who undertake structural adjustment programs. According to the enabling legislation, Food for Progress was "designed to expand free enterprise elements of the economies of developing countries through changes in commodity pricing, marketing, import availability, and increased private-sector involvement."[27] In other words, food is once again being used as a lever to open markets for U.S.-based corporations. While Food for Progress was originally targeted at the third world, the emphasis soon shifted: In 1996, thirty-seven of the thirty-eight donations made under this program went to former socialist countries in Eastern Europe,[28] the newest frontier in market opportunities for U.S. food exporters. Food for Progress shipments accounted for one-seventh of the food donated that year.[29]

The remaining category of food aid, Title II, consists of food that is donated either to support specific development projects or for emergency relief, generally in poor countries, and it accounted for slightly more than half of the food shipped in 1996.[30] These, finally, are the proverbial shiploads that we imagine being sent to the poor in third world countries. Yet even this food often has less than positive impacts.

Title II development food aid is usually distributed through so-called "food-for-work" programs that hire the jobless to provide manual labor for road improvement, irrigation development, and other infrastructure projects, in exchange for food. In theory, society as a whole benefits from this sort of program—the jobless get to eat, while the rest of society gains from the public works projects. Yet a careful examination shows that food-for-work benefits the well-off disproportionally, while the poor receive no long-term gains.

An example from Haiti, where so many people are deprived of enough to eat, makes this clear. In a particular village, one family controlled the local government and community offices.[31] When a U.S. relief agency came to the village with a food-for-work program, this same family was chosen to administer it. Jobless villagers built roads and tended the gardens of a well-to-do village leader, which took them away from their lands five days a week. The wealthy family gained benefits through the improvement of their lands, better access to markets for their produce, and increased patronage power. The workers gained temporary work, which provided food during the slack agricultural season, at the cost of not attending to their own plots, but they did not gain long-term, fundamental changes or a sustainable lessening of their poverty and hunger. Similar stories dot the landscape of food-for-work programs.[32]

Fourth, food aid can actually forestall agricultural development that could otherwise alleviate hunger. The inflow of food aid—even in many emergency cases—has proved time and again to be detrimental to local farm economies. Cheap, subsidized, or free U.S. grains undercut the prices of locally produced food, driving local farmers out of business and into cities.

Somalia is only one case in point. When a civil war began in 1991, domestic transportation was interrupted, precipitating a food crisis in large regions of the country. The UN estimated that almost 4.5 million people—over half of the estimated total population of the country—were threatened by severe undernutrition and malnutrition-related diseases at that time.[33]

Yet in December of 1992, when U.S. troops landed under the UN banner to distribute food and achieve a cease-fire among hostile factions, the worst of the famine was already over. The death rate had dropped from three hundred per day to seventy, and good crops of rice, sorghum, and corn from the agricultural regions of Afgoye and the Shebell River valley had already been harvested.[34] Nonetheless, food aid poured in, driving down the prices received by local farmers for their harvest by a whopping 75 percent. Sometimes they couldn't sell their crops even at the lower prices. Mrs. Faaduma Abdi Arush, a Somali farmer, tried to sell her corn to six relief agencies. None would buy it, as the U.S. government only provided them with funds to buy American food from U.S. companies. Many Somali farmers, unable to make a living by selling their produce, were forced to abandon their farms and join the lines for handouts of imported food.[35]

Nonemergency Title II food aid is sometimes used to support activities such as mother and child health, nutrition, and education programs.[36] The cash for the programs is raised by selling food aid in the recipient country. Or the food is used for lunch programs as an incentive for children to stay in school, or mothers at health centers receive food when they bring their babies to be treated.

While many of these activities seem at first glance to be laudable, we need to look deeper. First and foremost, this kind of food aid is still about the injection of food into the economy of recipient countries, which results in the distortion of food markets. Just as it does with other forms of food aid, this distortion weakens the local food system, drives farmers off the land, and ultimately creates long-term dependency on imported U.S. agricultural commodities.[37] These effects remain whether we are talking about food-for-work, health, or school programs.[38] That is not to say that all programs supported by food aid are misguided. Rather, other ways are needed to carry them out.

For example, mother and child health and nutrition programs can offer substantial benefits to recipients. The alternative to using imported food for these programs should be to purchase food from surrounding areas.[39] This system would strengthen farmers, local merchants, and the economy of the country, as local expertise, knowledge, and resources are utilized to produce the food. As income is generated internally, communities become self-sufficient and sustainable.

However, food aid–based development projects continue to depend on foreign expertise, knowledge, and outside resources to generate income. These projects are not self-sufficient, nor are they sustainable when the aid ends. Not surprisingly, food aid–based development projects have historically been failures. Says former food-aid manager Michael Maren, "Africa is littered with the ruins of such projects."[40]

Fifth, through military aid, the United States contributes directly to armed conflicts around the world—which are a major cause of hunger and famine. Since the end of the Cold War, U.S. military aid has declined, yet in 1998 it still totaled $6 billion, outweighing development assistance by a six-to-one ratio.[41] Arms sales add significantly to the impact of our military aid. Needing to cope with an overproduction problem in the post–Cold War era, American defense contractors have aggressively sought overseas markets, usually with government subsidies to do so. U.S. arms sales in the early 1990s exceeded those of all other nations combined.[42] Global military expenditure by governments is estimated at $1 trillion annually,[43] and that doesn't take into account illicit arms trafficking to nongovernmental belligerents. For every four weapons involved in such trafficking, three are estimated to come from the United States, many of them originally via aid or credits.[44]

Between 1985 and 1995, the belligerent parties in forty-five conflicts around the globe obtained $42 billion worth of weapons from the United States. In 90 percent of the fifty most significant conflicts in 1993–94, one or more parties received U.S. weapons or military technology.[45] Through trafficking, arms sales, and military aid, the United States helps keep dozens of civil wars and other armed conflicts around the world alive and kicking. This is particularly alarming in light of our conclusion in chapter 3 that contemporary episodes of famine are often the product of armed conflicts like that which took place in Somalia. U.S. arm sales and military aid make that possible.

Sixth, "good" aid projects serve a public relations, "window dressing" or "fig leaf" function that obscures an uglier reality. Focusing on the best projects funded by USAID can be misleading as to the overall impact of foreign aid. There are no doubt some projects that when viewed outside of the larger context appear unambiguously positive— but in the final analysis they really facilitate the far more common programs that have net negative impacts, simply because the "best projects" make the very idea of aid more palatable.

In the 1990s "humanitarian relief" missions, festooned with journalists and slick publicity, have been key to building a positive image of USAID—even though such activities represent a tiny proportion of the agency's budget and have ample problems of their own as described above. Environmental projects can also play a public relations role.

One of us had the opportunity to work with such an environmental effort during the 1980s and early 1990s, the Integrated Pest Management Project for Central America. Initially funded with $5 million from USAID, the project's laudable goal was to reduce pesticide use among small farmers in Central America. Who could argue with that? Nevertheless, our experience makes us think twice whenever we see something from USAID that seems too good to be true.

The project suffered from a typical design flaw, namely, a top-down conception of technological change. Project scientists—mostly Ph.D.-trained expatriates—were to research alternatives to pesticides and then train national "experts" in each country, who were to train local extension agents, who would then transmit the new information to farmers. Of course, this rarely happened—because of kinks in the long chain of collaborating institutions and individuals and because the alternatives finally presented to farmers rarely fit their reality.

The initial funding was approved at the tail end of the "basic needs" period of U.S. foreign assistance, so the project was said to be targeted at small farmers growing food crops, but project implementation coincided with the new emphasis in the 1980s on structural adjustment and related export promotion. Thus, USAID functionaries continually pressed project staff and the host institution to switch our focus to export crops and larger farmers. The host institution and staff held out against these changes, eventually leading USAID to discontinue its support for the project and redirect its funds to more pliable host organizations.[46]

Before the project's funding was terminated, an incident occurred that would be comical if it were not so sad. Congress passed a new requirement that USAID projects incorporate both "women and men" as beneficiaries, in response to criticisms that assistance favored men and left women out. This regulation was imposed when the project came up for renewal. A memo went out from USAID headquarters instructing all field staff to be sure to incorporate the new requirement in future funding requests. In response, the project leader had a secretary do a universal "search and replace" in her word processor. Each time the words "people," "persons," "farmers," "students," "beneficiaries," etc., were used in the renewal request they were replaced with, or preceded by, "women and men." Thus, one section read that "24 women and men farmers will be invited to the field day." No other changes were made to the proposal, which was approved without comment. In subsequent congressional hearings, USAID staff were able to argue that gender was now an integral component of development aid.

But these details about the project actually miss the real reason its overall impacts have been negative. The project was frequently used by USAID to show policy makers, journalists, Central American government functionaries, and others the friendly face of U.S. policy in the region. Even though it accounted for a tiny fraction of USAID money spent during the 1980s, it had a high profile. Thus, it served as a fig leaf hiding the true thrust of aid spending in the region: the overthrow of the revolutionary Sandinista government in Nicaragua[47] and the structural adjustment of the region's other economies.[48] In the end, its real function in the larger scheme of things was to make the overall U.S. presence in Central America more palatable, thus indirectly facilitating less beneficent ends.

Finally, even most "development assistance" fails to help the poor and hungry. Only 18 percent of U.S. bilateral aid is even called development assistance. How is this development aid spent? During the 1960s and early 1970s, much of it went to install infrastructure (power plants, transportation and communication facilities, and the like) benefiting mainly businessmen, landlords, and others in an economic position to take advantage of such facilities. In the late 1970s and early 1980s, the trend was more toward smaller-scale projects, including agricultural credit programs and the development of small and medium-size businesses. But even these smaller-scale projects failed to reach the poorest, concluded a major study by the World Bank and the International Monetary Fund.[49]

This general finding was borne out by USAID's own program evaluations. One report reviewing twelve years of small-farm credit programs noted that benefits were "highly skewed against the small farmer and the landless poor."[50] The reasons for this failure were clear enough—very few of the poor had titles to farms large enough to satisfy the requirements of a credit application. Since the majority of rural poor in most third world countries are landless, even the best farm credit program could never help them.

In the 1980s and 1990s a major trend has been to promote nontraditional exports. In Central America, for example, USAID has been pushing farmers into hopelessly competing for volatile niche markets by promoting new export crops. These Non-Traditional Agricultural Exports (NTAEs) range from passion fruit and broccoli to macadamia nuts and melons and have been vigorously advanced through massive foreign aid subsidies and fierce pressure on local governments. Central American farmers and governments now find themselves saddled with risky agricultural ventures that have destabilized traditional production of food crops for local consumption. The net result is deepening poverty and economic insecurity in agricultural communities throughout Central America. In stark contrast to USAID's stated aim of stabilizing Central America's economies, NTAE programs have intensified the inequities between small farmers and wealthy landowners.[51]

A 1983 USAID project in the Guácimo district of Costa Rica offers a poignant yet not atypical case in point. Investing money, credit, technical assistance, and marketing expertise, USAID encouraged poor farmers at the El Indio land settlement to switch from traditional yellow corn production to cocoa, tuber crops, and ayote squash for export to the growing Latino market in the United States. In the project's first season, farmers were provided with imported, disease-free seed, a full-time extension agent, and an advance purchase contract. The incomes of the farmers who participated soared in the first year, up to forty times more per acre than their neighbors who continued growing corn.

But just one year later, the El Indio venture began to unravel. The NTAE project no longer provided seeds, there was no marketing contract, and the extension agent was employed only part-time. Still, enticed by the previous year's success, more farmers took the plunge. The results were disastrous. Crop prices dropped as global competition heightened. Due to the low-grade seeds used the second year, much of the harvest was hit by disease—discouraging buyers from all but a small portion of the crops. Half of the farmers defaulted on their credit, and the forty who persisted defaulted in the following year.[52]

The El Indio experience and many others like it provide a cautionary tale of the pitfalls of pushing exports at all costs. Promoting capital-intensive crops for unproven markets, NTAE projects are a high-stakes gamble for peasants. Small farmers face hurdles at every step along the way.

In Guatemala, for example, the initial investment to plant nontraditional export crops ranges from five to fifteen times higher than that for traditional corn and beans.[53] Crossing this barrier means taking out risky credit and loans that frequently have interest rates biased against poor farmers and can easily lead to losing the farm after a bad harvest.[54]

The fate of small farmers in the nontraditionals industry has been similar to their fate with traditional exports and in the Green Revolution. Nontraditionals are expensive to produce—requiring enormous quantities of pesticide, fertilizer, and technical expertise, favoring larger, better capitalized producers. Because these are perishable products, small farmers are often unable to place their produce in Northern markets with quality standards, giving the edge to the giant fruit companies.

Unable to compete with better-financed growers, and heavily in debt because of high production costs, many small farmers have been driven out of business by trying to produce nontraditional exports. At the same time, chemical pesticides and fertilizers have seriously degraded the productive capacity of the soil in many regions and contaminated the environment.[55]

Growing corn and other basic staples is no longer profitable either, due to the flooding of local markets with cheap grain via free trade, and to cutbacks in price supports and marketing imposed by structural adjustment programs. As a result, small farmers have migrated to cities and to developed countries in huge numbers, fleeing the policy-driven collapse of rural livelihoods. The winners under current policies have been, first and foremost, international companies able to compete in the emerging global food system, and the net losers have clearly been the rural poor and the environment.

While the poor may not be the chief beneficiaries of development assistance projects, one group that does benefit handsomely includes the U.S. corporations, consulting companies, and universities that get USAID contracts. An independent study found that 29 percent of U.S. development assistance was 100 percent tied to purchases from companies in the United States—an amount greater than the total of U.S. assistance to sub-Saharan Africa.[56]

Funds for aid pass though many hands before reaching the supposed beneficiaries. So the question we must ask is, How likely is it that resources channeled through the *powerful* will help the *powerless*?

The already better off are positioned to capture a disproportionate share of any economic gains offered by development aid. And with their new resources, they can often further tighten their grip over land and other productive resources, thereby worsening the plight of the poor. Thanks to a bribe to a technician, an irrigation pump earmarked for a cooperative of poor farmers in Bangladesh winds up belonging to the village's richest landowner; he graciously allows his neighbors water from the new well in exchange for a third of their harvests. The pump and the added revenue give the "waterlord" the incentive to take over more land by foreclosing on the small farmers in debt to him. Thanks to his heightened prosperity, the landowner can now buy an imported tractor, eliminating desperately needed jobs for the village's landless families.

This and similar scenarios, endlessly repeated, entrench the already well off and add to their incentive to fight demands for democratic control over productive resources. In many countries, rich landowners are known to hire thugs to intimidate and even murder villagers who dare to protest or organize self-help cooperatives.

Only projects that reinforce the poor's initiatives to tackle the extreme inequalities in power within the village have a chance of improving the lives of the majority. However, most governments are unlikely to look kindly on such activities, for fear of antagonizing powerful elites.

But we hesitate even to use this space to question the possibility of government-sponsored development projects helping the poor within elite-dominated societies. To do so may mislead, for it is so easy to lose sight of the big picture.

142

No matter how sensitively designed the aid project, prospects for the poor majority—whether they will have land, jobs, food, and economic security—hinge largely on forces *outside* their villages. To whom is their government accountable? To whom are international bankers who make loans to their government accountable? And what about the corporations dominating trade in their country's exports? Such questions point us to what we call the iceberg. Foreign aid is only the tip.

The Iceberg

Focusing only on official aid can blind us to many other ways we citizens of the United States are linked to the lives—and hopes—of the hungry. We need to take responsibility not just for what our government does in the name of "aid" and otherwise—but also for what corporations and other institutions based in our country do (often supported directly or indirectly by our "aid" and other subsidies).

The iceberg is the action of the private sector—transnational corporations, investors, and currency speculators—and the less visible actions of the United States and other Northern governments to support their free rein in the third world. Some forty thousand corporations control two-thirds of global trade in goods and services, and most of that is in the hands of only a few hundred corporate giants.[57] In 1995, for example, General Motors' sales were greater than the gross national product of 169 countries, including Saudi Arabia, South Africa, Malaysia, and Norway.[58]

In the last few years, there has been a tremendous increase in private foreign investment, concentrated in the wealthier developing countries. The World Bank reports that the overall volume of private-capital flows to developing countries quadrupled in the first half of the 1990s, accounting for three-quarters of all long-term flows to developing countries.[59] While governments are backing out, private investors are taking their place. Private investment has become the main source of external financing for many middle-income countries, though the majority of low-income countries still rely primarily on official sources of financing.[60] That may yet change as corporations seek virgin territory for new investments.

In 1996 the Clinton administration announced plans to boost the 8 percent U.S. share of the sub-Saharan Africa market, meager in comparison to Europe's 40 percent share.[61] The United States is using free-trade language to argue that Africa, the "last frontier of American business,"[62] should open up to greater U.S. trade and investment.[63] Key, high-profit sectors of African economies, such as infrastructure (roads, telecommunications) and mining are targeted.[64] In June of 1997, at the G-8 Africa Summit in Denver, reminiscent of the famous 1883 Berlin Conference scramble for Africa, the future of African trade was discussed by the Northern countries, in the conspicuous absence of African delegates.[65]

Over and above its foreign aid program, through numerous other public channels (not to mention covert ones like the CIA), the U.S. government supports policies that promote business interests, often in ways diametrically opposed to the interests of the hungry.

U.S. government agencies like the Export-Import Bank (EXIMBANK) and the Overseas Private Investment Corporation (OPIC) can have a greater impact on the economy and policies of a third world country than official U.S. foreign aid, although few Americans have ever heard of them. Both offer financing and loan guarantees—backed by U.S. taxpayers—to finance exports of goods and services. In accordance with the turn toward greater private capital flows relative to official aid, EXIMBANK loans, guarantees, and insurance rose from $12 billion in 1980 to $53 billion in 1995,[66] more than five times greater than total U.S. foreign assistance.[67] In more than one case of corporate welfare, EXIMBANK largely backs the efforts of transnational corporations like Boeing, General Electric, and Westinghouse to penetrate overseas markets and outcompete local companies. Small U.S.-based businesses receive only 12–15 percent of EXIMBANK financing.[68] In the mid-1990s OPIC supported $84 billion of investments by U.S. corporations in 140 countries and played a key role in the corporate takeover of the former Soviet bloc countries in Eastern Europe.[69]

How Aid Could Benefit the Hungry

Whether U.S. foreign aid can benefit the hungry depends on how our government defines our national interest. Thus, a first step in putting ourselves on the side of the hungry is to work to *change our government's definition of our national interest.* Less control—less striving to make the world conform to the U.S. model and respond to U.S. fears—would actually mean more security for all.

After years of studying our foreign aid program, we have learned that foreign aid is only as good as the recipient government. *Foreign aid only reinforces the status quo.* It cannot transform an antidemocratic process working against the majority into a participatory government shaped in its interests. Where the recipient government answers only to a narrow economic elite or foreign corporations, our aid not only fails to reach the hungry, it girds the very forces working against them.

We do not suggest that we simply abolish foreign aid. The accumulated debt "owed" to the third world by Northern countries for centuries of unbridled profit taking through conquest, colonialism, mineral and other natural resource extraction, unequal trade, labor exploitation, and other forms of corporate pillage is too great to say nothing should be sent back.[70]

The problem is *how* to give something back, since as we've seen in this chapter, even the best-intentioned humanitarian aid can have negative consequences if the recipient government is based on elite local and foreign interests.

An immediate step that we as citizens can take is to tell our representatives that the best use for our money is not supporting the status quo but alleviating the largest economic barrier to true development in the third world—its foreign debt.

The combined debt of third world countries reached almost $2 trillion in 1996.[71] The bulk was accumulated largely as a result of Northern banks—flush with the "petrodollars" deposited with them by oil-producing countries in the 1970s—needing to place an unprecedented volume of loans. Once developed countries were "borrowed out," the banks turned to the third world, like snake-oil salesmen, selling huge loans for megaprojects that many knew would never pan out. The structural adjustment programs of the 1980s and 1990s have been designed in part to induce the third world to pay off that debt; the IMF and World Bank acting out the role of debt collectors for private banks. In various refinancing agreements, the debt owed to private banks has been assumed by agencies like the IMF, who are ultimately funded by taxpayers, and to whom much of the debt is now owed.[72]

That debt—for which the lenders bear as much or more responsibility than the borrowers, is now stifling economic development and social services throughout the third world. Repayments from Zambia to the IMF between 1991 and 1993 were $335 million, compared to $37 million spent on primary education. In Honduras, annual debt payments exceed the amount spent on health and education combined.[73]

In fact, annual interest payments alone by all third world countries amounted to $81 and $85 billion in 1994 and 1995, respectively, roughly equal to the $80 and $90 billion they received in total direct foreign investment and easily outstripping the $48 and $64 billion they received in total development assistance from Northern countries. Total debt payments (principal plus interest) were $190 and $213 billion in the same years, greater than the sum of investment plus assistance.[74]

Our institute and two hundred other organizations have joined together in the 50 Years is Enough Campaign against the IMF and the World Bank. These two institutions, which celebrated their fiftieth anniversaries in 1994, play key roles in policing the third world's debt. The campaign calls for debt relief for third world countries. Aid dollars could be made into something positive and noninterventionist if they were spent on debt relief—as long as they were not tied to structural adjustment–like conditions, which are so onerous for the poorer majorities.

One could argue that such unconditional debt relief might not end up benefiting the hungry, either—because most third world governments do not truly represent their poor majorities. This is a legitimate concern—yet, in the end, if we have learned anything, it is that real change starts with people themselves. Our job is to not block that change through conditional aid, or equally conditioned debt relief, that mandates the strengthening of a status quo in which the rich get more powerful and the poor more marginalized. If we allow our government and major lending institutions to "get a foot in the door" by agreeing that debt relief be conditioned—with our conditions, of course—we will most likely see the conditions distorted to meet ends other than those we support, just as has happened with originally well-intentioned foreign aid.

Rather, we must make our government and corporations stop blocking change—that is perhaps the most important step in making real change possible in third world countries. As individuals, and through the organizations we belong to, we can also support the movements of local people to bring about change on their own terms. We should not think or act as though we know better than they—or that we can or should tell them what to do or how to do it.

Understanding the nature of U.S. foreign aid—that it does not, and in most countries, cannot, help the hungry—does not lead necessarily to a there's-nothing-I-can-do dead end. It is actually the first step in perceiving the many and varied actions open to all who are determined to end world hunger. In our concluding essay, and in the other publications of our institute, we offer suggestions as to how to seize the opportunities all around us.

CHAPTER 11

Myth 11:
We Benefit from Their Hunger

with Fuyuki Kurasawa

MYTH: No matter how much Americans may think we would like to help end hunger, deep down we know that hunger benefits us. Because hungry people will work for low wages, we can buy everything from coffee to computers, bananas to batteries, at lower prices. Americans would have to sacrifice too much of their standard of living for there to be a world without hunger.

OUR RESPONSE: This myth presumes that our interests are opposed to those of the hungry, that acting to alleviate hunger will mean sacrificing our own well-being. In fact, we are coming to see that the opposite may be true—that the biggest threat to our own well-being is not the advancement but the continued deprivation of the hungry.

In the 1960s and 1970s, a revolutionary change in consciousness began to take shape as the concept of ecology eroded a mechanistic worldview in which separate parts could be isolated. All the natural processes of our unique planet came to be seen as organically connected, and ecology opened our eyes to the intricate ways in which life actually shapes life. From crickets to whales, from ragweed to human beings, we take the form we do through interplay with one another.

147

What would it mean to push this understanding one step further—to understand that we have created a world system as intricately tied together as a natural ecosystem? Doesn't it suggest that humanity's fate is just as intimately interwoven? We think the answer is yes.

With this understanding, everything changes. We no longer think of doing for the poor for their good. We realize that genuine, and very legitimate, self-interest cannot be separated from compassion for others. Such an understanding is the opposite of that implied in the myth. The myth leads us to believe that we would have to do the nearly impossible—forgo our own interests—in order to respond to the needs of those who go hungry. It therefore deepens our despair; everyone knows that people don't wittingly act against their own interest.

Self-interest is legitimate. The problem is that most of us are currently supporting economic and political arrangements that are neither in the interests of the hungry *nor in our own interests*. Changing these arrangements so that hunger can be ended would not undercut the majority in the so-called rich countries, but would benefit them.

This perspective is hard to hold on to. We know, because we have doubts ourselves when eyebrows are raised even among some of our colleagues each time we make this case. Why are citizens of rich nations so willing to see ourselves as competitors rather than natural allies with the world's hungry majority?

For many in the United States, American culture tells us we can only care about others after we overcome our own interests. Second, we get confused by appearances. The third world leaders we see on television often wear our kind of clothes, live in houses like ours, and may even speak our language. The same goes for businessmen from third world countries whom we may meet here in the North. Naturally, we come to identify with them. It is hard to keep in mind that they represent a tiny fraction of their countries' people, and to imagine that our real allies may be an Indian peasant in a white dhoti, a landless Brazilian worker, and a masked descendant of the Mayas in Chiapas. Finally, our government's rhetoric of dominance, telling us that the United States must be number one, encourages us to identify our well-being with winning out over others.

The idea that most Americans—and citizens of other Northern countries—have common interests with the hungry is not widely shared. Nevertheless, in this chapter we are asking you to consider such an alternative framework.

A Smaller World

In the past few years, with all the political, economic, and social changes going on around us, the world has become a much smaller place. A truly global society has emerged, one in which the old divisions between first and third worlds, between "us" and "them," are becoming less and less meaningful. We are part of the same world, and our lives are being affected by similar forces wherever we live. Today, most Americans, Europeans, and even Japanese are being made poorer by the same structures keeping people hungry in Africa, South America, the Caribbean, and Asia.

We have entered the age of globalization, a time in which an economic system beyond the borders of individual countries has emerged. Whereas the world used to be made up of separate national economies that traded with one another, it is increasingly becoming a single economic zone tied together by production networks literally spanning the globe. Trade agreements like NAFTA and organizations like the World Bank, the International Monetary Fund, and the World Trade Organization (WTO), are playing important roles in supporting this new global economy.

However, the real beneficiaries of this trend are not countries but big multinational or transnational corporations that can be headquartered in any country and control offices and plants in many others. Their names are familiar to billions of people: American Express, General Electric, IBM, Royal Dutch–Shell, Sony, and Toyota, for example. Multinationals have revenues that dwarf the GNPs of many countries. Controlling more than 70 percent of world trade, they are the big players in the world economy.[1]

With globalization, multinationals are now able to produce and sell goods as well as offer services anywhere in the global marketplace. Garment and electronics sweatshops are found in New York City and Los Angeles, not just in San Salvador and Mexico City. Parts of India and China are now considered prime locations to find large pools of low-wage engineers and computer programmers.[2] Companies do not depend on specific locations, nor do they have any sense of loyalty to communities here or abroad; overnight, they can close up shop and reopen across the country or across the world. In the Northern countries, as much as in the South, nations, regions, and cities are in what, as we mentioned earlier, writer Holly Sklar calls a "race to the bottom":

149

competing against one another to attract corporate investment by promising larger tax breaks, lower wages, and weaker environmental standards than anywhere else.[3] For example, American cities vying for a new factory are likely to come up against rivals in China and Mexico—and they will all be forced to engage in downward bidding.

"Global competitiveness," the catchphrase of business for the 1990s, actually means that workers and communities have to accept the lowest common denominator in the world economy: Who will give up the most in order to be "rewarded" by a company's investment? What is certain is that because of globalization, most members of our global society are worse off than before, working in poorly paid jobs and experiencing deteriorating working conditions. Contrary to what some want us to believe, ordinary people in the United States and abroad are coming out on the short end of globalization.

Hunger and Violence

While hunger is itself a quiet form of violence, we too are the victims of the violence that sustains it. As corporations silently take over control of the economy and decision making, governments become both weaker and less accountable. The interests they are likely to respond to are the interests of the big corporations, since they are locked into a desperate competition with other countries for investment. They may be more likely to use violent repression against their own citizens organizing for basic rights than take action to guarantee those rights.

These changes are not readily apparent, neither are they easy to grasp for the average citizen, and people in many countries go on reacting with nationalistic pride to their government's propaganda, believing that they must win out over others.

But this has never been the case. As others are increasingly impoverished, and we ourselves are thrown into competition with them for scarce jobs in the global economy—competition in which what counts is who will work for less—we lose too. We are beginning to actually see the consequences in the deterioration of salaries, the recomposition of the job market, and the spread of insecurity, homelessness, poverty, and hunger in the United States.[4]

Because our government identifies U.S. interests with protecting the business-as-usual status quo, even when that status quo means hunger, we Americans pay a heavy price—directly in tax dollars and indirectly in the undermining of our economy's health. Post–Cold War U.S. foreign policy continues to be geared to militarism. Violence is no longer directed at so-called communist regimes, however, but toward whoever opposes the ongoing process of concentration of wealth.

In spite of the disappearance of the "communist threat" since 1989, the U.S. Department of Defense maintains its expenditure on arms and military equipment at 90 percent of the average Cold War level, with a force of 1,543,000 uniformed servicemen and women.[5] In 1997 the military was expected to consume 53 percent of all discretionary federal spending, with the percentage to increase in future years.[6] Furthermore, military aid to foreign countries costs an estimated 6 billion taxpayers' dollars annually.[7] This aid not only keeps the arms race alive, but is all too often used to repress protesters or striking workers, or maintain inequalities that themselves cause hunger.[8]

Throughout this century, the United States has consistently backed governments representing wealthy elites against poor and peasant majorities and has overthrown those attempting genuine reforms. The post–World War II list includes Iran, Guatemala, the Dominican Republic, Indonesia, Nigeria, Greece, Chile, Nicaragua, Grenada, and so many others we cannot list them all here.

How do we as a people wind up helping to quell social struggle for justice and basic rights? Once the poor become the enemy, war no longer means only military against military. We are appalled by terrorism, especially when innocent civilians are the targets. Yet when our government supports regimes killing thousands of noncombatants, as we did in El Salvador,[9] or arms rebels notorious for barbaric treatment of civilians, as we did in Nicaragua,[10] is not our government's credibility and effectiveness as an opponent of terrorism destroyed?

Surely, both the hungry and we are hurt as long as our governments pretend that stability is possible where people are made to go hungry. In the long run, hunger can be maintained only by violence, and violence begets more violence. As long as there is hunger, *working for stability means working to make room for change.*

Hunger and Our Job Security

Since the 1970s, globalization has gone hand in hand with a major phase of domestic corporate restructuring, variously referred to as flexible specialization, just-in-time production, post-Fordism, and postindustrialism. These changes are redefining the nature of work in the United States. In an attempt to reduce production costs and increase profits, U.S. companies have been putting two strategies into action. The first one, alluded to above, consists of shutting down operations in northeastern cities and moving them to rural areas either in the U.S. South or overseas. This tendency has been particularly strong in the manufacturing sector, where millions of workers have been laid off as "runaway shops" have relocated to take advantage of cheaper, nonunionized labor. Hardest hit by this wave of deindustrialization is the Midwest, where once-booming industrial cities like Cleveland and Pittsburgh now form the heart of what has come to be known as the Rust Belt.

The second corporate strategy has been imposed through a series of reorganizations of the workplace. Under the banner of flexibility, owners and managers have created a two-tier workforce, which consists of a small core of full-time, highly skilled workers and a large pool of contingent, flexible workers. The latter group accounts for the swelling number of poorly paid, part-time, and temporary jobs now being created around the world—jobs that are disproportionately held by women, people of color, and immigrants. Already, 25 percent of the American workforce is employed on a part-time basis, and Manpower Inc., a personnel supply agency, has become the largest private employer in the country.[11] Disposable jobs—and disposable workers—are a trend of the future that corporate America is only too happy to foster.

In an effort to cut costs, companies have largely given up on the idea of doing everything in house. Instead, they have built contracting pyramids that crisscross the globe; outside contractors provide a growing share of all types of parts and services, from security and cleaning to computer and automobile components. This has even given birth to "hollow corporations," like Benetton and Nike, which do little or no direct production but simply stamp their names and market products made by their subcontracting networks. Workers who used to hold secure, unionized jobs inside a corporation have been replaced by low-cost workforces hired by contracting firms. These categories of workers, often drawn from the most vulnerable segments of society, are highly exploited and disposed of at will by contractors.

Full-time, secure, high-wage, unionized jobs, which were a staple of postwar American life, are becoming an endangered species. "McJobs" are now the norm. In fact, throughout the 1980s and 1990s, some of the occupations with the largest job growth in the United States have been cashier, janitor, truck driver, waiter, wholesale trade sales worker, and retail salesperson.[12] More than ever, what counts for corporations is the bottom line; the old story of profits over people is being replayed again.

Of course, these global economic transformations have not occurred in a political vacuum. On the contrary, they have been supported by the rise of what is called "neoliberalism" on a worldwide scale. Neoliberalism means basically a return to policies of free markets and free trade at all costs. In Asia, Africa, and South America, this has taken the form of rampant privatization and the removal of barriers to trade, via structural adjustment programs imposed on third world governments by the World Bank and the International Monetary Fund. In the United States, supply-side economics, or "Reaganomics" (the terms used to describe those policies here at home) continued essentially uninterrupted under the Bush and Clinton administrations. In England it was called "Thatcherism" but has continued virtually uninterrupted under the "new Labor" government.

Regardless of where it has taken place, the onslaught has been remarkably similar: debts and deficits accumulated through military overspending and tax cuts to the rich are being repaid on the backs of the poor, women, people of color, immigrants, and workers—in other words, the majority of the population. The choices made by governments beholden to the wealthy are clear: lower taxes and regulations on big corporations, increase military and prison budgets, cut back on funding to schools, relax environmental standards, privatize everything in sight, and shred the social safety net that once ensured a decent standard of living for all citizens.

Governments are operating with what can only be described as a double standard. In the 1980s, the tax share of the top 1 percent of the U.S. population was reduced by 14 percent, while that of the bottom 10 percent increased by 28 percent.[13] Social programs such as Aid to Families with Dependent Children (AFDC), unemployment insurance, Social Security benefits, and food stamps have been slashed. Between 1970 and 1992, average monthly AFDC benefits per family fell 39.8 percent in real terms.[14] With welfare reform, general assistance benefits have been drastically cut or simply eliminated in many states. More and more people are left completely unprotected after falling through the system's cracks. At the same time, corporate welfare is alive and well. Federal and state governments are throwing huge sums of money at private companies—to the extent that business and agricultural subsidies currently equal half of the federal deficit.[15]

The mirage of the American Dream is slowly fading away. Today, more than ever before in our history, we share many of the problems and challenges faced by other societies. For instance, the child mortality rate for African-American infants is higher than those national averages for Bulgaria and Cuba.[16] In fact, over the past thirty years, the U.S. population has witnessed a steady erosion of its standard of living. The Index of Social Health, published by the Fordham University Institute for Innovation in Social Policy as a measure of national social well-being, has plummeted to an all-time low in the 1990s; four indicators—children in poverty, health insurance coverage, average weekly earnings, and the gap between rich and poor—reached their worst levels in 1995.[17]

The middle class is disappearing quickly in the United States, as economic insecurity touches traditionally privileged segments of society. Between 1973 and 1993, the real wages of college-educated workers declined by 7.5 percent.[18] Although less severely affected than other groups, white men have seen their incomes fall about 7 percent since 1978.[19] To their dismay, even professionals and middle managers are feeling the squeeze: More than 12.2 million white-collar workers lost their jobs between 1987 and 1991; those who found new jobs took a 30 percent average pay cut.[20] Blue-collar workers have not been spared either. The inflation-adjusted weekly earnings of production and non-supervisory workers have fallen by 15 percent since 1973.[21] Moreover, the real value of the minimum wage declined 23 percent between 1979 and 1992;[22] a person holding a full-time, year-round, minimum-wage job now lives well below the poverty line. This has given rise to a widespread problem, as more and more workers join the ranks of the "working poor."

An extensive cross-national study conducted by the Organization for Economic Cooperation and Development (OECD) concluded that the United States has, by far, the most unequal income distribution of any industrialized country.[23] More worrisome, income and wealth inequalities have been steadily worsening since the late 1970s. During the 1980s, trickle-up economics came alive: The share of wealth held by the top 1 percent of the population went up 5 percent, while that of the bottom 80 percent of the population declined 4 percent.[24] Today, the top 1 percent of wealth holders control 39 percent of total household wealth, whereas the bottom 80 percent control only 15 percent. The gap between rich and poor is greater than at any other time since 1929—the year the Great Depression hit the country.[25]

Inequalities have reached absurd proportions: The income gap in Manhattan is worse than that in Guatemala, while U.S. CEOs earn on average 157 times what factory workers do.[26] The Bill Gateses, Michael Eisners, and Lee Iacoccas of the nation make hundreds of millions of dollars while most of their compatriots struggle just to make ends meet.

Although they affect everyone, these inequalities disproportionately hit women and people of color. Full-time, year-round working women still are paid only 72 cents for every dollar men are paid.[27] African-American workers are paid only 77 percent of what their white counterparts get, while per capita income for African-Americans is less than 60 percent that of whites.[28] In 1989, the year for which the most recent figures are available, the median family income was $35,975 for whites, $20,209 for African-Americans, and $23,446 for Latinos.[29]

Clearly, a healthy U.S. economy—affording work opportunities at livable wages for all—cannot be achieved by squeezing workers to make wage and other concessions just to keep their jobs. Is there another course, one recognizing the common interests of the American people with workers in the third world who face even greater obstacles? We believe there is.

Since its inception in 1994, workers on both sides of the Rio Grande have been working jointly to oppose NAFTA. This has helped create awareness of the need for collective mobilization across sectors and across national borders. In 1997, organized labor in the United States joined forces with the environmental community, consumer groups, and religious groups, as well as human rights groups to oppose Fast Track authority to expand NAFTA throughout the hemisphere and prevent its approval in the U.S. Congress.[30]

In a global economy, our own jobs, wages, and working conditions will be protected only when working people in every country establish their rights to organize and protect their interests. Working to wrench U.S. government props out from under repressive regimes abroad may be just as critical to achieving the goals of organized labor in this country as organizing workers here. If we allow our government to help drive wages down elsewhere, our own wages will soon follow. If, on the other hand, we support improving living standards abroad, those will help push our own back up.

A global corporation that isn't accountable to a workforce or to a national economy has workers and governments at its mercy. U.S. workers take pay cuts just to keep their jobs, while the government walks away from the minimum wage and health, safety, and environmental protection standards. And it fails to support strong collective bargaining rights for workers—all with the excuse of keeping the United States competitive.[31]

Hunger and the Debt Crisis

We briefly discussed the debt crisis at the end of the last chapter. While major international banks bear much of the moral responsibility for placing excessive loans they knew could never be paid back in full, it is the majority of the people in the third world and in Northern countries like the United States—taxpayers—who end up paying the price for unaccountable and undemocratic lending institutions.[32]

By the early 1980s, when the global recession cut into their export earnings, many third world nations found it hard even to make interest payments on the excessive loans they had been persuaded to take. Mexico, for example, has entered into technical insolvency three times between 1982 and 1995, and it has escaped default only by repeated borrowing, further expanding its total debt.[33] In this process multilateral lenders like the IMF have acquired debt that was once owed to private banks. Since the IMF is government—and thus taxpayer—funded, the risk of bad debts has been passed from foreign banks to ordinary citizens, as the Asian bailout crisis of the late 1990s amply demonstrated.

While major U.S. banks still expect hefty profits from their third world lending (as long as borrowing governments continue to pay interest), what if something goes wrong? U.S. bankers know they have us, the taxpayers, to bail them out. The precedent is clear from the federal government's $4.5 billion bailout of the Continental Bank of Illinois in 1984: the U.S. government will not let a major bank collapse.[34] It is also clear that we will not let Wall Street investors lose billions in a major third world default—thus, the U.S. Treasury Department has rushed to use taxpayers' contributions to bail out Mexico and many Asian countries during the 1990s.[35]

Almost $2 trillion in loans to the third world over two decades have strengthened the forces that generate poverty and hunger while undermining the capacity to repay the loans. Ordinary citizens in the third world as well as in the United States and other creditor countries pay the costs. We therefore share a common interest in restructuring financial institutions to include responsibility to majority concerns, and, specifically, in unconditional debt relief (see chapter 10).

Hunger and Our Food Security

Hunger in the third world generates agricultural exports that undercut U.S. farmers and threaten U.S. food safety and security.

How can this be? Aren't third world countries the major food *importers* and a boon to U.S. farmers?

Not really. The United States and other industrial countries are the world's major food importers, importing 71 percent of the total value of food items in world trade.[36] Even as the world's leading agricultural exporter, the United States imports 54 percent more in farm commodities than it exports,[37] much of it from countries where the majority lack a healthy diet.

Throughout our book we have suggested the logic behind this flow of food from the hungry to the well fed. As elites tighten their hold on the land and other productive resources, more and more of their compatriots are dispossessed, becoming too impoverished to make their need for food felt in the marketplace. Landowners therefore shift production toward those who can pay: better-off foreign consumers. At the same time, in the United States and other industrial countries, agribusiness corporations—wholesale food brokers, food processors, commodity firms, and supermarket chains—seek the cheapest sources of supply. They find third world landowners make ready partners.[38]

In the process, U.S. producers of certain crops are undercut by both third world producers and multinational agribusiness. The U.S. Department of Agriculture conservatively estimates that in 1996, 1,088 jobs were lost due to U.S.-Mexico agricultural trade.[39] Mexico's share of the U.S. market for winter tomatoes in the 1995–96 season reached 50 percent, while Florida's has shrunk after NAFTA from 56 percent to 35 percent.[40] Lest we think for a moment that Mexico received all the benefits, Mexican corn producers—often the poorest of the poor—have been very hard hit by imports of cheap corn from the United States.[41]

But don't U.S. consumers gain in cheaper produce? After adding in profits to the big growers and multinational marketers, plus transportation costs and tariffs, there is no evidence that we do.[42] The winners are integrated, "agrifood" corporations, not consumers.

Imports of produce from the third world also pose an invisible threat to U.S. consumers. U.S. chemical corporations routinely export pesticides to the third world that have been banned or severely restricted in the United States. Since most are used on export crops, they wind up as residues on the food we import. At our institute we call this insidious threat the "circle of poison."[43] Concern is growing about tainted imported fruits and vegetables.[44]

Hunger and Immigration

Neither we nor the third world's poor benefit if they are made economic or political refugees, forced to flee their homelands to find safety and opportunity.

As a result of the import of cheap grain under free-trade policies, thousands of Mexican farmers have been forced out of business and have no other alternative than migrating to where the work is: Mexican cities and often the United States. In 1996, the U.S. Immigration and Naturalization Service (INS) apprehended 1.5 million people trying to cross the border illegally. Most of the economic refugees who are not detained end up harvesting and processing U.S. food in often dangerous and low-wage conditions.[45]

People should have the right to a decent life in their homeland; and in the United States, people understandably want immigrants to our country to come for positive, not negative reasons. Thus, we share common interests with the hungry in the third world also on the question of immigration—we must stop our government and multinational corporations from undercutting the ability of people to make a living in their home countries.

The Third World Comes Home

In our response to this myth, we suggest just a few of many ways in which present international economic institutions fail to serve the interests of both the majority in the third world and the majority of U.S. citizens.

Don't some Americans gain from third world poverty? What about all the corporations and banks with lucrative investments? Our answer is yes, of course, some do gain. But they are not the majority. Half of the American people live in households earning less than $35,500 a year—not enough money for most people to buy a home, much less invest in the stock market.[46]

Once we looked at world development from the perspective of common interests, we also came to realize that economies governed by

158

world-spanning economic institutions inevitably *begin to look alike*. Within an overriding, antidemocratic financial system, we can't expect individual societies to remain democratic. In our opening chapter, we defined democracy as a principle of accountability—decision makers kept accountable to those whose lives are affected by their decisions. Such a principle applies equally well to economic as to political life.

If our economic life is governed by fewer and fewer antidemocratic corporate structures with a global reach, we are inevitably thrown into competition with societies in which the majority have virtually no voice. It's no coincidence, then, that in our economic life the voice of the majority is becoming weaker.

Many people now refer to the United States as two Americas; our society looks like a pyramid whose base is widening and top is narrowing, making it increasingly difficult for those of us in the middle and on the bottom to find job security and make a decent living.

When people are poor, they can't afford the basic necessities that should be available to all. The struggle to keep a roof overhead is day by day, often ending in failure. The loss of a job or a costly hospital stay is enough to force many people onto the streets of our cities and towns. No wonder between 5 and 9 million people experienced homelessness in the latter half of the 1980s,[47] and emergency shelter requests grew by 13 percent in the 1990s.[48] Here again, stereotypes don't hold water: Families with children represent 39 percent (and the fastest-growing segment) of the homeless population, while 19 percent of the homeless are employed but don't earn enough to afford housing.[49]

Pictures of starving babies in war-torn Somalia come to mind when people in the United States think of hunger. We often overlook the fact that every day, people right here at home lack sufficient food. Hunger is an epidemic in the United States. Second Harvest, the largest hunger relief organization in the country, serves almost 26 million people annually. That is 10.4 percent of the U.S. population.[50] Many are turned away each day for lack of food; to meet the actual demand, food donations would have to be increased by 15.7 percent.[51]

Hunger is not an individual problem. According to the United States Conference of Mayors, 64 percent of emergency food requests come from families.[52] Holding a job doesn't even guarantee that one is adequately fed in the United States today: 60.2 percent of hungry households include at least one employed member, and at least one full-time worker is found in 48.4 percent of hungry households.[53] The most shocking figures are found when we look at the condition of children.

Almost one in three (13.6 million) children under the age of twelve are hungry or at risk of hunger in the United States.[54]

Finally, where the majority have little voice in matters of economic life, they are made to sacrifice in times of crisis. We have described how the poor pay for the third world's debt, and the pattern holds here too, where the poor and middle class have borne the brunt of the infamous "cutbacks" of the 1980s and 1990s. We return to this point in the next chapter when we explore the meaning of freedom as it relates to economic life.

All of these trends suggest that the very character of our society is changing. With high-tech alarms and guarded streets, the wealthy here create walled enclaves much like the ones seen in Latin American cities, even as our government builds a giant wall and militarizes the U.S.-Mexico border. Fear rules rich and poor alike.

Beyond Scapegoating

When things take a turn for the worse, people look for easy targets to blame. The poor, the homeless, unions, government, women, immigrants, people of color, gay men and women—every group in society is labeled responsible for our current social and economic ills. But there are no scapegoats: Whether it be in Asia, Africa, South America, Europe, the Caribbean, or right here in the United States, everyone but a small global elite is being hurt.

Rather than pointing fingers at each other, we need to build alliances across borders and around the globe. Multinational corporations have made this one world, but we have to stop the vicious circle they have created by pitting communities and countries against one another, driving down living standards to unprecedented levels. People everywhere face similar challenges and problems.

As we have seen, in a global society our well-being is tied to that of others in so many ways. We are not sacrificing our well-being for that of others, since our fate is inseparable from that of all. The only way to solve our problems, here and abroad, is to create social movements that give power to ordinary people, not big corporations. Like-minded people must go global and unite around a common agenda, which should include the meeting of basic needs (food, clothing, shelter, health care, education) for every human being, the protection of the environment, decent working conditions for all, and an end to discrimination. Many of these "economic and social human rights" are already enshrined in the Universal Declaration of Human Rights, ratified by most of the world's countries and described in chapter 7. Our institute is part of an international network: the FoodFirst Information and Action Network (FIAN), with chapters or chapters-in-formation in nineteen countries. FIAN is a leader in the global battle to meet these basic human rights, and you can join this crucial fight. The U.S. chapter is carrying out a campaign for these rights here in our own country called "Economic Human Rights: The Time Has Come!"[55]

These global social movements are already taking shape before our very eyes. New communication technologies have made the world a smaller place for grassroots groups, as information is becoming available faster and to more people than ever before. Transnational support for events and causes can be mobilized in a matter of seconds, and the weaving together of multiple-issue global coalitions is being fostered through these changes.

More important, we are not starting from scratch. The scaffolds of a new global society already exist, and we can build on the many existing foundations. From the opposition to building of megadams in India to protesting against French nuclear testing in the South Pacific, a planetary consciousness has been pioneered by the environmental and peace movements. The women's movement strongly advocates for global gender solidarity, as was demonstrated at the Non-Governmental Organization Forum of the Fourth World Conference on Women in Beijing, China. For their part, unions are beginning to tap into the possibilities of cross-national strategies, such as the organizing of southern and northern workers employed in the same industry or even the same multinational company.

Women, people of color, small farmers, the poor and middle classes of all countries—who are, after all, the vast majority of the world's population—have to stand up and collectively say, "enough is enough!" The world can't go on tolerating or ignoring hunger, poverty, exploitation, and discrimination.

Governments and multinational corporations need to listen to us: The world economy has to serve people instead of the other way around. In this country, many of the things that have immeasurably improved our lives came about when ordinary people demanded change through collective struggle: civil rights, women's right to vote, legislation against sexual harassment, environmental regulations, the right to join unions, etc. Today, we need to hold on to those gains and broaden their scope through existing institutions and emerging networks of nongovernmental organizations. By bringing local issues to

161

the table of global society, our common experiences and problems as world citizens can serve as a basis to generate support throughout the world. This is how a just, peaceful, and ecologically sound global society can come about.

Building Solidarity:
Self-Interest and Compassion

Having focused on some of the ways people in the United States are hurt by a global economy that generates hunger for so many, we can also state our response in the positive. Only as the poor in the third world achieve decent livelihoods and dignity can we achieve economic and national security ourselves.

Because some might misread this chapter as an appeal to materialistic self-interest, we want to reiterate our very different perspective. Legitimate self-interest and compassion for others need not and *cannot* be separated.

What do we mean by "legitimate self-interest"? We assume that most of us, like most people everywhere, want to be free from institutions that violate our deepest values—fairness, protection of innocent lives (especially children), accountability of decision makers, and opportunity for all—just as we desire the basic security and stability needed to pursue our own goals.

Compassion is just as central. Without compassion we cannot put ourselves into the shoes of others, which is required if we are truly to grasp the many parallels and interconnections suggested in this chapter. But compassion too easily slides into pity for the less fortunate. And pity leads us to believe that we have to do for, rather than work side by side with, those struggling for dignity and security in the world.

Thus, the first step in working toward a more life-serving world is a leap of consciousness. We no longer see the hungry as a threat or a burden to us but understand that they are struggling for a liberation that is essential to our own. If we don't struggle with them to raise their living standards, ours will continue to be dragged down. Once we have shifted to this perspective, virtually every time we pick up the newspaper we will uncover new ties linking our fate to that of the hungry. We are also called upon to seek out alternative sources of information, some of which we suggest at the end of this book.

But this chapter still begs one critical question: Why have we acquiesced to the creation of global economic institutions that are neither in our best interests, nor in the interests of the majority in the third world? Why have we let it happen?

To answer that we are victims of the tightening concentration of political and economic power is at best partial. We must go deeper. To understand why so many Americans give in to such usurpation of our own and others' rights requires that we probe our most deeply held beliefs. In our concluding essay, we suggest that we cannot answer why unless we are willing to challenge the role of received economic dogma of both of the world's giant "isms": capitalism and statism. Taken as dogma, both subvert the most fundamental human values that we profess. Widespread hunger is the most tragic evidence of this subversion.

But first, it is necessary to take a close look at what we mean by one of those values: freedom.

CHAPTER 12

Myth 12:
Food vs. Freedom

MYTH: For hunger to be eliminated it is clear that a society would have to undergo radical changes. Many of its citizens would see their freedoms curtailed. A tradeoff between freedom and ending hunger is unfortunate, but it appears to be a fact of life. People have to choose one or the other.

OUR RESPONSE: Taking freedom to mean civil liberties, we can think of no theoretical or practical reason that it should be incompatible with ending hunger. In fact, there are good reasons to expect greater progress toward ending hunger in societies where civil liberties are protected. Freedom of the press and freedom to organize, for example, are critical vehicles through which citizens make a government accountable to their needs or change it for one that is.

Clearly, the problem lies in the definition of freedom. We may begin by asking the most basic question: Freedom for whom, and for what? Do we mean freedom to speak our minds, to organize and be free from repression, from exploitation, from unfair discrimination, even freedom from hunger itself? Or do we mean the freedom to do whatever we please, regardless of its impact on others, and the freedom to choose among thirty brands of breakfast cereal and twenty of shampoo?

Ending hunger is not at all incompatible with the first group of freedoms. But it may require limiting the second kind.

The myth that food and freedom are incompatible points to fundamental value questions that are worthy of debate and reflection. In one sense, the assumption embodied in this myth is absolutely correct. One definition of freedom is both theoretically and practically incompatible with ending hunger. It is not the definition of freedom expounded by our nation's founders but that extolled by political leadership beholden to corporate interests and the almighty dollar. It is not the definition embedded in religious traditions but that promoted by a minority of well-heeled, vocal Americans. Let us explain what we mean.

Freedom as Unlimited Accumulation

President Reagan declared in the early 1980s that the distinctive feature of American society is that here anyone is free to become a millionaire. The right to take all one can is one definition of freedom. The core protector of such freedom is the right to unlimited accumulation of wealth-producing property and the right to use that property however one sees fit. We hold that this definition of freedom *is* in fundamental conflict with ending hunger.

Once society starts to operate from this understanding of freedom—the right to unlimited private accumulation—certain consequences follow. Because money makes money and wealth begets wealth, economic power becomes increasingly concentrated. From the late 1970s to the mid-1990s, the average inflation-adjusted incomes of the highest-income families in the United States rose by 30 percent. Over the same period middle-class families saw their average income drop by $700, while low-income families with children saw their incomes fall by more than 20 percent.[1] Even during the economic recovery later in the 1990s, poverty failed to decline and the income of the poorest fifth of American families dropped further. By the end of 1996 only the top fifth of the U.S. population had achieved income above prerecession levels. That high-income group receives 49 percent of all the national income, virtually what is earned by the remaining 80 percent of families combined.[2] Concentration of income in the United States is as bad as in some third world countries, as we mentioned in the previous chapter. Yet income is only part of the story. The wealthiest 2.7 million Americans—who are each "worth" $2.35 million or more—now have as much accumulated wealth as the other 240 million of us, who are each worth $346,000 or less![3]

Why is ending hunger incompatible with such economic concentration? The answer is easiest to grasp in terms of a finite resource like farmland. Where a few can accumulate vast acreage, many are left with no land from which to provide for themselves, as we have suggested throughout our book.

Perhaps even more important, ending hunger is incompatible with economic concentration because along with economic power comes political power. Those with little or no income have little or no political clout. Protecting citizens' access to life-giving necessities, such as food and shelter, becomes difficult if not impossible. Perhaps never has this fact of economic life been more evident than in the past few decades, during which the tax rate paid by the richest Americans has been cut almost in half.[4] Due to changes in Social Security taxes, a family with an income of $37,800 pays 7.65 percent in Social Security tax, while a family with an income ten times higher pays 1.46 percent and one with an income a hundred times higher pays only 0.1 percent.[5] Finally, welfare legislation passed in 1996 cut the incomes in absolute terms of 11 million households, 10 percent of all U.S. families, more than 8 million of them with children.[6]

Many Americans believe that the right to unlimited accumulation is the guarantor of liberty. They fail to understand that "income-producing property is the bulwark of liberty only for those who have it,"[7] as Yale University economics philosopher Charles Lindblom coolly reminds us in his classic *Politics and Markets*. In the third world only a tiny minority have such a bulwark to their liberty. And as we saw in the previous chapter, most Americans don't have it either.

Security as the Basis of Freedom

Fortunately, this understanding of freedom—the freedom of unlimited accumulation—is not the only one. Nor, as we've said, is it consistent with the vision of our nation's founders. They too perceived a link between property and freedom, but they believed that such a link could be positive only when ownership of socially productive property is widely dispersed.

After a conversation on a country road with a desperately poor single mother trying to support two children with no land of her own, Thomas Jefferson wrote to James Madison in 1785, "Legislators cannot invent too many devices for subdividing property." The misery of Europe, he concluded, was caused by the enormous inequality in land-holding.[8] Benjamin Franklin endorsed the community's right to redistribute what he called superfluous property,[9] and Jefferson further believed that land should be redistributed every generation. "Man did not make the earth," declared Tom Paine, "[and] he had no right to locate as his property, in perpetuity, any part of it."[10]

Many dismiss Jefferson's vision of a small-farm–dominated democracy as naive and irrelevant to modern America. But such presumption misses Jefferson's and Franklin's critical insight that the economic security of citizens is the guarantor of our liberty. In their day, as well as for many in the third world today, economic security naturally would entail a plot of land, but their insight applies equally well to the industrial era. Translated into the late twentieth century, economic security would also mean the right to a remunerative job, and, if unable to work, the right to life's necessities.

Many political theorists of Jefferson's day and of the seventeenth century believed that unless people were economically independent— that is, had economic security, including access to food—they could not be full citizens of a democracy because they could not act independently. Both Oliver Cromwell and the Levellers in seventeenth-century England, for example, agreed that "if there be anything at all that is a foundation of liberty it is this, that those who shall choose the lawmakers shall be men freed from dependence upon others."[11] Here we find an echo of Plato's view that the essence of freedom is being self-directed.

Such a notion has been largely lost, but might not this age-old insight still be relevant? Because the right to employment is not protected, one might question how free are, say, employees of arms contractors to think independently about the military budget. Unsure of alternative employment, would they not feel compelled to push their representatives to vote for arms spending despite possible reservations about the arms race? In the third world, with jobs even more scarce and workers' rights often unprotected altogether, pressure to keep one's views to oneself is even more intense.

Not only is our freedom of action as citizens constrained by economic insecurity, so is our personal freedom. Franklin Roosevelt summed up this insight when he declared, "Necessitous men are not free men." In 1944, he therefore called for a second bill of rights centering on the right to remunerative employment. More recently, University of Maryland philosopher Henry Shue has offered a helpful exploration of precisely

167

why subsistence rights—particularly the right to an adequate diet and health care—are basic to freedom.

Shue likens such subsistence rights to the right to physical security—the right not to be subjected to murder, torture, mayhem, rape, or assault. How do we justify the right to physical security? In part by the fact that no other right can be enjoyed without it. Shue argues that subsistence rights are just as basic:

> No one can fully, if at all, enjoy any right that is supposedly protected by society if he or she lacks the essentials for a reasonably healthy and active life. Deficiencies in the means of subsistence can be just as fatal, incapacitating, or painful as violations of physical security. The resulting damage or death can at least as decisively prevent the enjoyment of any right as can the effects of security violations.[12]

Shue goes so far as to argue that the right to the essentials of survival is even more basic than the right to be protected from assault. For it is much easier to fight back against an assailant than to challenge the very structure of the social order that denies one access to food.

Such a view of freedom—rooted in security to permit full functioning as a human being—builds, we believe, on our religious and cultural heritage. It contrasts sharply with the much more recent notion of freedom defined as unfettered accumulation of property. Once again, the former definition is clearly compatible with, indeed essential to, ending hunger; the latter is not.

Freedom: Finite or Infinite?

But we want to probe this myth still further. Behind it lies the fear that freedom is finite, that ensuring everyone's right to eat will require expanding the freedom of some while shrinking the freedom of others, that freedom is a zero-sum equation.

As long as we focus our definition on the freedom to own or control property, this view holds considerable truth. But reducing the concept of freedom to mean unfettered control of property drastically curtails our vision. We can begin to embrace the vast breadth and depth of the concept of freedom only by asking the oft-forgotten question: What is the *purpose* of freedom?

For many people—and in most religious traditions—freedom is not an end in itself. Rather, its purpose is the development of the uniquely

168

human and individually unique potential of each person—be it intellectual, physical, artistic, or spiritual.[13] Freedom of expression, religion, and participation, and more basically freedom from physical assault (both direct and through deprivation of life's necessities) are prerequisites to such development.

Freedom so understood is not finite. My artistic development need not detract from yours. Your intellectual advances need not reduce my ability to develop my own intellectual powers. And, most pertinent to this chapter, assurances of my protection from physical assault, including my right to subsistence, need not prevent you from enjoying equal protection. This is true because, as we have shown throughout our book, sufficient resources already exist in virtually all countries to guarantee subsistence rights for everyone.

Not only is freedom so defined not a zero-sum equation, we see it as a rare case in which the sum truly is greater than its parts. For not only does your freedom to develop your unique gifts not have to limit my expression, my development in part *depends on* your freedom. How, for example, can I deepen my appreciation and enjoyment of music unless you, with much greater musical talent, are free to develop your gift? Or how can you develop your full potential physical health unless someone else, with talents in science and medicine, is free to cultivate those gifts?

Having thus expanded our understanding of freedom, we can now return our focus to hunger. Here in the United States the freedom of the poor is being thwarted by poverty and hunger, *and so is the freedom of those who are well fed.* The failure of our society to protect subsistence rights means that all of its members are deprived of the intellectual breakthroughs, spiritual insights, musical gifts, and athletic achievements of those whose development has been blocked by poverty and hunger. Denied the potential inspiration, knowledge, example, and leadership of those who are directly deprived, all of us experience a diminution of our freedom to realize our fullest potential.

So in this broader sense we conclude that the protection of the right to food is not in conflict with freedom but essential to its maximum realization throughout society.

Freedom: Our Responsibility

We hope we have said enough in our response to this myth to make clear that freedom carries more than one definition. This alone should make us wary of those attempting to impose their definition on others. When the president of the United States calls on people to support "freedom fighters" abroad, we might appropriately ask whose definition of freedom they are fighting for.

Since true freedom can be achieved only by a people for themselves, is not our responsibility to other peoples limited to the challenges addressed in the preceding two chapters? We can make sure that our tax dollars and our government's influence are not used to shore up foreign governments that deny their people's rights. And, through knowledge exchange, financial help, and joint campaigns on matters of common concern, we can work in concert with those in other societies who are themselves striving for greater freedom.

Here at home, does not a commitment to freedom require that we bring forth into public debate the profoundly conflicting definitions of freedom now held in our society—and clarify how radically the current property-accumulation definition diverges from our cherished heritage? Obviously, we hope that in such a debate our book will contribute to a renewed appreciation of the positive link between economic security and freedom, so that people who love liberty will want to expand it by establishing the right of every citizen to the resources necessary to live in dignity.

Beyond the Myths of Hunger:
What We Can Do

Some approaches to world hunger elicit our guilt (that we have so much) or our fear (that they will take it from us). Others imply impossible tradeoffs. Do we protect the environment or grow needed food? Do we seek a just or an efficient food system? Do we choose freedom or the elimination of hunger?

But our search for the roots of hunger has led us to a number of positive principles that neither place our deeply held values in conflict nor pit our interests against those of the hungry. We offer the following principles as working hypotheses, not to be carved in stone but to be tested through experience:

- Since hunger results from human choices, not inexorable natural forces, the goal of ending hunger is obtainable. It is no more utopian than the goal of abolishing slavery was, not all that long ago.
- While slowing population growth in itself cannot end hunger, the very changes necessary to end hunger—the democratization of economic life, especially the empowerment of women—are key to reducing birth rates so that the human population can come into balance with the rest of the natural world.
- Ending hunger does not necessitate destroying our environment. On the contrary, it requires protecting it by using agricultural methods that are both ecologically sustainable and within the reach of the poor.

- Greater fairness does not undercut the production of needed food. The only path to increased production that can end hunger is to devise food systems in which those who do the work have a greater say and reap a greater reward.
- We need not fear the advance of the poor in the third world. Their increased well-being can enhance our own.

These and other liberating principles point to possibilities for narrowing the unfortunate rifts we sometimes observe among those concerned about the environment, population growth, and world hunger.

Understanding Democracy and Freedom

Americans have always thought of our country as a beacon of hope for the world's oppressed. But as we travel throughout the third world, we sense a change. We fear our example is becoming increasingly irrelevant to the poor majority abroad.

While our government extols the virtues of democracy and freedom, America's present version of these two values appears unrelated to the concerns of the hungry—food, access to land, and jobs.

If amid our nation's fantastic food bounty, poor American children are stunted by malnutrition, what example of hope do we offer to children in the third world? If, with an unparalleled industrial and service economy, millions go without work even during a period of economic growth, and millions more work full-time yet remain in poverty, what hope do we offer the impoverished and jobless in the third world?

We fear the answer is very little as long as Americans' understanding of democracy and freedom fail to address the most central concerns of the poor.

This realization suggests that we can contribute to ending world hunger not only by helping to remove obstacles in the way of change in the third world but also by what we do right here at home. In the preceding chapter, we quoted philosopher Henry Shue, who argues that subsistence rights—what we call economic rights—are just as central to freedom as is the right to security from physical assault.

We would add only that until we expand our understanding of democracy and freedom to include economic rights—a job for all those able to work and income with dignity for those not able—the United States can't be an example of hope in the eyes of the world's poor.

Moreover, unless we so enlarge our understanding of democracy here at home, we doubt our government's capacity to understand or tolerate attempts for such change in the third world.

Beyond Economic Dogma

What would be required to expand our understanding of freedom and democracy, necessary both to end hunger here and to allow our nation to open the way to change in the third world?

First and foremost, a willingness to challenge the grip of economic dogma. In the opening essay of this book, we pinpointed what we see as the root of hunger—the antidemocratic concentration of power over economic resources, especially land and food.

But why have we allowed such concentration of power to continue, even at the price of untold human suffering? We began by answering that myths block our understanding. Here we want to probe deeper. We believe the answer lies in our externally and self-imposed powerlessness before economic dogma.

Seventeenth-century intellectual breakthroughs forced us to relinquish the comforting notion of an interventionist God who would put the human house aright. And what a frightening void we then faced! Running from the weighty implication that indeed human beings are responsible for society-inflicted suffering, we've desperately sought a substitute concept. We've longed for overriding laws we could place above human control, thus relieving us of moral responsibility.

With Newton's discovery of laws governing the physical world and with Darwin's parallel discovery in the realm of nature, we became convinced that there must indeed be laws governing the social world. And we thought we had found them! Here we'll mention two such "absolutes" that relate most directly to the causes of hunger. Though they are human creations, our society has made them sacred.

The first is the market. Who can deny that the market is a handy device for distributing goods? As we stated in chapter 7, societies that have attempted to do away with the market have run up against serious stumbling blocks. But once transformed into dogma, this useful device can become the cause of great suffering. As such, we are made blind to even the most obvious shortcomings of the market—its ability to respond only to the demands of wealth, not to the needs of people, its inability to register the real resource costs of production, and its inherent tendency to concentrate power in ever fewer hands.

Facing up to these shortcomings does not mean that we throw out the market in favor of another dogma, such as top-down state control. It means that we approach the market as a useful device, asking ourselves, under what circumstances can the market serve our values? In chapter 7, we set forth the very simple proposition that the more widely purchasing power is distributed, the more the market will respond to actual human needs.

But within a market system in which everything—land, food, human skills—is bought and sold with no restrictions, how can we work toward a more equal distribution of buying power? The answer is we cannot. Yet if we agree that tossing out the market would be foolish, what do we do?

In answering this question, we face the second major stumbling block posed by the prevailing economic dogma, the notion of unlimited private control over productive property.

Taken as economic dogma, the right to unlimited private control over productive property allows many Americans to accept as fair and inevitable the accelerating consolidation of our own farmland in fewer hands and the displacement of owner-operated farms, just as we have seen in much of the third world.

Although many Americans believe that the right to unlimited private control over productive property is the essence of the American way, this was certainly not the vision of many of our nation's founders, as we pointed out in the preceding chapter. In their view, property could serve liberty only when ownership was widely dispersed, and the right to property was valid only when it served society's interests. This view was widely held well into the nineteenth century. "Until after the Civil War, indeed, the assumption was widespread that a corporate charter was a privilege to be granted for purposes clearly in the public interest," writes historian Alan Trachtenberg.[1]

But by 1986, Ford executive Robert A. Lutz could declare without apology that his "primordial duty" is to his shareholders, while lamenting that his company's investment decisions meant the loss of tens of thousands of jobs.[2] Lutz seemed unaware that the notion that a corporation is responsible to its shareholders but not to its workers or to the larger society is in fact a very new idea.

More accurately, Lutz's view is the revival of a once discarded idea. When our nation's founders rejected monarchy, their cry was no taxation without representation. It was a demand for the accountability of governing structures. Applied to the much altered economic world of the twentieth century, their demand seems especially appropriate vis-à-vis our major corporations. Corporations now can have more impact on the lives of more people than the government of many a town, city, province, or state, notes Yale political scientist Robert A. Dahl.[3] Thus, today's claim by corporations of an unfettered right to allocate wealth we all helped to create may be closer to the concept of the divine right of kings than it is to the principles of democracy.[4]

Ownership with Responsibility

Working against hunger requires a fundamental rethinking of the meaning of ownership, certainly when applied to the productive resources on which all humanity depends. Such effort would be a first step in breaking free of the constraints of dogma.

In this rethinking, we believe Americans would be well served by going back to our roots, to the concept of property-*cum*-responsibility held by our nation's founders and to that of the original claimants to these soils, the American Indian nations. Because the community endures beyond the lifetime of any one individual, the Native American concept of community tenure carried within it an obligation to future generations as well.[5]

Ownership of productive resources, instead of an absolute to be placed above other values, should become a cluster of rights and responsibilities at the service of our deepest values. We should seek neither the rigid capitalist concept of unlimited private ownership nor the rigid statist concept of public ownership.

We introduced our discussion of property rights in response to the question, What would be required to achieve a dispersion of economic power such that the market could reflect human needs rather than the demands of wealth? Part of the answer, we have suggested, lies in rethinking property rights as a device to serve higher values, not as ends in themselves.

What Can We Do? Down to the Most Personal Question

Believing in the possibility of ending hunger means believing in the possibility of real change. Ironically, the greatest stumbling block of all is the notion held by many Americans that in the United States we have achieved the best that can be—no matter how flawed it may appear. Why is this ironic? Because as Americans we have a very different heritage. Near his death, the father of the Constitution, James Madison, said of our newborn nation, "[America] has been useful in proving things before held impossible."[6] Thus, the belief that indeed something new is always possible is our very birthright.

But how is it possible to believe that those who are poor and downtrodden—those who have so much working against them—can construct better lives? Observing ourselves and others, we've come to appreciate how hard it is to believe that others can change unless we experience change ourselves. With this realization, the crisis of world hunger becomes the personal question, How can I use my new knowledge to change myself so that I can contribute to ending hunger? The answer lies in dozens of often mundane choices we make *every day*.

These choices determine whether we are helping to end world hunger or to perpetuate it. Only as we make our choices conscious, do we become less and less victims of the world handed to us, and more and more its creators. The more we consciously align our life choices with the vision of the world we are working toward, the more powerful we become. We are more convincing to ourselves and more convincing to others.

How Do We Begin?

A first step is getting alternative sources of information. As we hope to have demonstrated, as long as we get only world news from television and the mainstream press, our vision will remain clouded by myths. That's why the resource section at the end of this book includes a list of useful periodicals that continually challenge prevailing dogma. Without a variety of independent sources, we can't fulfill our role as citizens to help reshape our government's definition of our national interest and its policies toward the poor in the third world and at home.

Then we must put that new knowledge to use. We are all educators—we teach friends, coworkers, and family. With greater confidence borne of greater knowledge, we can speak up effectively when others repeat self-defeating myths. Letters to the editor, letters to our representatives, letters to corporate decision makers all count too.

Perhaps the most important step, however, in determining whether we will be part of the solution to world hunger is the choice of a job—for those of us who have the luxury of choice. The challenge is to think through just how we apply our skills in jobs that confront, rather than accept, a status quo in which hunger and poverty are inevitable.

To have a real choice of career path or to contemplate involvement in social change, we also have to decide what level of material wealth we need for happiness. Millions of Americans are discovering the emptiness of our society's pervasive myth that material possessions are the key to satisfying lives. They are learning that the less they believe they need, the more freedom of choice they have in where to work, in where to live, in learning experiences.

In every community in America, people go hungry and lack shelter. Through our churches, community groups, trade unions, and local government, we can help address immediate needs and participate in generating a new understanding of democracy—not as a vote one casts every few years but as active participation in community planning for more and better jobs, affordable housing, and environmental protection. Working to elect officials committed to addressing the roots of hunger is essential to such change.

Where and how we spend our money—or don't spend it—is also a vote for the kind of world we want to create. For example, in most communities we can now choose to shop at food stores that offer less-processed and less-wastefully-packaged foods, stores managed by the workers themselves, instead of conglomerate-controlled supermarkets. And we can choose to redirect our consumer dollars in support of specific product boycotts, such as the successful boycotts of Nestlé that alerted the world to the crisis of infant deaths caused by the corporate promotion of infant formula in the third world, and of Campbell Soup that forced the company to sign a landmark contract with the Midwest farmworkers union, as well as the divestment campaign that helped bring majority rule to South Africa.

But little is possible by oneself. We need others to push us and to console us when we are overwhelmed by the enormity of the problems we face. The points we make about the myth of the passive poor in chapter 9 apply equally well to "passive" nonpoor. We, too, need the example of others. *The Quickening of America* is a book that offers inspiring glimpses into local initiatives for change in America.[7] We can become activists, and we can join activist organizations. When we are with others, we are stronger. Social movements brought women the vote, brought us landmark civil rights legislation, and helped end the war in Vietnam. They can end hunger too, if we lend them our energy and our commitment.

At the end of this book, we have included a selected list of some of the organizations working at a number of levels; all are part of the growth in understanding necessary to end hunger.

The Essential Ingredient

Our capacity to help end world hunger is infinite, for the roots of hunger touch every aspect of our lives—where we work, what we teach our children, how we fulfill our role as citizens, where we shop and save. But whether we seize these possibilities depends in large measure on a single ingredient. You might expect us to suggest that the needed ingredient is compassion for the millions who go hungry today. As we have pointed out, compassion is indeed a profoundly motivating emotion. It comes, however, relatively easy. Our ability to put ourselves in the shoes of others makes us truly human. Some even say it's in our genes and that we deny our innate compassion only at great peril to our own emotional well-being. There is another ingredient that's harder to come by. It is moral courage.

At a time when the old "isms" are clearly failing, many cling even more tenaciously to them. So it takes courage to cry out, "The emperor wears no clothes! The world is awash in food, and all of this suffering is the result of human decisions!"

To be part of the answer to world hunger means being willing to take risks, risks many of us find more frightening than physical danger. We have to risk being embarrassed or dismissed by friends or teachers as we speak out against deeply ingrained but false understandings of the world. It takes courage to ask people to think critically about ideas so taken for granted as to be like the air they breathe.

And there is another risk—the risk of being wrong. For part of letting go of old frameworks means grappling with new ideas and new approaches. Rather than fearing mistakes, courage requires that we continually test new concepts as we learn more of the world—ever willing to admit error, correct our course, and move forward.

But from where does such courage come? Surely from the same root as our compassion, from learning to trust that which our society so often discounts—our innate moral sensibilities, our deepest emotional intuitions about our connectedness to others' well-being. Only on this firm ground will we have the courage to challenge all dogma, demanding that the value of human life be paramount. Only with this new confidence will we stop twisting our values so that economic dogma might remain intact while millions of our fellow human beings starve amid ever greater abundance.

Notes

Beyond Guilt and Fear

1. Peter Uvin, "The State of World Hunger," in *The Hunger Report: 1995,* eds. Ellen Messer and Peter Uvin (Amsterdam: Gordon and Breach Publishers, 1996), 1–17, table 1.6; estimates vary; see chapters 1 and 5 of this book.

2. United Nations Children's Emergency Fund (UNICEF), *The State of the World's Children 1993* (Oxford: Oxford University Press and UNICEF, 1993), "statistical note," unnumbered. See also Richard A. Hoehn, "Introduction," in *Hunger 1997: What Governments Can Do* (Silver Spring, MD: Bread for the World Institute, 1996), 1.

3. Charles Clements, *Witness to War* (New York: Bantam, 1984), 104.

4. For discussion of the nuances of gender and food production, see Judith Carney, "Contracting a Food Staple in the Gambia," chapter 5 in *Living Under Contract: Contract Farming and Agrarian Transformation in Sub-Saharan Africa,* eds. Peter D. Little and Michael J. Watts, (Madison: University of Wisconsin Press, 1994); Beverly Grier, "Pawns, Porters and Petty Traders: Women in the Transition to Export Agriculture in Ghana," African Studies Center, Boston University, *Working Papers in African Studies,* no. 144, 1989; Gita Sen and Caren Grown, *Development, Crises and Alternative Visions: Third World Women's Perspectives* (New York: Monthly Review Press, 1986); and Carmen Diana Deere

and Magdalena León, eds., *Rural Women and State Policy: Feminist Perspectives on Latin American Agricultural Development* (Boulder: Westview Press, 1987).

5. Rehman Sobhan, *Agrarian Reform and Social Transformation* (London: Zed Books, 1993), table 1.

6. Mark S. Langevin and Peter Rosset, "Land Reform from Below: The Landless Workers Movement in Brazil," *Food First Backgrounder* (Institute for Food and Development Policy) no. 3, vol. 4 (1997): 1–4, 3.

7. United Nations Conference on Trade and Development, *Handbook of International Trade and Development Statistics 1994* (New York and Geneva: United Nations, 1995), table A2.

8. Michael E. Conroy, Douglas L. Murray, and Peter M. Rosset, *A Cautionary Tale: Failed U.S. Development Policy in Central America* (Boulder: Lynne Rienner/Food First Development Studies, 1996), figure 4.4.

9. For examples see *Structural Adjustment and the Spreading Crisis in Latin America* (Washington, DC: Development Gap for Alternative Policies, 1995); and Walden Bello with Shea Cunningham and Bill Rau, *Dark Victory: The United States, Structural Adjustment and Global Poverty* (London: Pluto Press/Food First Books/Transnational Institute, 1994).

MYTH 1: There's Simply Not Enough Food

1. Calculated from Food and Agriculture Organization, *1992 FAO Production Yearbook,* vol. 46 (Rome: FAO, 1993). Thirty-eight percent of the world's grain supply is now fed to livestock (*World Resources 1996–97,* [New York: Oxford University Press, 1996] table 10.3). Most of the land and other resources now used to produce feed grain could be used to grow grain and other foods for human consumption. Feed grains are grown because better-off consumers prefer livestock products, making feed grains more profitable than food grains. While daily calorie requirements vary greatly and are notoriously difficult to estimate, it seems reasonable to use the FAO figure of 2,450 per day for the average person (see P. R. Payne, "Measuring Malnutrition," *IDS Bulletin* 21, no. 3, July 1990). Calories adequate to cover energy needs are generally sufficient to meet protein needs, except for people (especially young children) subsisting on low-protein roots, tubers, and plantains.

2. Food and Agriculture Organization, *FAO Production Yearbook 1995,* vol. 49 (Rome: FAO, 1996).

3. Calculated from *FAO Time Series for State of Food and Agriculture,* (Rome: FAO, 1994).

4. Donald O. Mitchell and Merlinda D. Ingco, *The World Food Outlook* (Washington, DC: World Bank, 1993).

5. Merlinda D. Ingco, Donald O. Mitchell, and Alex F. McCalla, *Global Food Supply Prospects,* World Bank Technical Paper no. 353, 1996.

6. Food and Agriculture Organization, *FAO Production Yearbook* 1966, 1974, 1984, 1995 (Rome: FAO), table 9. See Philip Raikes, *Modernising Hunger: Famine, Food Surplus & Farm Policy in the EEC & Africa* (London: Catholic Institute for International Relations, 1988). Raikes argues that the FAO statistics seriously underestimate African production because, among other things, often only products sold through official marketing channels are counted. He suggests that there has been a decline in the proportion of production sold through such channels, as farmers sell elsewhere in response to artificially low prices.

7. Lisa C. Smith, Science, Engineering and Diplomacy Fellow, American Association for the Advancement of Science, *The FAO Measure of Chronic Undernourishment: What Is It Really Measuring?* (Washington, DC: U.S. Agency for International Development, Office of Population, Health and Human Development, June 1997), 6–7.

8. Thomas T. Poleman, "Quantifying the Nutrition Situation in Developing Countries," *Food Research Institute Studies* 18, no. 1: 9. This article is a good discussion of the multifaceted problems of most agricultural and nutritional statistics. (See also Donald McGranahan et al., *Measurement and Socioeconomic Development* [Geneva: United Nations Research Institute for Social Development, 1985]).

9. *Handbook of International Trade and Development Statistics* (New York and Geneva: United Nations Conference on Trade and Development, 1995), table 3.2. Data for food items include beverages, tobacco, and edible oil seeds.

10. Calculated from Food and Agriculture Organization, *1994 FAO Trade Yearbook,* vol. 48 (Rome: FAO, 1994), tables 7, 8. Classification of lowest-income countries according to the *World Development Report, 1992* (Washington, DC: World Bank).

11. According to the FAO, 21 percent of Indians, or about 185 million people, are undernourished (*Mapping Undernutrition: An Ongoing Process,* poster, 1996, Food and Agriculture Organization, Rome). However, in *The FAO Measure* cited above, Lisa Smith argues that this number is a

gross underestimation, as it is calculated not from real surveys but from projections based on food production and imports, and thus does not reliably take into account food distribution and access. A better index of the prevalence of hunger, she suggests, is the percent of children who are malnourished, which is calculated from surveys and represents the outcome of food availability *and* access. The FAO estimate for percent of children under five who are malnourished in India is 61 percent, the second highest in the world (*The Sixth World Food Survey*, FAO, 1996, appendix 2, table 8), suggesting that the total number of hungry people is probably far higher than the 21 percent or 185 million figures reported.

12. FAOSTAT Database (Rome: Food and Agriculture Organization, 1990–97).

13. James K. Boyce, "Agricultural Growth in Bangladesh, 1949–50 to 1980–81: A Review of the Evidence," *Economic and Political Weekly* 20, no. 13 (March 30, 1985): A31–A43.

14. FAOSTAT Database.

15. World Bank, *Bangladesh: Economic and Social Development Prospects*, report no. 5409 (Washington, DC: World Bank, April 1985), 18.

16. Food and Agriculture Organization, *FAO Production Yearbook 1995*, vol. 49 (Rome: FAO, 1996), table 17.

17. Steve Jones, "Agrarian Structure and Agricultural Innovation in Bangladesh: Panimara Village, Dhaka District," in *Understanding Green Revolutions*, ed. Tim Bayliss-Smith and Sudhir Wanmali (New York: Cambridge University Press, 1984), 194.

18. UNDF, *Human Development Report 1994* (New York: United Nations Development Program, 1994), table 2.

19. Food and Agriculture Organization, *FAO Trade Yearbook 1995*, vol. 49 (Rome: FAO, 1996) 13. See also UNDF, *Human Development Report 1994*, 134.

20. Lisa Smith, *The FAO Measure*, appendix A, table A1. See also *Food Security in Africa*, GAO testimony, United States General Accounting Office, Statement of Harold J. Johnson, associate director, International Relations and Trade Issues, National Security and International Affairs Division, Washington, DC, 1996.

21. Per Pinstrup-Andersen, "World Trends and Future Food Security," *Food Policy Report* (Washington, DC: International Food Policy Research Institute, March 1994), 9–10.

22. Calculated from Food and Agriculture Organization, *1994 FAO Trade Yearbook,* table 8. When all agricultural products are taken into account, the figure rises to twenty countries (Ibid., table 7). Note that the increase of imports in a specific country may reflect an increase in food aid received by it. Calculations of imports include food aid, according to James Hill, senior economist at the North American UN FAO Liaison Office, Washington, D.C., interviewed by Joseph Collins in May 1986.

23. Calculated from *1984 FAO Trade Yearbook.* For Chad, Niger, Mauritania, Mali, Burkina Faso, and Senegal, years of net exports were 1980, 1982, and 1983. Years of net imports were 1981 and 1984 due to exceptionally high imports into Senegal and Niger those two years.

24. Reports from two of the Sahelian countries, Niger and Burkina Faso (formerly Upper Volta), estimate that traders smuggle out as much as half the grain produced to sell elsewhere to customers able to pay more. (Interview with chief economist, U.S. Agency for International Development Mission, Ouagadougou, Upper Volta on January 17, 1977).

25. During the comparatively less severe drought of 1982–85, the value of food exported by these countries was three-fourths that of food imported, Chad, Mali, and Niger being net exporters (calculated from *FAO Trade Yearbook 1985,* table 7).

26. *FAO Production Yearbook* 1966, 1974, 1984, 1990, tables 9 and 10.

27. Calculated from FAOSTAT Database, data on production, consumption, availability, and imports of cereal products in 1995, September 17, 1997.

28. Sara S. Berry, "The Food Crisis and Agrarian Change in Africa: A Review Essay," *African Studies Review* 27, no. 2 (June 1984): 59–97. See also Jane Guyer, "Women's Role in Development," in *Strategies for African Development,* ed. Robert J. Berg and Jennifer Seymour Witaker (Berkeley: University of California Press, 1986), esp. 393–396. Also see *Modernising Hunger.*

29. Lisa Smith, *The FAO Measure,* pp. 15–16. The much reported but, she argues, inaccurate FAO estimate of chronic undernourishment for sub-Saharan Africa is 43 percent, while it is only 22 percent for South Asia. Yet the percent of children under five who are malnourished, a better index of hunger (see note 8 above), is 53 percent in South Asia, almost double that of sub-Saharan Africa (30 percent).

30. Donald L. Plucknett, "Prospects of Meeting Future Food Needs through New Technology," in *Population and Food in the Early Twenty-*

First Century: Meeting Future Food Demand of an Increasing Population, ed. Nurul Islam (Washington, DC: International Food Policy Research Institute, 1995).

31. Gerhard K. Heilig, "How Many People Can Be Fed on Earth?" in *The Future Population of the World: What Can We Assume Today?* ed. Wolfgang Lutz (Laxenburg, Austria: International Institute for Applied Systems Analysis, 1996, revised edition).

32. See Stephen K. Commins et al., eds., *Africa's Agrarian Crisis: The Roots of Famine* (Boulder: Lynne Rienner, 1985); Nigel Twose, *Fighting the Famine* (San Francisco: Food First Books, 1985); Michael Watts, "Entitlements or Empowerment? Famine and Starvation in Africa," *Review of African Political Economy*, no. 51 (1991): 9–26.

33. Paul Harrison, *The Greening of Africa: Breaking Through in the Battle for Land and Food* (Nairobi: Academy Science Publishers, 1996). See also Eric R. Wolf, *Europe and the People Without History* (Berkeley: University of California Press, 1982). See also Barbara Dinham and Colin Hines, *Agribusiness in Africa: A Study of the Impact of Big Business on Africa's Food and Agricultural Production* (Trenton, NJ: Africa World Press, 1984).

34. Paul Richards, "Ecological Change and the Politics of African Land Use," *African Studies Review* 26, no. 2 (June 1983). See also Paul Richards, *Indigenous Agricultural Revolution* (Boulder: Westview Press, 1985).

35. See Bill Rau, *Feast to Famine* (Washington, DC: Africa Faith and Justice Network, 1985), esp. chapter 6. See also Bonnie K. Campbell, "Inside the Miracle: Cotton in the Ivory Coast," in *The Politics of Agriculture in Tropical Africa*, ed. Jonathan Barker (Beverly Hills: Sage, 1984), 154–168.

36. World Resources Institute, *World Resources, 1994–1995* (New York: Oxford University Press, 1994), 48–49. For examples of the nuances of gender, policy, investment, and food production, see Judith Carney, "Contracting a Food Staple in the Gambia," in *Living under Contract: Contract Farming and Agrarian Transformation in Sub-Saharan Africa*, ed. Peter D. Little and Michael J. Watts (Madison: University of Wisconsin Press, 1994); Beverly Grier, "Pawns, Porters and Petty Traders: Women in the Transition to Export Agriculture in Ghana," African Studies Center, Boston University, *Working Papers in African Studies*, no. 144, 1989.

37. Independent Commission on International Humanitarian Issues, *Famine: A Man-Made Disaster?* (New York: Vintage Books, 1985), 85–89.

38. See *Africa, Make or Break: Action for Recovery* (London: Oxfam UK, 1993); and John Mihevc, *The Market Tells Them So: The World Bank and Economic Fundamentalism in Africa* (Penang, Malaysia, and Accra, Ghana: Third World Network, 1995).

39. Mihevc, *The Market Tells Them So;* and Manfred Bienefeld, *Structural Adjustment and Rural Labor Markets in Tanzania* (Geneva: International Labor Organization, 1991).

40. Mihevc, *The Market Tells Them So.*

41. Calculated from FAOSTAT Database.

42. A typical ad appearing in an African newspaper in the early 1970s, cited in Jean-Yves Carfantan and Charles Condamines, *Vaincre la Faim, C'est Possible* (Paris: L'Harmattan, 1976), 63.

43. Gunilla Andrae and Björn Beckman, *The Wheat Trap: Bread and Underdevelopment in Nigeria* (London: Zed Books, 1985).

44. Joel E. Cohen, *How Many People Can the Earth Support?* (New York: W. W. Norton, 1995), esp. appendix 3.

45. Ben Wisner, "The Limitations of 'Carrying Capacity,'" *Political Environments* (Winter/Spring 1996): 1, 3–6.

46. Cohen, *How Many People Can the Earth Support?* See appendix 3.

47. UN Department for Economic and Social Information and Policy Analysis, Population Division, *World Population Prospects: The 1996 Revision. Annex 1: Demographic Indicators,* table A2.

48. According to the *1994 Human Development Report,* by the United Nations Development Program (UNDP New York and Oxford University Press, 1994), the average per capita calorie supply for China in the early 1990s was 12 percent above minimum requirements. See also Elizabeth Croll, *The Family Rice Bowl: Food and the Domestic Economy in China* (Geneva: UN Research Institute for Social Development, 1982). Though Lester Brown of the WorldWatch Institute recently created a media frenzy when he argued that China's future grain consumption would grossly deplete the food available to the rest of the world (Lester R. Brown, *Who Will Feed China? A Wake-Up Call for a Small Planet,* New York: W. W. Norton, 1995), calmer heads responded by recalculating his data, as well as furnishing new data that clearly demonstrates China's ability

to produce sufficient grain for its future needs. See Vaclav Smil, *Who Will Feed China? Concerns and Prospects for the Next Generation* (Fourth Annual Hopper Lecture, University of Guelph, 1996); Jikun Huang et al., *China's Food Economy to the Twenty-First Century: Supply, Demand, and Trade* (Washington, DC: International Food Policy Research Institute, Food, Agriculture and the Environment Discussion Paper no. 19, 1997); Feng Lu, *Grain versus Food: A Hidden Issue in China's Food Policy Debate* (China Center for Economic Research, Peking University, Working Paper no. E1996003); Xiaoguang Kang, *Excerpts of "How Chinese Feed Themselves"— Reply to Lester R. Brown's "Who Will Feed China?"* (Chinese Academy of Sciences, Research Center for Eco-Environmental Sciences, Department for the Study of National Conditions, 1997).

49. In 1994, the United States had 1.6 ha/per capita of cropland and China had 0.4 ha/per capita (calculated from FAOSTAT Database).

50. *Hunger, 1997. What Governments Can Do,* Seventh Annual Report on the State of World Hunger (Silver Spring, MD: Bread for the World Institute, 1996), 114–15, tables 5, 6.

51. World Food Programme. INTERFAIS Internet information system, September 19, 1997.

52. Calculations based on the 1994 figure for hungry children under twelve years of age. *Hunger, 1997,* p. 114, table 5.

MYTH 2: Nature's to Blame

1. *Church Perspective,* San Francisco Council of Churches (February 1986).

2. For an excellent interpretation of the Irish potato famine see Rick Crawford, "The Laws of Nature, or the Limitations of Ideology: Why Starvation Killed One Million in the Richest Nation on Earth," *Voices: Sierra Club Journal of the Environmental Justice Network* 2, no. 3 (Autumn 1997): 15, 19, 32, 36.

3. John MacHale, *Letter to Lord Russell* (1846), cited in Cecil Woodham-Smith, *The Great Hunger: Ireland 1845–9* (New York: Harper & Row, 1962). For more recent scholarship see Joel Mokyr, *Why Ireland Starved: A Quantitative and Analytical History of the Irish Economy, 1800–1850* (Boston: Allen & Unwin, 1983); and Cormac O'Grada, *Ireland Before and After the Famine: Explorations in Economic History 1800–1925,* 2nd edition (Manchester: Manchester University Press, 1993).

4. Anders Wijkman and Lloyd Timberlake, *Natural Disasters: Acts of God or Acts of Man?* (London and Washington, DC: Earthscan, 1984).

5. *Disaster History Report* (Washington, DC: U.S. Office of Foreign Disaster Assistance, April 1997).

6. Interview by Michael Scott of Oxfam America, Boston, 1979.

7. Amartya Sen, *Poverty and Famines* (Oxford: Clarendon Press, 1981).

8. Ibid., 151, table 10.1.

9. Betsy Hartmann and James Boyce, *A Quiet Violence: View from a Bangladesh Village* (San Francisco: Food First Books, 1983), 189.

10. Talk by Mahmood Mandani, dean of social sciences, Makerere University, Kampala, Uganda, March 19, 1985). Following the speech he was stripped of his citizenship and deported. Abridged version printed in *Dollars and Sense*, no. 109 (September 1985): 6, 7, 15.

11. The exception was mineral-rich Mauritania, which has very little land suitable for cultivation. Information from Marcel Ganzin, director, Food Policy and Nutrition Division, FAO, Rome, December 18, 1975.

12. Calculated from Food and Agriculture Organization, *FAO Trade Yearbook 1975* (Rome: FAO, 1975). For further background on famine in the Sahel, see Richard Franke and Barbara Chasin, *Seeds of Famine* (Totowa, NJ: Rowman and Allenheld, 1980); Rolando V. García, *Nature Pleads Not Guilty: Drought and Man: The 1972 Case History* (New York: Pergamon Press, 1981), 181–195; and Michael Lofchie, "Political and Economic Origins of African Hunger," *Journal of Modern African Studies* 13, no. 4 (1975): 551–567.

13. Michael Watts, *Silent Violence: Food, Famine and Peasantry in Northern Nigeria* (Berkeley: University of California Press, 1983).

14. Telephone interview by Joseph Collins with John Sutter, a Rural Poverty Program officer at Ford Foundation, Dakar, Senegal, February 1986.

15. During the past three decades, rainfall in the Sahel has been 20 to 40 percent less than it was during the three previous decades. M. B. K. Darkoh, "Desertification: Its Human Costs," *Forum for Applied Research and Public Policy* 11, no. 3 (Fall 1996): 13.

16. Ibid., 13–14. See also Tesfaye Teklu, Joachim von Braun, and Elsayed Zaki, *Drought and Famine Relationships in Sudan: Policy Implications*, Report no. 88 (Washington, DC: International Food Policy Research

Institute, 1991); and Peter Rosset, John Gershman, Shea Cunningham, and Marilyn Borchardt, "Myths and Root Causes: Hunger, Population and Development," *Food First Backgrounder* 1, no. 1 (Institute for Food and Development Policy, 1994): 1–8.

17. Nigel Twose, *Fighting the Famine* (San Francisco: Food First Books, 1985), 18.

18. Michael Watts, personal communication, May 21, 1986.

19. John Scheuring, International Crops Research Institute for the Semi-Arid Tropics (ICRISAT), Bamako, Mali, personal communication to authors dated January 8, 1986. See also Watts, *Silent Violence*, 373–465.

20. For an introduction to the problems of famine and the environment of the region, see Jeremy Swift, "Disaster and a Sahelian Nomad Economy," in *Drought in Africa*, ed. David Dalby and R. J. Harrison (London: Centre for African Studies, 1973), 71–79; Douglas L. Johnson, "The Response of Pastoral Nomads to Drought in the Absence of Outside Intervention," paper commissioned by the United Nations Special Sahelian Office, December 19, 1973; F. Fraser Darling and M. Taghi Farvar, "Ecological Consequences of Sedentarization of Nomads," in *The Careless Technology*, ed. M. Taghi Farvar and John P. Milton (Garden City, NJ: Natural History Press, 1972); and Wijkman and Timberlake, *Natural Disasters*, 23.

21. Independent Commission on International Humanitarian Issues, *Famine: A Man-Made Disaster?* (New York: Vintage, 1985), 86–87.

22. Ibid.

23. Calculated from Food and Agriculture Organization, *1984 FAO Trade Yearbook* (Rome: FAO, 1985).

24. See Michael Watts, "Entitlements of Empowerment? Famine and Starvation in Africa," *Review of African Political Economy* 51 (1991): 9–26.

25. Because many of our sources for the material on Ethiopia are still working in that country and fear government reaction against them, they have asked to remain anonymous.

26. Interview with Guido Gryseels, vice director for International Livestock Center for Africa, Addis Ababa, January 21, 1985.

27. *Facts on File* 45, no. 2303 (January 1985): 1–11.

28. Rene Lefort, *Ethiopia: An Heretical Revolution?* (London: Zed Press, 1983), esp. 18–36; Jason Clay and Bonnie Holcomb, *Politics and the Ethiopian Famine, 1984–1985* (Cambridge, MA: Cultural Survival, 1985), 5–23; and Pranab Bardhan, "Method in the Madness? A Political Economy Analysis of the Ethnic Conflicts in Less Developed Countries," *World Development* 25, no. 9 (1997): 1381–1398.

29. Eiichi Shindo, "Hunger and Weapons: The Entropy of Militarization," *Review of African Political Economy* 33 (August 1985): 6–22.

30. Robin Luckham and Dawit Bekele, "Foreign Powers and Militarism in the Horn of Africa," *Review of African Political Economy* 30 (September 1984): 16, citing figures in U.S. Arms Control and Disarmament Agency, *World Military Expenditures and Arms Transfers, 1971–1980.* Some analysts of Ethiopia cite even higher figures for arms imports. See, for instance, Hailu Lemma, "The Politics of Famine in Ethiopia," *Review of African Political Economy* 33 (August 1985): 51.

31. In 1980 to 1981, the government farms absorbed 80 percent of the agricultural credit, 82 percent of fertilizer imports, and 73 percent of the improved seeds, as well as consuming large amounts of imported oil running their 3,500 tractors. See World Bank, *Ethiopia: Agricultural Sector,* 20–21.

32. Data are from 1984. See Graham Hancock, *Ethiopia* (London: Victor Gollancz, 1985), 52. For comparison with other nations, see tables for third world nations in *South* (September 1985).These figures apparently do not include Ethiopia's sizable air force.

33. Estimate taken from Clay and Holcomb, *Politics and the Ethiopian Famine,* 8.

34. For a good history of the conflict see Rodolfo Stavenhagen, *Ethnic Conflicts and the Nation-State* (New York: St. Martin's Press and UNRISD, 1996).

35. Letter from Michael Glantz, Center for Atmospheric Research, Boulder, Colorado, May 6, 1986. In March 1986, the United Nations Office for Emergency Operations in Africa noted that in four of the five African countries still affected by famine (Ethiopia, Angola, Mozambique, and Sudan) the resolution of armed conflicts is the essential condition for ending the famines. See *Status Report on the Emergency Situation in Africa,* Report no. OEOA/3/7 (New York: United Nations, March 1986). See also Patrick Webb, Joachim von Braun, and Yisehac

Yohannes, *Famine in Ethiopia: Policy Implications of Coping Failure at National and Household Levels*, Report no. 92 (Washington, DC: International Food Policy Research Institute, 1992).

36. Within a period of three months in 1994, an estimated 500,000 to 800,000 people were killed, over 2,000,000 fled to neighboring countries, and maybe half as many became internally displaced within Rwanda. (Steering Committee of the Joint Evaluation of Emergency Assistance to Rwanda, *Joint Evaluation of Emergency Assistance to Rwanda* [Copenhagen, March 1996], 4. Available on the web at www.ingenioeren.dk/danida/rwanda.htm.)

37. For example, among the literally hundreds of articles from the popular press are: Nicholas D. Kristoff, "Rwandans, Once Death's Agents, Now Its Victims" *New York Times* (April 13, 1997); James C. McKinley, Jr., "New Rwanda Killings Dim Hopes for Amity" *New York Times* (February 17, 1997). The notion that ethnicity and ethnic conflict stem from human nature is thoroughly debunked by John Vandermeer in *Reconstructing Biology: Genetics and Ecology in the New World Order* (New York: John Wiley & Sons, 1996).

38. *Joint Evaluation*, 4.

39. *Joint Evaluation*, 17.

40. Government estimates in 1990 showed that 81 percent of rural households "earned money from informal activities such as brickmaking, carpentry and sewing, and almost everyone was active in the parallel or 'black' economy, if only from time to time. This included cross-border trade and barter, or smuggling, with neighboring countries" (The Economist Intelligence Unit, 1995, quoted in *Joint Evaluation*, 16).

41. In 1995, 91.3 percent of the economically active population belonged to the agricultural sector (*FAO Production Yearbook 1995* [Rome: FAO, 1996], table 3). The economy has almost exclusively been built around two export crops: coffee and tea. Before the upheavals, important industrial subsectors included beverages and food, detergents, textiles, and agricultural tools such as hoes and machetes (World Bank figures, *Joint Evaluation*, 18).

42. Coffee accounted for more than two-thirds of Rwanda's foreign exchange revenues (ibid., 36).

43. Ibid.

44. Moderate debt, a moderate inflation rate and a higher than average growth rate for sub-Saharan Africa during the 1980s (at least up to the second half of the decade) made the World Bank and others consider it a successful African economy (*Joint Evaluation*, 33).

45. Ibid., 37.

46. Ibid.

47. See G. Vassall-Adams, *Rwanda: An Agenda for International Action* (Oxford: Oxfam Publications, 1994); S. Marysse and T. de Herdt, *L'Ajustement Structurel en Afrique: Les Expériences du Mali et du Rwanda* (Antwerp: UFSIA/Centre for Development Studies, 1993); and S. T. Marysse, T. de Herdt, and E. Ndayambaje, *Rwanda: Appauvrissement et Ajustement Structurel* (Brussels: CEDAF/L'Harmattan, 1994), quoted in *Joint Evaluation*.

48. Defined as consumption of less than one thousand calories a day (*Joint Evaluation*, 36).

49. J. Maton, *Développement Économique et Social au Rwanda entre 1980 et 1993, le Dixième Dicile en Face de l'Apocalypse* (Gent: UG/Unité d'Enseignement et de Recherche au Développement, 1994), quoted in *Joint Evaluation*.

50. Marysse and de Herdt, *L'Ajustement Structurel en Afrique*.

51. *Joint Evaluation*, 4; also see Pranab Bardhan, "Method in the Madness?" 1384.

52. Estimates vary from 500,000 to 800,000 deaths (*Joint Evaluation*).

53. In the early 1990s, farmers' real income decreased as a result of the decline in the price of their produce and inflation produced by devaluations and deficit financing. The "benefits" of the devaluation were not passed on to coffee farmers (*Joint Evaluation*). See also Marysse, et al. Rwanda, 1994; World Bank, *Rwanda: Country Strategy Paper* (Washington, DC, 1992); and World Bank, *Implementation Completion Report: Rwandese Republic: Structural Adjustment Credit* (Washington, DC, 1995).

54. Public wages were affected by the restructuring package, and while some employees were able to compensate by participating in increased private-sector activity, others had their fears about the future compounded in view of the overall economic and political deterioration (*Joint Evaluation*, 38).

55. The number of internally displaced persons, many in camps, was estimated at about 1 million, and the number of Rwandan refugees in other countries at about 2 million (UNHCR [U.N. High Commission for Refugees], Special Unit for Rwanda and Burundi, March 1995, quoted in *Joint Evaluation*, 54).

56. *Joint Evaluation*, 19.

57. Tourism, for example, was a flourishing source of income. Rwanda ranked third in tourism earnings in the continent (*Joint Evaluation*, 19, 47).

58. See Vassall-Adams, *Rwanda*, 1994.

59. Ellen Messer, "Hunger as a Weapon of War in 1994," in *The Hunger Report: 1995*, ed. Ellen Messer and Peter Uvin (Amsterdam: Gordon and Breach Science Publishers, 1996), 19–48.

MYTH 3: Too Many Mouths to Feed

1. Ben J. Wattenberg, "The Population Explosion Is Over," *The New York Times Magazine* (November 23, 1997): 60–63.

2. Shrinking populations can lead to an age distribution dominated by elderly people, with increasing numbers of middle-aged, childless couples.

3. Unless indicated otherwise, all population growth and fertility figures in this chapter come from *World Population Prospects: The 1996 Revision*, the conservative and most widely accepted set of population data and projections, produced periodically by the highly regarded Population Division of the Department for Economic and Social Information and Policy Analysis, United Nations, New York. The projections produced by the division are known popularly as the "UN Projections."

4. Thomas Merrick et al., "Population Dynamics in Developing Countries," in *Population and Development: Old Debates, New Conclusions*, ed. Robert Cassen (Transaction Publishers, New Brunswick, NJ, 1994), 79–105.

5. *World Population Prospects*, various projections throughout.

6. Merrick et al., "Population Dynamics," 82.

7. *World Population Prospects*, annex 1, 10–11.

8. Tomas Frejka, "Long-Range Global Population Projections: Lessons Learned," in *The Future Population of the World*, ed. Wolfgang Lutz (London: Earthscan Publications, 1996), 5, table 1.1.

9. "End of World Population Growth Projected for 21st Century," *International Institute for Applied Systems Analysis News Release* (October 9, 1996), 1.

10. Paul Ehrlich, *The Population Bomb* (New York: Sierra Club/Ballantine, 1968).

11. A similar reiteration of arguments over time, never borne out by subsequent history, can be seen in the following works by Lester R. Brown: "The World Outlook of Conventional Agriculture," *Science* 158 (1967):604–611; *By Bread Alone* (New York: Praeger, 1974); *State of the World 1990* (New York: W. W. Norton); and *Tough Choices: Facing the Challenge of Food Security* (New York: W. W. Norton, 1996), among others.

12. Paul Ehrlich, *The Population Explosion* (New York: Simon and Schuster, 1990).

13. A good summary of the evidence for fertility decline can be found in *The Future Population of the World: What Can We Assume Today?* ed. Wolfgang Lutz (London: Earthscan Publications, 1996).

14. For example, see the many publications of the Population Council available on the web at www.popcouncil.org. See also Rockefeller Foundation, *High Stakes: The United States, Global Population and Our Common Future* (New York: Rockefeller Foundation, 1997).

15. 1990 hectares-per-capita values are: Trinidad and Tobago 0.09, Guatemala 0.20 (World Resources Institute, *World Resources 1992–93* [New York: Oxford University Press, 1992], table 18.2). 1987 prevalence-of-stunted-children values are: Trinidad 5.0, Guatemala 57.9 (Food and Agricultural Organization, *The Sixth World Food Survey* [Rome: FAO, 1996], table 8, appendix 2).

16. Per capita cropland from the World Resources Institute, *World Resources 1992–93* (New York: Oxford University Press, 1992), table 18.2. Life expectancy from World Bank, *Human Development Report 1994* (New York: Oxford University Press, 1994), table 2.

17. Per capita cropland from *World Resources 1992–93*, table 18.2.

18. Calculated from *World Resources*, table 18.2; Bread for the World Institute *Hunger, 1997: What Governments Can Do* (Silver Spring, MD, 1996), table 4; and World Bank, *Human Development Report, 1994*, table 13.

19. Per capita, the Netherlands has only about one-thirteenth the cropland of the United States. Yet if the people of the Netherlands consumed

all they produce (i.e., did not export food), almost five thousand calories of food would be available per person, not even counting imports. Calculated from Food and Agriculture Organization, *FAO Food Balance Sheets, 1992–1994* (Rome: FAO, 1995).

20. Frederick H. Buttel and Laura T. Raynolds, "Population Growth, Agrarian Structure, Food Production, and Food Distribution in the Third World," in *Food and Natural Resources,* ed. David Pimentel and Carl W. Hall (New York: Academy Press, 1989), 325–361.

21. John Vandermeer, *Reconstructing Biology: Genetics and Ecology in the New World Order,* (New York: John Wiley & Sons, 1996), ch. 14. In his now classic 1980 study, another ecologist, William W. Murdoch, found much the same thing—namely, that inequality was the key determinant of population growth *The Poverty of Nations: The Political Economy of Hunger and Population* (Baltimore: Johns Hopkins University Press, 1980).

22. Planned Parenthood Federation of America, *Echoes from the Past* (New York: Planned Parenthood, 1979), 181.

23. M. T. Cain, "The Economic Activities of Children in a Village in Bangladesh," *Population and Development Review* 3 (1977): 201–228, cited in Murdoch, *Poverty of Nations,* 26.

24. M. Nag, B. White, and R. C. Peet, "An Anthropological Approach to the Study of the Economic Value of Children in Java and Nepal," *Current Anthropology* 19 (1978): 293–306.

25. Murdoch, *Poverty of Nations,* 45.

26. Frances Moore Lappé and Rachel Schurman, *Taking Population Seriously* (San Francisco: Food First Books, 1990), 26–27.

27. See Lant H. Pritchett, "Desired Fertility and the Impact of Population Policies," *Population and Development Review* 20, no. 1 (March 1994): 1–55. See also Paul Schultz, "Human Capital, Family Planning, and Their Effects on Population Growth," *American Economic Review* 84, no. 2 (May 1994): 255–260. While some birth control advocates have criticized this view (for example, James C. Knowles et al., "The Impact of Population Policies: Comment," *Population and Development Review* 20, no. 3 [1994]: 611–615; and John Bongaarts, "The Impact of Population Policies: Comment," *Population and Development Review,* 20, no. 3 [1994]: 616–620), the weight of evidence supports the position that under the vast majority of circumstances people have the number of children they want (see Lant H. Pritchett, "The Impact of Population

Policies: Reply," *Population and Development Review* 20, no. 3 [1994]: 621–630). Some studies purport to show that the presence of family planning programs is the key element leading to fertility decline; nevertheless, their own data generally support the view that people take advantage of these programs when they want them, in order to have the number of children that make sense from the point of view of economic development and improved education and economic opportunity for women (see, for example, Paul J. Gertler and John W. Molyneaux, "How Economic Development and Family Planning Programs Combined to Reduce Indonesian Fertility," *Demography* 31, no. 1 [1994]: 33–63, 57–58, 60). The editors of a recent volume comparing four cases of fertility decline conclude that "fertility change occurs with or without access to modern contraception" (*Understanding Reproductive Change: Kenya, Tamil Nadu, Punjab, Costa Rica,* ed. Bertil Egerö and Mikael Hammarskjöld [Lund, Sweden: Lund University Press, 1994], 20).

28. Lappé and Schurman, *Taking Population Seriously,* 26.

29. Ibid., 29.

30. U.S. Agency for International Development, *Sri Lanka: The Impact of PL 480 Title I Assistance, AID Project Impact Evaluation,* Report no. 39 (Washington, DC: U.S. Agency for International Development, October 1982), C-8.

31. *World Population Prospects: The 1996 Revision,* 378, annex 2 and 3.

32. Medea Benjamin, Joseph Collins, and Michael Scott, *No Free Lunch: Food and Revolution in Cuba Today* (New York: Grove Press/Food First Books, 1986), 26.

33. Ibid., 92. In 1983, in fact, the Organization of American States reported that Cuba ranked second in per capita food availability in Latin America. See also Peter Rosset and Medea Benjamin, ed., *The Greening of the Revolution: Cuba's Experiment with Organic Agriculture* (Melbourne: Ocean Press, 1994), 10, table 1.

34. *World Population Prospects: The 1996 Revision,* 154, annex 2 and 3.

35. S. Kumar, *The Impact of Subsidized Rice on Food Consumption in Kerala,* Research Report no. 5 (Washington, DC: International Food Policy Research Institute, 1979).

36. A. V. Jose, "Poverty and Inequality: The Case of Kerala," in *Poverty in Rural Asia,* ed. Azizur Rahman Khan and Eddy Lee (Bangkok:

International Labour Organization, Asian Employment Programme, 1983), 108.

37. John Ratcliffe, "Social Justice and the Demographic Transition: Lessons from India's Kerala State," in *Practicing Health for All,* ed. D. Morley, J. Rohde, and G. Williams (Oxford: Oxford University Press, 1983), 65. See also John Ratcliffe, "Toward a Social Justice Theory of Demographic Transition: Lessons from India's Kerala State," *Janasamkhya* (Kerala University, June 1983) 1.

38. Lappé and Schurman, *Taking Population Seriously,* 58–59.

39. Richard W. Franke and Barbara H. Chasin, *Kerala: Radical Reform as Development in an Indian State,* 2nd ed. (Oakland: Food First Books, 1994), ii.

40. World Bank, *World Development Report 1984,* table 28.

41. U.S. Agency for International Development, *Women of the World: A Chartbook for Developing Regions* (Washington, DC: Bureau of the Census, 1985), 30–33.

42. Paul Schultz, "Human Capital, Family Planning, and Their Effects on Population Growth," *American Economic Review* 84, no. 2 (May 1994): 255–260.

43. Matthew Lockwood, "Development Policy and the African Demographic Transition: Issues and Questions," *Journal of International Development* 7, no. 1 (1995): 1–23, tables 1, 3.

44. Ibid. See also Gilbert Arum and Wahida Patwa Shah, *Towards a Comprehensive Population Policy. A Review of Population Policies in Kenya* (Nairobi: KENGO Policy Study Series, 1994).

45. Lockwood, "Development Policy," 15.

46. Locoh, quoted in Lockwood, "Development Policy," 16.

47. See, for example, Jonathon Porritt, "Birth of a Brave New World Order," *Manchester Guardian,* September 11, 1994.

48. Wim Dierckxsens, "Costa Rica—The Unfinished Demographic Transition," 135–163 *Understanding Reproductive Change* (Lund, Sweden: Lund University Press, 1994), 137–138.

49. An example of this kind of thinking can be found in Porritt, "Birth of a Brave New World Order."

50. D. J. Hernández, *Success or Failure? Family Planning Programs in the Third World* (Westport, CT: Greenwood Press, 1984), 133. See also In-

terdisciplinary Communications Program, "The Policy Relevance of Recent Social Research on Fertility," *Occasional Monograph Series*, no. 2 (Washington, DC: Smithsonian Institution, 1974).

51. W. Parker Mauldin, Bernard Berelson, and Zenas Sykes, "Conditions of Fertility Decline in Developing Countries, 1965–1975," *Studies in Family Planning* 9, no. 5 (1978): 121. See also W. Parker Mauldin and Robert J. Lapham, "Contraceptive Prevalence: The Influence of Organized Family Planning Programs," *Studies in Family Planning* 16, no. 3 (1985).

52. Pritchett, "Desired Fertility," and Schultz, "Human Capital."

53. See discussion in Murdoch, *Poverty of Nations*, 56–57.

54. World Health Organization, *Injectible Hormonal Contraceptives: Technical Aspects and Safety* (Geneva: WHO, 1982), 17–23. WHO Collaborative Study of Neoplasia and Steroid Contraceptives, "Invasive Cervical Cancer and Depot-medroxy-progesterone Acetate," *Bulletin of the World Health Organization* 63, no. 3 (1985): 508; L. C. Powell and R. J. Seymour, "Effects of Depot-Medroxyprogesterone Acetate as a Contraceptive Agent," *American Journal of Obstetrics and Gynecology* 110 (1971): 36–41. See also Asoka Bandarage, *Women, Population and Global Crisis. A Political-Economic Analysis* (London: Zen Books, 1997), 83–84; and Betsy Hartmann, *Reproductive Rights and Wrongs: The Global Politics of Population Control*, revised edition (Boston: South End Press, 1995), 200–207.

55. Bandarage, *Women, Population and Global Crisis*, 84.

56. Ibid., 86.

57. Ibid., 70–80.

58. Ibid., 71.

59. Asoka Bandarage, "A New and Improved Population Control Policy?" *Sojourner: The Women's Forum* 20, no. 1 (1994): 17–19.

60. Hartmann, *Reproductive Rights and Wrongs*, 247–248.

61. Ibid. See also Vandermeer, *Reconstructing Biology*, 370.

62. Vandermeer, *Reconstructing Biology*, 370.

63. *La Operación*, produced by Ana María García, CINGLD, 1982.

64. Bandarage, *Women, Population and Global Crisis*; and Hartmann, *Reproductive Rights and Wrongs*.

65. *Maquiladora* factories assemble imported components into goods for re-export and pay very low wages. See Laura Eggertson, "It's Pregnancy

Tests—or Else—in Mexico: Women Undergo Forced Exams, and If the Result Is Positive, Goodbye," *San Francisco Examiner,* November 16, 1997.

66. Bandarage, *Women, Population and Global Crisis,* 85–86.

67. Ibid., 163–167.

68. Population Council, "Do Family Planning Programs Affect Fertility Preferences?" *Population Council News Release* (March 24, 1997).

69. Hartmann, *Reproductive Rights and Wrongs,* 235–241.

70. Pritchett, "Desired Fertility," 35–39.

71. Ibid., 38.

72. Ibid., 37.

73. Hartmann, *Reproductive Rights and Wrongs,* 236.

74. Ibid., 224.

75. See Bandarage, *Women, Population and Global Crisis,* 78–80.

76. John Ratcliffe, "China's One Child Policy: Solving the Wrong Problem?" (unpublished manuscript, 1985), 38.

77. From 1960 to 1980 total fertility fell by an average of 0.12 percent per year. Since 1980 it has fallen by an average 0.09 percent per year. Calculated from *World Population Prospects,* 140–141, annex 2 and 3.

78. For example, see Mary Tiffen, Michael Mortimore, and Francis Gichuki, *More People, Less Erosion: Environmental Recovery in Kenya* (New York: John Wiley & Sons, 1994).

MYTH 4: Food vs. Our Environment

1. Staff of the Interim Secretariat for the UN Convention to Combat Desertification, "The Convention to Combat Desertification: Actions to Date in Africa and the Mediterranean," *The Arid Lands Newsletter,* no. 40 (Fall/Winter 1996).

2. John Vandermeer and Ivette Perfecto, *Breakfast of Biodiversity: The Truth About Rain Forest Destruction* (Oakland: Food First Books, 1995), 20. Table 2.1

3. 4.7 billion tons of active ingredient; Natural Resources Defense Council (NRDC), *Summary of EPA Data* (May 1996).

4. Calculated from World Health Organization estimate, cited by David Pimentel and Anthony Greiner, "Environmental and Socio-

Economic Costs of Pesticide Use," in *Techniques for Reducing Pesticide Use. Economic and Environmental Benefits*, ed. David Pimentel (Chichester: John Wiley and Sons, 1997), 52.

5. For background on African agriculture and the impact of colonialism, see Paul Richards, *Indigenous Agricultural Revolution: Ecology and Food Production in West Africa* (Boulder: Westview Press, 1985), chapters 1–3; Robert Chambers, *Rural Development: Putting the Last First* (London: Longman, 1983), chapters 3–4; Walter Rodney, *How Europe Underdeveloped Africa* (Washington, DC: Howard University Press, 1981); and Bill Rau, *From Feast to Famine* (Washington, DC: Africa Faith and Justice Network, 1985).

6. Richard Franke and Barbara Chasin, "Peasants, Peanuts, Profits and Pastoralists," *The Ecologist* 11, no. 4 (1981): 162. For a more complete picture by the same authors, see *Seeds of Famine: Ecological Destruction and the Development Dilemma in the West African Sahel* (Totowa, NJ: Rowman and Allanheld, 1980).

7. Randall Baker, "Protecting the Environment Against the Poor," *The Ecologist* 14, no. 2 (1983): 56.

8. Franke and Chasin, *Seeds of Famine*, chapter 3.

9. W. P. Pritchard, "Veterinary Education in Africa, Past, Present and Future," *Journal of Veterinary Medical Education* 15 (1988): 13–16.

10. Aggrey Ayuen Majok and Calvin W. Schwabe, *Development Among Africa's Migratory Pastoralists* (Westport, CT: Bergin & Garvey, 1996), 4.

11. Majok and Schwabe, *Development*, 5.

12. Majok and Schwabe, *Development*, 8. See also J. L. Dodd, "An Assessment of the Desertification/Degradation Issue in Sub-Saharan Africa," *BioScience* 44 (1994): 28–34.

13. Mary Tiffen, Michael Mortimore, and Francis Gichuki, *More People, Less Erosion: Environmental Recovery in Kenya* (New York: John Wiley & Sons, 1994); and Mary Tiffen, Michael Mortimore and Francis Gichuki, "Population Growth and Environmental Recovery: Policy Lessons from Kenya," International Institute for Environment and Development, *Gatekeeper Series*, no. 45 (1994): 1–26.

14. Colin Maher, 1937, quoted in Tiffen, Mortimore, and Gichuki, *More People, Less Erosion*, 3 (Rhodes House: Maher, 1937: 3. Rhodes House Library, Oxford).

15. *World Population Prospects: The 1996 Revision* (New York: Population Division of the Department for Economic and Social Information and Policy Analysis, United Nations), annex 2 and 3, table A.32.

16. Tiffen, Mortimore, and Gichuki, *More People, Less Erosion,* 272, figure 16.2.

17. "Convention to Combat Desertification," 1.

18. David Pimentel, "Environmental and Economic Costs of Soil Erosion and Conservation Benefits," *Science* 267 (1995): 1117–1123.

19. Ibid., 1119.

20. Ibid., 1117.

21. Paul Faeth and John Westra, "Alternatives to Corn and Soybean Production in Two Regions of the United States," in *Agricultural Policy and Sustainability: Case Studies from India, Chile, the Philippines and the United States,* ed. Paul Faeth (Washington, DC: World Resources Institute, 1993), 74.

22. U.S. Department of Agriculture 1996 Farm Bill, "Regulatory File" in *Farm Chemicals Handbook '97* (Willoughby, OH: Meister Publishing Company, 1997), D-68.

23. Vandermeer and Perfecto, *Breakfast of Biodiversity,* 3.

24. *Tropical Forests: A Call for Action, Part I: The Plan, Report of an International Task Force of the World Resources Institute, the World Bank and the United Nations Development Program* (Washington, DC: World Resources Institute, 1985), 3. See also John Vandermeer and Ivette Perfecto, "Re-thinking Rain Forests," *Food First Backgrounder* (Summer 1995).

25. Vandermeer and Perfecto, *Breakfast of Biodiversity,* 20.

26. Ibid., 20, table 2.1.

27. Ibid.

28. Ibid.

29. Susanna Hecht and J. C. Tucker, "Sacred Groves and Sacrifice Zones" (unpublished manuscript, 1998). See also Susanna Hecht and Alexander Cockburn, *The Fate of the Forest: Developers, Destroyers and Defenders of the Amazon* (New York: Harper Perennial, 1990).

30. See, for instance, "Multilateral Banks and Indigenous Peoples," *Cultural Survival Quarterly* 10, no. 1 (1986). The entire issue is devoted

to the impact of large development projects—many of which involve massive deforestation schemes—on indigenous peoples. See also "Statement of Brent H. Millikan before the Subcommittee on Natural Resources, Agricultural Research, and Environment" of the Committee on Science and Technology, U.S. House of Representatives, Washington, D.C., September 19, 1984, 12–14; Teresa Hayter and Catherine Watson, *Aid: Rhetoric and Reality* (London: Pluto Press, 1985), 192; and Patricia Adams and Lawrence Solomon, *In the Name of Progress* (Toronto: Energy Probe Research Foundation, 1985), 20–21.

31. Brent Millikan, *Políticas públicas e Desenvolvimento em Rondônia* (Report to the World Bank, Washington, D.C., 1997).

32. Susanna Hecht, "Colonist Attrition in Amazonia," *World Development* (in press, 1998).

33. Interview by Peter Rosset with Dr. Susanna Hecht, University of California at Los Angeles, School of Public Policy and Social Research, December 6, 1997.

34. Hecht, interview.

35. World Resources Institute, *World Resources 1994–95: A Guide to the Global Environment* (New York: Oxford University Press, 1994), 294–295, table 18.2.

36. Comparison based on the 1985 IBGE (Instituto Brasilero do Geografia e) Agricultural Census and the *Atlas Fundiário Brasileiro*.

37. *Atlas Fundiário Brasileiro*, 1996.

38. Ibid.

39. These data are reported by Instituto Brasileiro de Geografia e Estatistica (IBGE), Censo Agricola, 1985.

40. *Boletim da Commissão Pastoral da Terra-CPT*, no. 136 (August 1996), 7, with 1996 data provided by the Documentation Sector of the *Commissão Pastoral da Terra*.

41. Mark S. Langevin and Peter Rosset, "Land Reform from Below: The Landless Workers Movement in Brazil," *Food First Backgrounder* (Fall 1997): 1–4.

42. *Boletim da Commissão Pastoral da Terra-CPT*, no. 7.

43. Langevin and Rosset, "Land Reform," 1.

44. Susanna Hecht and J. C. Tucker, "Who Clears Forests in Bolivia?" (unpublished manuscript 1998).

45. Vandermeer and Perfecto, *Breakfast of Biodiversity*.

46. See, for example, Nicholas D. Kristoff, "Asian Pollution Is Widening Its Deadly Reach," *New York Times* (November 29, 1997); see also John Stackhouse, "Indonesia's Forest-Clearing Policy Backfires," *Toronto Globe and Mail* (November 13, 1997); and Lawrence Pintak, "New Fires Add to Pall over Indonesia," *San Francisco Chronicle* (February 27, 1998).

47. Kristoff, "Asian Pollution."

48. Stephen Schwartzman, *Fires in the Amazon: An Analysis of NOAA-12 Satellite Data, 1996–1997* (Washington, DC: Environmental Defense Fund, December 1, 1997).

49. Kristoff, "Asian Pollution."

50. Ibid.

51. Susanna Hecht interview. Even without the fires, she points out, virtually all of this logging is unsustainable, and in Brazil about 80 percent is carried out illegally.

52. Stackhouse, "Indonesia's Forest-Clearing Policy."

53. Leslie Weiss, "Burning for Your Dollar: You Might Be Partly Responsible for the Forest Fires in Indonesia—and What You Can Do about It," *MoJo Mother Jones Newswire* (November 18, 1997; www.mojones.com/news_wire/indofires.html).

54. Leslie Weiss, "A Timber Tycoon's Trophies," *MoJo Mother Jones Newswire* (November 18, 1997; www.mojones.com/news_wire/hasan.html).

55. Schwartzman, *Fires in the Amazon*.

56. Food and Agriculture Organization, *FAO Trade Yearbook 1995*, vol. 49 (Rome: FAO, 1996), 160, table 12.

57. Weiss, "Burning for Your Dollar."

58. Susanna Hecht and Alexander Cockburn, *Amazon's End* (Verso Books, London 1998, in press).

59. See note 3.

60. In 1995, 1.25 billion lbs. of active ingredient alone were sold within the U.S. (NRDC, *Summary of EPA Data*, May 1996, National Resource

Defense Council). However, other estimates of usage put the amount of pesticides at slightly less than 1 billion lbs. (See David Pimentel and David Khan, "Environmental Aspects of 'Cosmetic Standards' of Foods and Pesticides" in *Techniques for Reducing Pesticide Use. Economic and Environmental Benefits,* 414). Even if we consider this low estimate, it is still more than 3 lbs. of pesticides per person.

61. Californians for Pesticide Reform (CPR) and Pesticide Action Network (PAN), *Rising Toxic Tide: Pesticide Use in California 1991–1995* (San Francisco: Californians for Pesticide Reform and Pesticide Action Network, 1997), v.

62. Ibid.

63. Charles M. Benbrook, *Pest Management at the Crossroads* (Yonkers, NY: Consumers Union, 1996), 1, figure 1.

64. Data are for 1990–91, and we know that the use has been increasing rapidly over the 1990s (EPA, *Pesticide Industry Sales and Usage: 1990 and 1991 Market Estimates*).

65. J. Jeyarathum, "Acute Pesticide Poisoning: A Major Health Problem," *World Health Statistics Quarterly* 43, no. 3 (1990): 139–144. Estimates vary widely. Many cases go unreported, partly because of growers' actively preventing reporting. The Guatemalan government, for example, estimated that only 23 percent of cases were reported. What official figures show is just the tip of the iceberg: When so many people are being acutely poisoned, many more will be exposed to smaller amounts of pesticide with less immediate but no less serious effects.

66. W. G. Hauserman, "The Legal Response to the Widespread Poisoning of Farmworkers from Pesticide Exposure," *Journal of Products and Toxics Liability* 17, no 1 (1995): 47–65.

67. W. S. Pease et al., *Preventing Pesticide Illness in California Agriculture: Strategies and Priorities* (Berkeley: California Policy Seminar, 1993).

68. U.S. Environmental Protection Agency, *Pesticide Question: National Pesticide Survey* (Washington, DC: EPA, 1990).

69. The real figures are elusive, since 74 percent of pesticides shipped out of the United States are not labeled in the shipping records. See *Exporting Risk: Pesticide Exports from U.S. Ports, 1992–1994* (Los Angeles: Foundation for Advancements in Science and Education, Spring 1996). During testimony before the Senate on June 5, 1991, the presi-

dent of the National Agricultural Chemical Association (NACA), Jay Vroom, stated that about 35 percent of the volume of all pesticides exported by NACA member producers have not been registered for use in the United States (U.S. Senate, Committee on Agriculture, Nutrition and Forestry, "The Circle of Poison: Impact on American Consumers," hearing on September 20, 1991, quoted in FASE, 5). It is important to note that this does not include numerous and uncountable exports of products that have been banned, suspended, severely restricted, or discontinued in the United States.

70. Michael E. Conroy, Douglas L. Murray, and Peter M. Rosset, *A Cautionary Tale: Failed U.S. Development Policy in Central America* (Boulder: Lynne Rienner, 1996), 146, table 6.3.

71. Vasanthi Arumugam, *Victims Without Voice: A Study of Women Pesticide Workers in Malaysia* (Penang, Malaysia: Tenaganita and Pesticide Action Network Asia and the Pacific, 1992), foreword.

72. Conroy, Murray, and Rosset, *A Cautionary Tale*, 139, table 6.1.

73. See Angus Wright, "Where Does the Circle Begin? The Global Dangers of Pesticide Plants," *Global Pesticide Campaigner* 4, no. 4 (1994): 1, 10–11.

74. David Weir, *The Bhopal Syndrome: Pesticide Manufacturing and the Third World* (Penang, Malaysia: International Organization of Consumers Unions, 1986).

75. Philip Shabecoff, "Pesticide Control Finally Tops EPA's List of Most Pressing Problems," *New York Times* (March 6, 1986).

76. For a summary of the evidence, see Martin Bourque and Ingrid Bekkers, "Silent Spring II? Recent Discoveries of New Threats of Pesticides to Our Health," *Food First Backgrounder* (1997): 1–8. See also Sandra Steingraber, *Living Downstream: An Ecologist Looks at Cancer and the Environment* (New York: Addison-Wesley, 1997); Theo Colborn, Dianne Dumanoski, and John P. Meyers, *Our Stolen Future: Are We Threatening Our Fertility, Intelligence and Survival? A Scientific Detective Story* (New York: Penguin USA, 1996); Ted Schettler, Gina Solomon, Paul Burns, and Maria Valenti, *Generations at Risk: How Experimental Toxins May Affect Reproductive Health in Massachusetts* (Boston: GBPSR and Mass PIRG, 1996; Dan Fagin, Marianne Lavelle, and the Center for Public Integrity, *Toxic Deception: How the Chemical Industry Manipulates Science, Bends the Law and Endangers Your Health* (New Jersey: Birch Lane Press, 1996).

77. Benbrook, *Pest Management at the Crossroads*, 1.

78. David Pimentel and Hugh Lehman, eds., *The Pesticide Question: Environment, Economics, and Ethics* (New York and London: Chapman & Hall, 1993), 226.

79. David Pimentel and Lois Levitan, "Pesticides: Amounts Applied and Amounts Reaching Pests," *Bioscience* 36, no. 2 (February 1986): 90.

80. David Pimentel, Jason Friedman, and David Khan, "Reducing Insecticide, Fungicide and Herbicide Use on Vegetables and Reducing Herbicide Use on Fruit Crops," in *Techniques for Reducing Pesticide Use*, ed. David Pimentel, 379.

81. Interview with Gary Ballard at the Environmental Protection Agency, Economic Analysis Branch, April 1986.

82. David Pimentel et al., "Benefits and Costs of Pesticides in U.S. Food Production," *BioScience* 28 (1978): 772, 778–783.

83. David Pimentel and David Khan, "Environmental Aspects of 'Cosmetic Standards' for Foods and Pesticides," *Techniques for Reducing Pesticide Use*, ed. David Pimentel, 415.

84. Communication from John Scheuring, International Crops Research Institute for Semiarid Tropics, Bamako, Mali, January 8, 1986.

85. Clara Ines Nicholls and Miguel A. Altieri, "Conventional Agricultural Development Models and the Persistence of the Pesticide Treadmill in Latin America," *International Journal of Sustainable Development and World Ecology* 4 (1997): 93–111, 94.

86. Douglas L. Murray, *Cultivating Crisis: The Human Costs of Pesticides in Latin America* (Austin: University of Texas Press, 1994).

87. Food and Agriculture Organization, *FAO Trade Yearbook 1995*, vol. 49 (Rome: FAO, 1995), 305, table 132.

88. For the whole story, see Murray, *Cultivating Crisis*, chapters 2 and 3.

89. Murray, *Cultivating Crisis*, 18, table 2–1.

90. See Robert G. Williams, *Export Agriculture and the Crisis in Central America* (Chapel Hill: University of North Carolina Press, 1986).

91. Ramachandra Guha, "The Malign Encounter: The Chipko Movement and Competing Visions of Nature" in *Who Will Save the Forest?*

Knowledge, Power and Environmental Destruction, ed. Tariq Banuri and Frédérique Apfell Marglin (London: Zed Books, 1993), 80–113. See also Anumpam Mishra, "The Forest Cover 'Chipko Movement' in North India" in *Readings on Poverty and Development* (Rome: FAO, 1980); Pandurang Ummayya and J. Bandyopadhyay, "The Trans-Himalayan Chipko Foot March," *The Ecologist* 13, no. 5 (1983).

92. Anthony Hall, "Did Chico Mendes Die in Vain? Brazilian Rubber Tappers in the 1990s" in *Green Guerrillas: Environmental Conflicts and Initiatives in Latin America and the Caribbean,* ed. Hellen Collinson (London: Latin America Bureau, 1996), 93–101. See also Susanna Hecht and Alexander Cockburn, *Fate of the Forest.*

93. Californians for Pesticide Reform, 49 Powell St. 5th floor, San Francisco, CA 94102, www.igc.org/cpr.

MYTH 5: The Green Revolution Is the Answer

1. See Yrju Halla and Richard Levins, *Humanity and Nature: Ecology, Science and Society* (London: Pluto Press, 1992); Christopher J. Baker, "Frogs and Farmers: The Green Revolution in India, and Its Murky Past" in *Understanding Green Revolutions,* ed. Tim Bayliss-Smith and Sudhir Wanmali (New York: Cambridge University Press, 1984), 40. The first major Green Revolution in the Indian Punjab, for example, took place over a hundred years ago when Punjabi farmers adopted three new varieties of sugar cane in a single generation, with striking results.

2. Bruce H. Jennings, *Foundations of International Agricultural Research: Science and Politics in Mexican Agriculture* (Boulder: Westview Press, 1988); John H. Perkins, "The Rockefeller Foundation and the Green Revolution, 1941–1956," *Agriculture and Human Values* 7, no. 3/4 (1990): 6–18.

3. For an analysis of the role of internationally funded agricultural research in this process, see Shripad D. Deo and Louis E. Swanson, "Structure of Agricultural Research in the Third World" in *Agroecology,* ed. C. Ronald Carroll, John H. Vandermeer, and Peter M. Rosset (New York: McGraw-Hill, 1990).

4. P. L. Pingali, M. Hossain, and R. V. Gerpacio, *Asian Rice Bowls: The Returning Crisis* (Wallingford, UK: CAB International, 1997), 4.

5. Peter A. Oram and Behjat Hojjati, "The Growth Potential of Existing Agricultural Technology," in *Population and Food in the Early Twenty-*

First Century: Meeting Future Food Demand of an Increasing Population, ed. Nurul Islam (Washington, DC: International Food Policy Research Institute, 1995), 167–189, table 7.8.

6. Christopher R. Dowsell, R. L. Paliwal, and Ronald P. Cantrell, *Maize in the Third World* (Boulder: Westview Press, 1996), 137.

7. Michael Lipton and Richard Longhurst, *New Seeds and Poor People* (Baltimore: Johns Hopkins University Press, 1989), 3.

8. Food and Agriculture Organization of the United Nations, "Lessons from the Green Revolution: Towards a New Green Revolution" in *World Food Summit: Technical Background Documents,* vol. 2 (Rome: FAO, 1996).

9. Agriculture and Rural Development Department, World Bank, "Agricultural Biotechnology: The Next 'Green Revolution'?" *World Bank Technical Papers* no. 133, 1991.

10. See, for example, part four of Frances Moore Lappé and Joseph Collins, *Food First: Beyond the Myth of Scarcity* (New York: Ballantine Books, 1977); Susan George, *How the Other Half Dies* (London: Penguin, 1976); George Kent, *The Political Economy of Hunger: The Silent Holocaust* (New York: Praeger, 1984); Keith Griffin, *The Political Economy of Agrarian Change: An Essay on the Green Revolution,* 2nd ed. (London: Macmillan, 1979); Keith Griffin and Jeffrey James, *Transition to Egalitarian Development: Economic Policies for Structural Change in the Third World* (New York: St. Martin's Press, 1981); Andrew Pearse, *Seeds of Plenty, Seeds of Want: Social and Economic Implications of the Green Revolution* (New York: Oxford University Press, 1980); Vandana Shiva, *The Violence of the Green Revolution: Third World Agriculture, Ecology and Politics* (Penang, Malaysia: Third World Network, 1991).

11. Husain was chairman of the Consultative Group on International Agricultural Research, quoted in *Bank's World* vol. 4 (1985) no. 12:1.

12. World Bank, *Poverty and Hunger: Issues and Options for Food Security in Developing Countries* (Washington, DC: World Bank, 1986), 49.

13. Lappé and Collins, *Food First,* 121.

14. Peter Uvin, "The State of World Hunger" in *The Hunger Report: 1995,* ed. Ellen Messer and Peter Uvin (Amsterdam: Gordon and Breach Publishers, 1996), 1–17, table 1.6.

15. Paul Lewis, "The Green Revolution Bears Fruit," *New York Times,* June 2, 1985.

16. World Bank, *Poverty and Hunger*, 1.

17. Uvin, "The State of World Hunger," table 1.6.

18. Calculated from table 3.2 in Nikos Alexandratos, "The Outlook for World Food and Agriculture to Year 2010" in Islam, *Population and Food in the Early Twenty-First Century*, 25–48.

19. Ibid.

20. See, for example, Gregg Easterbrook, "Forgotten Benefactor of Humanity," *The Atlantic Monthly* 279, no. 1 (January 1997): 75–82.

21. Uvin, "The State of World Hunger," calculated from table 1.6. China reduced the number of hungry people by 53 percent, while the number rose a combined 27 percent in sub-Saharan Africa, South Asia, and South America.

22. Ibid.

23. Ibid. In all fairness, we should point out that the number of hungry people also fell in East Asia and in the Near East, though the numbers are nowhere as dramatic as in China. It is also worth remembering that Chinese policy toward hunger was undoubtedly strongly influenced by the terrible famine that struck that country in the early 1960s.

24. John E. Pluenneke and Sharon Moshavi, "A Revolution Comes Home to Roost . . . Leaving Hunger in the Midst of Plenty," *Business Week*, November 6, 1994.

25. Balanced historical treatments of the Green Revolution debate can be found in Frederick H. Buttel and Laura T. Raynolds, "Population Growth, Agrarian Structure, Food Production, and Food Distribution in the Third World" in *Food and Natural Resources*, ed. David Pimentel and Carl W. Hall (New York: Academic Press, 1989), 341–351; and Anthony Bebbington and Graham Thiele, *Non-Governmental Organizations and the State in Latin America: Rethinking Roles in Sustainable Agricultural Development* (London: Routledge, 1993), chapter 4.

26. See, for example, Clifton R. Wharton, Jr., "The Green Revolution: Cornucopia or Pandora's Box," *Foreign Affairs* 47 (1969): 464–476; and K. Griffin, *The Political Economy of Agrarian Change: An Essay on the Green Revolution* (London: Macmillan, 1974).

27. Green Revolution supporter Walter Falcon cautioned in 1970 that Green Revolution success in some regions was counterbalanced by poor results in marginal areas, and that the new varieties and associ-

ated technologies were accompanied by increasing pest, crop disease, and weed problems (he felt that better pesticide programs were the solution). While he argued that these would prove to be "short-run issues," they remain with us three decades later. See Walter P. Falcon, "The Green Revolution: Generations of Problems," *American Journal of Agricultural Economics* 52 (1970): 698–710; and Magnus Jirström, *In the Wake of the Green Revolution: Environmental and Socio-Economic Consequences of Intensive Rice Agriculture—The Problems of Weeds in Muda, Malaysia* (Lund, Sweden: Lund University Press, 1996), 35.

28. See, for example, M. Perelman, *Farming for Profit in a Hungry World* (Montclair, NJ: Allanheld, Osmun, 1977); W. Ophuls, *Ecology and the Politics of Scarcity* (San Francisco: Freeman, 1977); P. R. Mooney, *Seeds of the Earth* (Ottawa: Inter Pares, 1979).

29. Lipton and Longhurst, *New Seeds and Poor People*, 118.

30. Bebbington and Thiele, *Non-Governmental Organizations and the State*, 64; J. Rigg, "The New Rice Technology and Agrarian Change: Guilt by Association?" *Progress in Human Geography* 13, no. 2: 374–399.

31. Buttel and Raynolds, "Population Growth, Agrarian Structure," 345–347, summarize what they call the "formidable counterattack" by defenders of the Green Revolution. See also FAO, "Lessons from the Green Revolution."

32. FAO, "Lessons from the Green Revolution"; Bebbington and Thiele, *Non-Governmental Organizations and the State*, 64–67.

33. Ibid.

34. Buttel and Raynolds, "Population Growth, Agrarian Structure," 345–347; Peter Hazell and James L. Garrett, "Reducing Poverty and Protecting the Environment: The Overlooked Potential of Less-Favored Lands," International Food Policy Research Institute, *2020 Vision Brief*, no. 39, 1996; FAO, "Lessons from the Green Revolution" (Washington, DC: IFRRI, 1996).

35. Keith Griffin, *Alternative Strategies for Economic Development* (New York: St. Martin's Press, 1989), 147.

36. See Perelman, *Farming for Profit*, for a historical treatment of how the agrochemical industry has worked with development agencies to promote their products through the Green Revolution.

37. International Food Policy Research Institute, "Donors to the 2020 Vision Initiative" in *A 2020 Vision for Food, Agriculture and the Environ-*

ment: The Vision, Challenge and Recommended Action (Washington, DC: IFPRI, 1995), 51.

38. Letter to Ambassador Robert O. Blake, chairman, Committee on Agricultural Sustainability for Developing Countries, from Jack Whelan, External Relations, International Fertilizer Industry Association, dated May 7, 1996, a copy of which was leaked to the authors.

39. See, for example, Robert Chambers, "Farmer-First: A Practical Paradigm for the Third Agriculture" in *Agroecology and Small Farm Development*, ed. Miguel A. Altieri and Susanna B. Hecht (Ann Arbor: CRC Press, 1990), 237–244; and Eric Holt-Gimenez, "The Campesino a Campesino Movement: Farmer-led, Sustainable Agriculture in Central America and Mexico," Institute for Food and Development Policy *Food First Development Report*, no. 10, (Oakland: Institute for Food and Development Policy, 1996).

40. Buttel and Raynolds, "Population Growth, Agrarian Structure," 345, n. 7; see also F. Bray, *The Rice Economies* (Oxford: Blackwell, 1986).

41. See George A. Collier with Elizabeth Lowery Quaratiello, *Basta! Land and the Zapatista Rebellion in Chiapas* (Oakland: Food First Books, 1994); and Peter Rosset with Shea Cunningham, "Chiapas: Social and Agricultural Roots of Conflict," *Global Pesticide Campaigner* 4, no. 2 (1994): 1, 8–9, 16. For a foreshadowing of these problems, written before the uprising, see George A. Collier, "Seeking Food and Seeking Money: Changing Productive Relations in a Highland Mexican Community," United Nations Research Institute for Social Development *Discussion Paper*, no. 10, 1990.

42. Donald K. Freebairn, "Did the Green Revolution Concentrate Incomes? A Quantitative Study of Research Reports," *World Development* 23, no. 2 (1995): 265–279. Despite the "maturation" of the Green Revolution in recent decades, later studies were just as likely to find heightened inequality as were studies carried out in the early years. Three "landmark" books that attempt to refute the argument that inequality has increased have been published in the 1990s by Green Revolution supporters. One of the most widely cited is a multi-investigator, village-level study provocatively named *The Green Revolution Reconsidered: The Impacts of High-Yielding Rice Varieties in South India*, edited by P. B. R. Hazell and C. Ramasamy (Baltimore and Washington: Johns Hopkins University Press and the International Food Policy Research Institute, 1991). The editors conclude that the

"Green Revolution had a favorable impact" in their study villages, including "increasing aggregate output," and "across-the-board gains in income, employment, and the quality of diet" (p. 251). Nevertheless, the team's anthropologist, John Harriss, observed a "remarkable stability" of social class relations over the course of the study, despite a good deal of social mobility, "rather more of it downward than upward" (p. 73). Rita Sharma and Thomas T. Poleman, in *The New Economics of India's Green Revolution: Income and Employment Diffusion in Uttar Pradesh* (Ithaca: Cornell University Press, 1993), take a look at the off-farm economic impacts of the Green Revolution. Massive investment in agriculture during the Green Revolution has generated a diversity of off-farm employment opportunities related to the storage, transport, processing, and marketing of farm production. Thus they conclude that "the Green Revolution can be a double-barreled blessing to India," providing both increased production and off-farm employment (p. 254). The weakness of their argument is that *any* agricultural growth, regardless of whether it is based on the Green Revolution, would have positive effects on the rest of the economy. The authors did not consider whether alternative development strategies could have generated more and/or better off-farm effects.

In the next chapter of this book, we argue for a different kind of rural development, based on social equity, which if the experiences of South Korea, Japan, and Taiwan are worth anything, can generate far more positive impacts on the off-farm economy than did the Green Revolution in India. Cristina C. David and Keijiro Otsuka, the editors of *Modern Rice Technology and Income Distribution in Asia* (Boulder and Manila: Lynne Rienner and International Rice Research Institute, 1994), take on the issue of regional equity. They ask: "What effect has technological change in the favorable rice-growing areas had on the welfare of people in the unfavorable areas bypassed by the new technology?" (p. 7). Their rather lukewarm conclusion is that Green Revolution adoption "is limited to irrigated and favorable rainfed environments, and thus the yield gap between favorable and unfavorable rice-growing areas has widened." Lest this conclusion generate concern, they offer that "when the indirect effects through labor, land, and product market adjustments are accounted for, differential adoption of modern varieties across production environments *does not significantly worsen income distribution*" (p. 427, emphasis added). The problem with this argument is that we need to significantly *improve* income distribution if we are to achieve the kind of broad-based development needed to attack the structural roots of hunger and poverty.

211

43. Summarized in Bebbington and Thiele, *Non-Governmental Organizations and the State in Latin America,* chapter 4.

44. Roy L. Prosterman, Mary N. Temple, and Timothy M. Hanstad, eds., *Agrarian Reform and Grassroots Development: Ten Case Studies* (Boulder: Lynne Rienner, 1990), Introduction, p. 1.

45. See, for example, Michael Lipton, "Inter-Farm, Inter-Regional and Farm Non-Farm Income Distribution: The Impact of the New Cereal Varieties," *World Development* 6, no. 3 (1978): 319–337; and R. Barker and V. G. Cordova, "Labor Utilization in Rice Production" in *Economic Consequences of the New Rice Technology,* ed. R. Baker and Y. Hayami (Los Banos, Philippines: International Rice Research Institute, 1978). In a more recent study by P. B. R. Hazell et al., "Economic Changes Among Village Households," pp. 29–56 in Hazell and Ramasamy, *The Green Revolution Reconsidered,* the authors found higher wages in new off-farm employment, though their "results suggest that the green revolution did little to increase total crop employment" (p. 37). In the editors' conclusions to the entire volume (chapter 11), they admit that they may not have detected an increase in the absolute poverty of the landless because "of migration from the villages to towns" (p. 252). In other words, the landless left the area if they could not find work, fueling rural-urban migration.

46. Lipton and Longhurst, *New Seeds and Poor People,* 401, 415. See also Michael Lipton, "Successes in Anti-Poverty," International Labour Office, Development and Technical Cooperation Department, *Issues in Development Discussion Paper,* no. 8, (Geneva: ILO, 1996), 66–71.

47. See, for example, Y. Hayami and V. W. Ruttan, *Agricultural Development: An International Perspective* (Baltimore: Johns Hopkins University Press, 1985), 341.

48. Tractor numbers in the third world have, however, continued to grow at a rapid clip, increasing by 68 percent between 1980 and 1994 (*FAO Production Yearbook 1990,* table 118 and *1995,* table 106).

49. Lipton, "Successes in Anti-Poverty," 63.

50. Lappé and Collins, "Food First," 174–177; for a case in the United States see John H. Vandermeer, "Mechanized Agriculture and Social Welfare: The Tomato Harvester in Ohio," *Agriculture and Human Values* 3, no. 3 (Summer 1986): 21–25; and Peter M. Rosset and John H. Vandermeer, "The Confrontation Between Processors and Farm Workers in the Midwest Tomato Industry and the Role of the Agricultural

Research and Extension Establishment," *Agriculture and Human Values* 3, no. 3 (Summer 1986): 26–32.

51. Azizur Rahman Khan and Eddy Lee, *Poverty in Rural Asia,* International Labour Organization and the Asian Employment Programme (Bangkok: International Labour Office, 1984), 126–130. See also Richard W. Franke and Barbara H. Chasin, *Kerala: Radical Reform as Development in an Indian State,* 2nd edition (Oakland: Food First Books, 1994).

52. Martin Ravallion, "Poverty and Growth: Lessons from 40 Years of Data on India's Poor," Development Economics Vice Presidency of the World Bank, *DEC Notes Research Findings No. 20,* 1996, figure 3 (Washington, DC: World Bank, 1996).

53. D. P . Singh, "The Impact of the Green Revolution," *Agricultural Situation in India* 13, no. 8 (1980): 323.

54. Lipton and Longhurst, *New Seeds and Poor People,* 128–133.

55. Ibid., 121–125.

56. Manfred Zeller, Gertrud Schrieder, Joachim von Braun, and Franz Heidhues, "Rural Finance and Food Security for the Poor: Implications for Research and Policy," *Food Policy Review* (International Food Policy Research Institute) 4 (1997): chapter 3. For an overview of how the availability of subsidized credit grew in the 1970s and shrank in the 1980s, see Willem C. Beets, *Raising and Sustaining Productivity of Smallholder Farming Systems in the Tropics* (Alkmaar, Holland: AbBé Publishing, 1990), 594–598.

57. Yujiro Hayami and Masao Kikuchi, "Directions of Agrarian Change: A View from Villages in the Philippines" in *Agricultural Change and Rural Poverty,* ed. John W. Mellor and Gunvant M. Desai (Baltimore: Johns Hopkins University Press, 1985), 132 ff.

58. Lipton and Longhurst, *New Seeds and Poor People,* 42–51.

59. Ibid., chapter 2.

60. In 1970 India used an average of 12.7 kg/ha of fertilizer; by 1995 the figure stood at 76.6. The ratio of agricultural production to fertilizer use was calculated by dividing the FAO Agricultural Production Index by the number of millions of metric tons of fertilizer used in India, giving a ratio of 24.4 in 1970 and 8.15 in 1995. Data from *Global Data Manager 3.0,* CD-ROM (Philadelphia: World Game Institute, 1996).

61. Pingali et al., *Asian Rice Bowls,* table 4.5.

62. For a discussion of pesticide dependency, see chapter 4 of this book. Hugh McGuinness, *Living Soils: Sustainable Alternatives to Chemical Fertilizers for Developing Countries* (Yonkers, NY: Consumer Policy Institute, 1993), discusses the hidden costs of fertilizer use.

63. See, for example, John Harriss, "What Happened to the Green Revolution in South India? Economic Trends, Household Mobility and the Politics of an 'Awkward Class,'" IFPRI/TNAU Workshop on Growth Linkages, International Food Policy Research Institute, Washington, DC 1986, 29–30. A very rough comparison of net farmer revenues from Philippine rice production in 1971 and 1986 can be made by comparing tables 3.1 and 3.7 in Pingali et al., *Asian Rice Bowls*, suggesting that net farmer profits per hectare may have fallen from U.S. $481 to $296, a 38 percent drop.

64. P. L. Pingali, "Diversifying Asian Rice Farming Systems: A Deterministic Paradigm" in *Trends in Agricultural Diversification: Regional Perspectives*, paper no. 180, ed. S. Barghouti, L. Garbux, and D. Umali (Washington, DC: World Bank, 1992).

65. Rosset and Altieri, "Agroecology versus Input Substitution," figure 3a–d.

66. Ibid., calculated from figure 2.

67. A. V. Krebs, *The Corporate Reapers: The Book of Agribusiness* (Washington, DC: Essential Books, 1992), 29.

68. For extensive discussion of this point, see Marty Strange, *Family Farming: A New Economic Vision* (San Francisco: Food First Books, 1988), and the following chapter of this book.

69. Not only can the biggest farms take advantage of bulk discounts in purchasing and premium prices for large volume sales, but they also benefit disproportionately from contracts with processors and from tax policies favoring large capital investments.

70. Rosset and Altieri, "Agroecology versus Input Substitution," figure 1.

71. Linda M. Lobao, *Locality and Inequality: Farm and Industry Structure and Socioeconomic Conditions* (Albany: State University of New York Press, 1990), table 2.1.

72. P. L. Pingali, M. Hossain, and R. V. Gerpacio, *Asian Rice Bowls: The Returning Crisis?* (Wallingford, UK: CAB International, 1997), chapters 4 and 5.

73. See, for example, Clara Ines Nicholls and Miguel A. Altieri, "Conventional Agricultural Development Models and the Persistence of the Pesticide Treadmill in Latin America," *International Journal of Sustainable Development and World Ecology* 4 (1997): 93–111; Peter M. Rosset and Miguel A. Altieri, "Agroecology versus Input Substitution: A Fundamental Contradiction of Sustainable Agriculture," *Society & Natural Resources* 10 (1997): 283–295; Douglas L. Murray, *Cultivating Crisis: The Human Cost of Pesticides in Latin America* (Austin: University of Texas Press, 1994); McGuinness, *Living Soils*, chapters 1, 2, and 3.

74. K. G. Cassman and P. L. Pingali, "Extrapolating Trends from Long-Term Experiments to Farmers' Fields: The Case of Irrigated Rice Systems in Asia" in *Agricultural Sustainability: Economic, Environmental and Statistical Considerations*, ed. Vic Barnett, Roger Payne, and Roy Steiner (London: John Wiley & Sons, 1995), 1: 67–68.

75. Ibid., figures 5.6 and 5.7; see also Pingali et al., *Asian Rice Bowls: The Returning Crisis?* figures 4.1 and 4.2.

76. K. G. Cassman and R. R. Harwood, "The Nature of Agricultural Systems: Food Security and Environmental Balance," *Food Policy* 20, no. 5 (1995): 439–454, 447–448; K. K. M. Nambiar, "Long-Term Experiments on Major Cropping Systems in India" in *Agricultural Sustainability*, ed. Vic Barnett et al., 133–170; D. Byerlee, "Technical Change, Productivity and Sustainability in Irrigated Cropping Systems of South Asia: Emerging Issues in the Post-Grain Era," *Journal of International Development* 4, no. 5: 477–496.

77. Cassman and Harwood, "The Nature of Agricultural Systems"; Cassman and Pingali, "Extrapolating Trends"; and Pingali et al., *Asian Rice Bowls*.

78. Pluenneke and Moshavi, "A Revolution Comes Home to Roost."

79. Pingali et al., *Asian Rice Bowls*, 26.

80. Chapter 8 in Michael Hansen, *Escape from the Pesticide Treadmill: Alternatives to Pesticides in Developing Countries* (Mount Vernon, NY: Institute for Consumer Policy Research, 1987), 134.

81. Ibid., 137–138.

82. Ibid., 138.

83. See Pingali et al., *Asian Rice Bowls*, 110–118, for a discussion of health problems associated with pesticide use in rice.

84. Hansen, *Escape from the Pesticide Treadmill*, 139.

85. Ibid., 143–148; PANUPS, "Farmer First: Field Schools Key to IPM Success," Pesticide Action Network North America Updates Service, August 16, 1994, San Francisco, CA: www.panna.org/panna; Peter E. Kenmore, *Indonesia's Integrated Pest Management: A Model for Asia* (Manila: FAO Intercountry IPC Rice Programme, 1991).

86. PANUPS, "Farmer First."

87. Pingali et al., *Asian Rice Bowls*, 267.

88. See, for example, Monica Moore, *Redefining Integrated Pest Management: Farmer Empowerment and Pesticide Use Reduction in the Context of Sustainable Agriculture* (San Francisco: Pesticide Action Network, 1995).

89. Holt-Gimenez, "The Campesino a Campesino Movement."

90. Dr. Prabhu Pingali, comments made at discussion workshops held as part of "The Keystone Center Workshop on Critical Variables and Long-Term Projections for Sustainable Global Food Security," Warrentown, VA, March 10–13, 1997.

91. Rosamond Naylor, "Herbicide Use in Asian Rice Production," *World Development* 22, no. 1 (1994): 55–70.

92. Jirström, *In the Wake of the Green Revolution*, 226–229. This 1996 study of the phenomenon concludes that "intensive Green Revolution agriculture is associated with a set of sustainability problems having effects which do not seem to be scale-neutral." The author, a Green Revolution supporter himself, warns that "there is little room for complacency about the distributional impacts of current technologies. . . . On the contrary, the present spread and adoption of labour-displacing technologies such as direct-seeding and herbicides may, unless the circumstances are right, pose a major threat to the less well-to-do."

93. See, for example, Chambers, "Farmer-First"; and Holt-Gimenez, "The Campesino a Campesino Movement."

94. Hiromitsu Umehara, "Green Revolution for Whom?" in *Second View from the Paddy*, ed. Antonio J. Ledsma, S. J. et al. (Manila: Institute of Philippine Culture, Ateneo de Manila University), 37.

95. Marty Strange, "Family Farming: Faded Memory or Future Hope?" *Food First Action Alert*, Institute for Food and Development Policy, 1989.

96. Jack Doyle, "The Agricultural Fix," *Multinational Monitor* 7, no. 4 (1986): 3.

97. See Perelman, *Farming for Profit*, for some history on this point.

98. Ravallion, "Poverty and Growth," 2 and figure 1.

99. Frederick H. Buttel and Randolph Barker, "Emerging Agricultural Technologies, Public Policy, and Implications for Third World Agriculture," *American Journal of Agricultural Economics* 67, no. 5 (1985): 1170–1175; and Jack R. Kloppenburg, *First the Seed: The Political Economy of Plant Biotechnology, 1492–2000* (Cambridge: Cambridge University Press, 1988).

100. Martin Kenney and Frederick Buttel, "Biotechnology: Prospects and Dilemmas for Third World Development," *Development and Change* 16 (1985): 61–91; Henk Hobbelink, *Biotechnology and the Future of World Agriculture: The Fourth Resource* (London: Zed, 1991); Vandana Shiva, *Monocultures of the Mind: Perspectives on Biodiversity and Biotechnology* (London: Zed and Third World Network, 1993).

101. Kristin Dawkins, *Gene Wars: The Politics of Biotechnology* (New York: Seven Stories Press, 1997), 31.

102. World Bank, "Agricultural Biotechnology: The Next 'Green Revolution'?"

103. Kenney and Buttel, "Biotechnology," 68. It is possible that some patented genes will be provided to third world countries on a donated or at least "favorable" license basis, according to Klaus M. Leisinger of the Ciba-Geigy Foundation for Cooperation in Development, a charitable foundation established by one of the world's largest pesticide and biotechnology companies (Klaus M. Leisinger, "Sociopolitical Effects of New Biotechnologies in Developing Countries," International Food Policy Research Institute, *2020 Vision Brief* No. 35, 1996, Washington, DC). Dr. Michael Hansen of the Consumer Policy Institute in New York, an expert on the biotechnology industry, told the authors of this book that if the industry decides that poor farmers in certain countries do not have sufficient resources to constitute a profitable market, some companies will provide genes free of charge purely for their advertising and public relations value.

104. Jane Rissler and Margaret Mellon, *Perils Amid the Promise: Ecological Risks of Transgenic Crops in a Global Market* (Cambridge, MA: Union of Concerned Scientists, 1993).

105. Bette Hileman, "Views Differ Sharply Over Benefits, Risks of Agricultural Biotechnology," *Chemical & Engineering News*, August 21, 1995 (http://pubs.acs.org).

106. Shiva, *Monocultures of the Mind.*

107. For an excellent philosophical discussion of the history of this mindset, see Edmund P. Russell III, "'Speaking of Annihilation': Mobilizing for War Against Human and Insect Enemies, 1914–1945," *Journal of American History* 82, no. 4: 1505–1529.

108. Shiva, *Monocultures of the Mind*, 67.

109. Ibid., 80.

110. Miguel A. Altieri, *Agroecology: The Science of Sustainable Agriculture*, 2nd edition (Boulder: Westview Press, 1995); Carroll et al., *Agroecology*; Jules N. Pretty, *Regenerating Agriculture: Policies and Practices for Sustainability and Self-Reliance* (London: Earthscan, 1995).

111. Miguel A. Altieri, "Why Study Traditional Agriculture?" chapter 20 in Carroll et al., *Agroecology.*

112. Rosset and Altieri, "Agroecology versus Input Substitution."

113. Tim P. Bayliss-Smith, "Energy Flows and Agrarian Change in Karnataka: The Green Revolution at Micro-scale," in Bayliss-Smith and Wanmali, *Understanding Green Revolutions*, 169–170. While types of energy are not strictly comparable, such comparisons are meaningful in designing agricultural systems appropriate to farmers with varying access to energy sources.

114. John Vandermeer, *The Ecology of Intercropping* (Cambridge, UK: Cambridge University Press, 1989); Donald Q. Innis, *Intercropping and the Scientific Basis of Traditional Agriculture* (London: Intermediate Technology Publications, 1997).

115. Vandermeer, *The Ecology of Intercropping.*

116. Miguel A. Altieri and M. Kat Anderson, "An Ecological Basis of the Development of Alternative Agricultural Systems for Small Farmers in the Third World, *American Journal of Alternative Agriculture* 1, no. 1 (1986): 33–34; Altieri, *Agroecology.*

117. Chambers, "Farmer-First"; and Holt-Gimenez, "The Campesino a Campesino Movement."

118. Shiva, *The Violence of the Green Revolution.*

119. Doyle, "The Agricultural Fix."

120. Innis, *Intercropping.*

121. For a useful discussion, see Paul Richards, "Ecological Change and the Politics of African Land Use," *African Studies Review* 26, no. 2 (1983). See also Kurt G. Steiner, *Intercropping in Tropical Smallholder Agriculture with Special Reference to West Africa* (Eschborn, Germany: GTZ, 1984); Lloyd Timberlake, *Africa in Crisis: The Causes, the Cures of Environmental Bankruptcy* (London: Earthscan, 1985); Sustainable Agriculture Networking and Extension, *An Agroecology Reader for Africa* (New York: UNDP-SANE, 1995).

122. Peter H. Freeman and Tomas B. Fricke, "Traditional Agriculture in Sahelia: A Successful Way to Live," *The Ecologist* 13, no. 6 (1983): 210–212.

123. FAO, "Lessons from the Green Revolution."

124. "Challenging the 'New Green Revolution,' Institute for Food and Development Policy, (Oakland, CA: *Food First News & Views* 19, no. 65, 1997: 1, 3); for an example of this model in Ethiopia, see the Letter to the Editor in the same issue, by Dr. Mario Pareja, food & livelihood security coordinator, CARE–East Africa.

125. Nigel Dudley, John Madeley, and Sus Stolton, eds., *Land Is Life: Land Reform and Sustainable Agriculture* (London: Intermediate Technology Publications, 1992).

126. Some proponents have recently made the claim that the Green Revolution offers the best way to protect the environment (see, for example, Dennis Avery, *Saving the Planet with Pesticides and Plastic: The Environmental Triumph of High-Yield Farming,* Indianapolis: Hudson Institute, 1995). They argue that by boosting yields on favorable lands it will be unnecessary to farm less favorable ones, which are more likely to be more important wildlife refuges or pristine forests, and can thus be saved. This argument is specious for several reasons: It recognizes only one way to boost production (their way), when in fact there are many; it fails to take into account the environmental destruction wrought by industrial-style farming; and it also fails to consider the greater compatibility with the environment offered by alternative farming methods. For a report that rebuts this argument, see Tracy Irwin Hewitt and Katherine R. Smith, *Intensive Agriculture and Environmental Quality: Examining the Newest Agricultural Myth* (Greenbelt, MD: Henry Wallace Institute for Alternative Agriculture, 1995).

127. National Research Council, *Alternative Agriculture* (Washington, DC: National Academy Press, 1989), 8, 10, 17.

128. Erik van der Werf, "Agronomic and Economic Potential of Sustainable Agriculture in South India," *American Journal of Alternative Agriculture* 8, no. 4 (1993): 185–191.

129. Robert Collier, "Cuba Turns to Mother Earth: With Fertilizers and Fuel Scarce, Organic Farming Is In," *San Francisco Chronicle*, February 21, 1998, A1, A6.

130. Peter Rosset and Medea Benjamin, *The Greening of the Revolution: Cuba's Experiment with Organic Agriculture* (Melbourne: Ocean Press, 1994).

131. Peter Rosset, "Alternative Agriculture and Crisis in Cuba," *Technology and Society* 16, no. 2 (1997): 19–25.

132. The Cuban government tried a short-lived experiment with farmers' markets in the 1980s, which were subsequently closed because the leadership felt that middlemen were taking a large share of the profits. For a thorough discusion of these and other food issues from the 1980s, see Medea Benjamin, Joseph Collins, and Michael Scott, *No Free Lunch: Food and Revolution in Cuba Today* (San Francisco: Food First Books, 1989).

133. N. Companioni, A. A. Rodríguez Nodals, Mariam Carrión, Rosa M. Alonso, Yanet Ojeda, and Ana María Viscaíno, "La Agricultura Urbana en Cuba: Su Participación en la Seguridad Alimentaria," pp. 9–13 in Asociación Cubana de Agricultura Urbana (ACAO), *III Encuentro Nacional de Agricultura Orgánica 14 al 16 de mayo de 1997, Universidad Central de las Villas, Villa Clara, Cuba. Conferencias* (Havana: ACAO, 1997). For an excellent discussion of the enormous potential that urban agriculture has worldwide, see Jac Smit, Annu Ratta, and Joe Nasr, *Urban Agriculture: Food, Jobs and Sustainable Cities* (New York: UNDP, 1996).

MYTH 6: Justice vs. Production

1. Instituto Brasileiro de Geografia e Estatística (IBGE), Brazil: *Censo Agrícola*, 1985.

2. See Rehman Sobhan, *Agrarian Reform and Social Transformation* (London: Zed, 1993), 78; William C. Thiesenhusen, *Broken Promises: Agrarian Reform and the Latin American Campesino* (Boulder: Westview Press, 1995), 8, 10, 12, 13, 26, 64, 76, 81, 155.

3. Small farms defined as having fewer than five acres. See Giovanni Andrea Cornia, "Farm Size, Land Yields and the Agricultural Produc-

tion Function: An Analysis for Fifteen Developing Countries," *World Development* (April 1985): 518.

4. Ibid., 531.

5. Christopher B. Barret, "On Price Risk and the Inverse Farm Size—Productivity Relationship," *University of Wisconsin–Madison, Department of Agricultural Economics Staff Paper Series* no. 369, 1993; Frank Ellis, *Peasant Economics: Farm Households and Agrarian Development,* 2nd edition (Cambridge: Cambridge University Press, 1993), chapter 10; Thomas P. Tomich, Peter Kilby, and Bruce F. Johnston, *Transforming Agrarian Economies: Opportunities Seized, Opportunities Missed* (Ithaca: Cornell University Press, 1995), 124–136; R. Albert Berry and William R. Cline, *Agrarian Structure and Productivity in Developing Countries* (Baltimore: Johns Hopkins University Press, 1979); Michael R. Carter, "Identification of the Inverse Relationship between Farm Size and Productivity: An Empirical Analysis of Peasant Agricultural Production," *Oxford Economic Papers,* no. 36 (1984): 131–145. Gershon Feder, "The Relationship between Farm Size and Farm Productivity," *Journal of Development Economics* 18 (1985): 297–313; Roy L. Prosterman and Jeffrey M. Riedinger, *Land Reform and Democratic Development* (Baltimore: Johns Hopkins University Press, 1987), esp. chapter 2.

6. Tomich, Kilby, and Johnston. *Transforming Agrarian Economies,* 133, figure 4.6; and 126, figure 4.1.

7. Robert Netting, *Smallholders, Householders* (Stanford: Stanford University Press, 1993); Gene Wilken, *Good Farmers: Traditional Agricultural Resource Management in Mexico and Central America* (Berkeley: University of California Press, 1987); Miguel A. Altieri, *Agroecology: The Science of Sustainable Agriculture,* 2nd edition (Boulder: Westview Press, 1995).

8. Sobhan, *Agrarian Reform;* Thiesenhusen, *Broken Promises;* Tomich, Kilby, and Johnston, *Transforming Agrarian Economies.*

9. Michael Lipton, "Successes in Anti-Poverty," Development and Technical Cooperation Department, International Labour Office, Geneva, *Issues in Development Discussion Paper* no. 8, 1996, 62–69.

10. According to 1985 Congressional Budget Office figures, U.S. farms in the smallest size class had 94 percent higher total output per acre (in dollars) and 85 percent higher net profit per acre than farms in the largest size class (calculated from data presented in chapter 5, table 3, of Marty Strange, *Family Farming: A New Economic Vision,* San Francisco: Food First Books, 1988).

11. See general arguments through Marty Strange, *Family Farming*, and A. V. Krebs, *The Corporate Reapers: The Book of Agribusiness* (Washington: Essential Books, 1991). See also Desmond A. Jolly, "The Small Farm: It's Innovative and Persistent in a Changing World," *California Agriculture* 47, no. 2 (1993): 19–22.

12. Netting, *Smallholders, Householders*, 124.

13. Most of the land is worked in whole or in part by sharecroppers and day laborers. See F. Tomasson Jannuzi and James T. Peach, "Report on the Hierarchy of Interests in Land in Bangladesh," University of Texas, Austin, for U.S. Agency for International Development, Washington, DC, September 1977.

14. Ibid., In Bangladesh, sharecroppers generally must hand over one-half to two-thirds of their harvest to landlords. Only rarely do landlords contribute to the purchase of seeds and fertilizers.

15. North Central Farm Management Research Committee, *Conservation Problems and Achievements on Selected Midwestern Farms* (Wooster: Ohio Agricultural Experiment Station, July 1951), cited in R. Burnell Held and Marion Clawson, *Soil Conservation in Perspective* (Baltimore: Johns Hopkins University Press, 1965).

16. Iowa studies by John F. Timmons and Wade Hauser of Iowa State University, cited in Erik Eckholm, *Dispossessed of the Earth: Land Reform and Sustainable Development*, Worldwatch Paper 30 (Washington, DC: Worldwatch Institute, 1979). The Iowa studies found twenty-one tons per acre per year losses on the tenant-operated farms compared to sixteen tons on the owner-operated farms.

17. U.S. Department of Commerce, Bureau of the Census, and U.S. Department of Agriculture, Economic Research Service, *Farm Population of the United States: 1981* (Washington, DC: U.S. Department of Agriculture, Farm Population Series P-27, no. 55, 1981), 4.

18. Peter M. Rosset, "Alternative Agriculture and Crisis," *Technology and Society Magazine* 16, no. 2 (1997): 19–25.

19. Radha Sinha, *Landlessness: A Growing Problem* (Rome: FAO, 1982), 73.

20. For more detail, see two books by Betsy Hartmann and James Boyce, *Needless Hunger: Voices from a Bangladesh Village* and *A Quiet Violence: View from a Bangladesh Village* (Oakland: Food First Books, 1982, 1983).

21. Percent calculated from *FAO Production Yearbook 1978*, vol. 32. Averaged 1969 to 1978.

22. A. C. Delgado, "Determinacion de Pesticidas Clorinados en Leche Materna del Departamento de Leon," Monografia, Departmento de Biologia, Facultad de Ciencias y Letras, Universidad Nacional Autonoma de Nicaragua, León, 1978.

23. Steve O'Neil, "Hancock Is Willing to Meet the LSP," *Land Stewardship Letter* (St. Paul, MN, The Land Institute, 1985), 1.

24. Keith Schneider, "As More Family Farms Fail, Hired Managers Take Charge," *New York Times*, March 17, 1985, 1.

25. Food and Agriculture Organization, *High Level Mission on the Follow-up to the World Conference on Agrarian Reform and Rural Development in Sri Lanka* (Rome: FAO, 1984), 21.

26. Foro Emaús, "The Price of Bananas: The Banana Industry in Costa Rica," *Global Pesticide Campaigner* 8, no. 1 (March 1998): 3–7.

27. Data from *Bargaining Position and Distribution of Gains in the Banana Exporting Countries, Especially Honduras and Panama* (Santiago de Chile: CEPAL, 1982), quoted in Tom Berry, *Roots of Rebellion: Land & Hunger in Central America* (Boston: South End Press, 1987), 77.

28. Walter Goldschmidt, "160-Acre Limitation: It's Good for Farmers—and the Nation," *Los Angeles Times*, December 4, 1977. Goldschmidt's classic 1940s study contrasting two California towns has been reprinted in Walter Goldschmidt, *As You Sow* (Totowa, NJ: Rowman and Allanheld, 1978). Studies carried out in California in the 1970s came up with similar findings. See Isao Fujimoto, "The Communities of the San Joaquin Valley: The Relationship between Scale of Farming, Water Use, and the Quality of Life," testimony before the House Subcommittee on Family Farms, Rural Development, and Social Studies, Sacramento, CA, October 28, 1977.

29. Calculated from *Food and Agriculture Organization Yearbook: Production 1990, 1995* (Rome: FAO), table 6.

30. Some of the U.S. corporations that have heavily invested in farm land include Dow Chemical, Monsanto, Union Carbide, Goodyear, and Coca-Cola; see Tracey Clunies-Ross and Nicholas Hildyard, "The Politics of Industrial Agriculture," *The Ecologist* 22, no. 2 (March–April 1992).

31. Total farm numbers in 1992 were 1,925,300, the lowest since 1850. Peak farm numbers were 6.8 million in 1935. From 1980 to 1986 almost

235,000 U.S. farms went out of business, along with 60,000 corresponding rural, main street businesses ("Farm count at lowest point since 1850: just 1.9 million," *New York Times*, November 10, 1994.

32. Calculated from U.S. Bureau of Census, *1987 Census of Agriculture*, vol. 3, Related Surveys, part 2, *Agricultural Economics and Land Ownership Survey 1988, Change Sheet* (Washington, DC: U.S. Government Printing Office, 1988), 225, table 66; and "Intercountry Comparisons of Agricultural Output and Productivity, *FAO Economic and Social Development Paper*, no. 112.

33. R. Albert Berry and William R. Cline, *Agrarian Structure and Farm Productivity in Developing Countries* (Baltimore: Johns Hopkins University Press, 1979), 132–133, table 5-1.

34. Ibid. See also Eckholm, *Dispossessed of the Earth*, for a good overview of the issues.

35. Sobhan, *Agrarian Reform*, 117.

36. Tania Krutscha, "Brazil's Large Landowners Brace to Resist Reform," *Latin America Press*, September 19, 1985, 1.

37. See Collins et al., *Nicaragua: What Difference Could a Revolution Make?* for an in-depth look at the attempts of large landowners in Nicaragua to resist reform. See also Thiesenhusen, *Broken Promises*, for examples of counterreform in other Latin American countries.

38. World Bank, *Land Reform: Rural Development Series* (Washington, DC: World Bank, July 1974, 62). For excellent overviews, see also Sobhan, *Agrarian Reform;* and Jeffrey D. Sachs, "Trade and Exchange Rate Policies in Growth Oriented Adjustment Programs" in *Growth-Oriented Adjustment Programs*, ed. Vittorio Corbo, Morris Goldstein, and Moshin Khan (Washington, DC: International Monetary Fund & World Bank, 1987), 291–325.

39. Measured in kilograms per hectare. Calculated from the *Food and Agriculture Organization Production Yearbook 1995*, vol. 49 (Rome: FAO, 1996), table 15.

40. World Bank, *Land Reform*, 62. For excellent overviews, see also Sobhan, *Agrarian Reform;* and Sachs, "Trade and Exchange Rate Policies."

41. *FAO Production Yearbook 1995*, table 15.

42. World Bank, *Land Reform*, 61. See also Eckholm, *Dispossessed of the Earth*, 22.

43. World Bank, *Land Reform*, 61. See also Sobhan, *Agrarian Reform*, 88–89; and Sachs, "Trade and Exchange Rate Policies."

44. Elizabeth Croll, *The Family Rice Bowl* (Geneva: Institute for Social Development, 1982). See also Croll's "Food Supply in China and the Nutritional Status of Children" (unpublished manuscript, 1985); and Paul B. Trescott, "Incentives Versus Equality: What Does China's Recent Experience Show?" *World Development* 13, no. 2 (1985): 205–217; Tomich et al., *Transforming Agrarian Economies*, 296–304.

45. See U.S. Department of Agriculture, Economic Research Service, "China's Agricultural Revolution," *Agricultural Outlook* (December 1985): 19.

46. From 1980 to 1990, output per capita increased almost 40 percent, and from 1990 to 1995, almost 25 percent (*FAO Production Yearbook, 1990, 1995*, vols. 44 and 49, table 10).

47. "Zimbabwe Success Holds Out Hope for Others in Africa," *Africa Emergency* 4 (September–October 1985): 3.

48. See Sobhan, *Agrarian Reform*, 73–74. See also Peter Rosset, John Gershman, Shea Cunningham, and Marilyn Borchardt, "Myths and Root Causes: Hunger, Population and Development," *Food First Backgrounder* (Winter 1994): 5.

49. Ronald Herring, "Explaining Anomalies in Agrarian Reform: Lessons from South India," *Agrarian Reform and Grassroots Development: Ten Case Studies*, 73.

50. See Richard Franke and Barbara Chasin, *Kerala: Radical Reform as Development in an Indian State* (Oakland: Food First Books, 1994), 58.

51. For recent studies, see Sobhan, *Agrarian Reform*; Lipton, "Successes in Anti-Poverty"; and Tomich et al., *Transforming Agrarian Economies*. See also Folke Dovring, "Economic Results of Land Reforms," *Spring Review of Land Reform* (Washington, DC: U.S. Agency for International Development, June 1970); Schlomo Eckstein et al., *Land Reform in Latin America: Bolivia, Chile, Mexico, Peru and Venezuela*, World Bank Staff Working Paper no. 275 (Washington, DC: World Bank, April 1978).

52. Lipton, "Successes in Anti-Poverty," 62.

53. Ibid., and Sobhan, *Agrarian Reform*, demonstrate this clearly.

54. Roger Burbach and Peter Rosset, "Chiapas and the Crisis of Mexican Agriculture," Institute for Food and Development Policy, *Food First*

Policy Brief no. 1, 1994; Tom Barry, *Zapata's Revenge: Free Trade and the Farm Crisis in Mexico* (Boston: South End Press, 1996). See also James D. Cockcroft, *Mexico: Class Formation, Capital Accumulation, and the State* (New York: Monthly Review Press, 1983), 177, 195.

55. Diskin, *Agrarian Reform in El Salvador*.

56. The best overview of these "fake" reforms is provided by Sobhan in *Agrarian Reform*.

57. Peter White, "A New Kind of Mexican Land Reform," *In These Times*, May 2, 1994.

58. Mariana Mora, María Elena Martínez, and Peter Rosset, "Report from the Front: Building Local Economy in Zapatista Territory," *Food First Backgrounder* (Winter 1997), 1–5.

59. Mark S. Langevin and Peter Rosset, "Land Reform from Below: The Landless Workers Movement in Brazil," *Food First Backgrounder* (Fall Season 1997), 1–4.

60. Michael E. Conroy, Douglas L. Murray, and Peter M. Rosset, *A Cautionary Tale: Failed U.S. Development Policy in Central America* (Boulder: Lynne Rienner/Food First Development Studies, 1996), 41, 59, table 2.5.

61. Sobhan, *Agrarian Reform;* Lipton, "Successes in Anti-Poverty," 62–66.

MYTH 7: The Free Market Can End Hunger

1. World Bank, *World Development Report 1992* (New York: Oxford University Press, 1992), table 11. Government expenditures are equivalent to 24 percent of gross national product in the United States, 53 percent in the Netherlands, 46 percent in Norway, and 49 percent in Belgium.

2. Mark Zepenzauer and Arthur Naiman, *Take the Rich off Welfare* (Tucson: Odonian Press, 1996), 6.

3. Donald J. Puchala and Jane Stavely, "The Political Economy of Taiwanese Agricultural Development" and Young Whan Kahn, "Politics and Agrarian Change in South Korean Rural Modernization by Induced Mobilization" in *Food, Politics and Agricultural Development: Case Studies in the Public Policy of Rural Modernization*, ed. R. Hopkins et al. (Boulder: Westview Press, 1979).

4. Cuba is one example. Although Cuba is the only country in the Western Hemisphere to have eliminated hunger, its experience provides no evidence that eliminating the market mechanism is necessary

to end hunger. When farmers' markets were tried and then eliminated in the 1980s, farmers and consumers suffered (Medea Benjamin, Joseph Collins, and Michael Scott, *No Free Lunch: Food and Revolution in Cuba Today*, New York: Grove Press/Food First Books, 1986).

5. For a detailed analysis of the impact of "free market" policies in Chile, see Joseph Collins and John Lear, *Chile's Free Market Miracle: A Second Look* (Oakland: Food First Books, 1995).

6. Matt Moffett, "Flour Power: Mexico's Campaign to Modernize Sparks Battle over Tortillas," *Wall Street Journal*, September 9, 1993, front page. See also Joel Millman, "Mexico's Billionaire Boom," *Washington Post*, November 27, 1994), 1C.

7. Data published by the *New York Times* and quoted by Noam Chomsky in "Rollback II: 'Civilization' Marches On," *Z Magazine* 8, no. 2 (February 1995): 20–31.

8. *FAO Production Yearbook 1995* (Rome: FAO, 1995).

9. David Pimentel et al., "The Impact of Energy Use on the Environment" in *Food, Energy, and Society*, revised edition, ed. David Pimentel and Marcia Pimentel (Niwot, CO: University of Colorado Press, 1996), 270.

10. Mort Hantman, *Export Agriculture: An Energy Drain*, Research Report (San Francisco: Institute for Food and Development Policy, 1984).

11. David Pimentel et al., "Environmental and Economic Costs of Soil Erosion and Conservation Benefits," *Science* 267 (February 1995): 1117, 1120. See also Pierre Crosson, "Soil Erosion Estimates and Costs," *Science* 269 (July 1995): 261–264, and Pimentel's response to it in the same issue.

12. Pimentel, et al., "Environmental and Economic Costs," 1120, table 4.

13. See A. V. Krebs, *The Corporate Reapers. The Book of Agribusiness* (Washington, DC: A. B. Krebbs, 1992), esp. chapters 1 and 2. See also James Wessel with Mort Hantman, *Trading the Future* (San Francisco: Food First Books, 1983); and Marty Strange, *Family Farming: A New Economic Vision* (San Francisco: Food First Books, 1988).

14. Data for 1979 showed that 65 percent of the land was secured by only 4 percent of holdings of over 450 hectares, whereas 10 percent of the land was secured by 81 percent of holdings of 3.5 hectares or less. The larger holdings continue to be in the hands of U.S.-owned plan-

tations and livestock ranches catering to U.S. markets. See Rehman Sobhan, *Agrarian Reform and Social Transformation: Preconditions for Development* (London: Zed Books, 1993), 53.

15. Data from U.S. Census of Agriculture, 1992, quoted in Rick Welsh, *The Industrial Reorganization of U.S. Agriculture: An Overview and Background Report*, Policy Studies report no. 6 (Greenbelt, MD: Henry A. Wallace Institute for Alternative Agriculture, April 1996), 2.

16. Marc Cooper, Peter Rosset, and Julia Bryson, "Warning: Corporate Meat and Poultry May Be Hazardous to Workers, Farmers, the Environment and Your Health," *Food First Backgrounder* 4, no. 1 (Spring 1997): 2.

17. Bill Turque, Deborah Rosenberg, and Todd Barrett, "Where the Food Isn't," *Newsweek* (February 24, 1992).

18. Ibid.

19. Judy Heany and Tamara Hayes, "Redlining Food: How to Ensure Community Food Security," *FIAN Fact Sheet* (Oakland: Institute for Food and Development Policy, 1996.)

20. Turque et al., "Where the Food Isn't"; and David Dante Trout, *The Thin Red Line: How the Poor Still Pay More* (San Francisco: West Coast Regional Office, Consumers Union, 1993).

21. Walden Bello, with Shea Cunningham and Bill Rau, *Dark Victory: The United States, Structural Adjustment and Global Poverty* (London: Pluto Press/Food First/Transnational Institute, 1994), chapters 4 and 8.

22. Bello, et al. *Dark Victory*, chapter 6. See also Duncan Green, *Silent Revolution: The Rise of Market Economics in Latin America* (London: Cassell/LARB, 1995).

23. Alicia Korten, "A Bitter Pill: Structural Adjustment in Costa Rica," *Food First Development Report no. 7* (1995): 46.

24. Ibid., 30, table 4.1.

25. A major source of *inequity* in purchasing power in contemporary Cuba, however, is access to dollars.

26. Rosset, "Alternative Agriculture and Crisis in Cuba." See also Peter Rosset and Medea Benjamin, *The Greening of the Revolution: Cuba's Experiment with Organic Agriculture* (Melbourne: Ocean Press, 1994).

27. John Ratcliffe, "Social Justice and the Demographic Transition: Lessons from India's Kerala State" in *Practicing Health for All*, ed. D. Morley

et al. (Oxford: Oxford University Press, 1983), 7–71; Richard W. Franke and Barbara H. Chasin, *Kerala: Radical Reform as Development in an Indian State*, 2nd edition (Oakland: Food First Books, 1994).

28. Roger Burbach and Peter Rosset, "Chiapas and the Crisis of Mexican Agriculture," *Food First Policy Brief*, no. 1 (1994); Krebs, *The Corporate Reapers*; Strange, *Family Farming*.

29. UN Department of Public Information, *Universal Declaration of Human Rights* (New York: United Nations, 1993), 13.

30. A. V. Jose, "Poverty and Inequality: The Case of Kerala" in *Poverty in Rural Asia*, ed. Azizur Rahman Khan and Eddy Lee (Bangkok: International Labour Organization, Asian Employment Programme, 1983), 107ff; see also Franke and Chasin, *Kerala*.

31. Mark B. Lapping and V. Dale Forster, "Farmland and Agricultural Policy in Sweden: An Integrated Approach," *International Regional Science Review* 7, no. 3 (1982): 297, 299.

32. Interview by Frances Moore Lappé with Tore Johansson of the Federation of Swedish Farmers, Stockholm, September 1982.

33. Michael Lipton and Martin Ravallion, "Poverty and Policy," *Policy Research Working Papers, Poverty and Human Resources*, no. 1130 (Washington, DC: World Bank, Policy Research Department, 1993), chapter 5.

MYTH 8: Free Trade Is the Answer

1. Latin America Commodities Report. CR-81-15, July 31, 1981.

2. Survey of Brazilian homes conducted by the Brazilian Institute of Economics with the consultation of the U.S. Department of Agriculture, cited in *The IMF and the Impoverishment of Brazil* (Rio de Janeiro: IBASE, December 1985), 17.

3. Calculated from *FAO Trade Yearbook 1995* (Rome: FAO, 1995), table 6; and *FAO Production Yearbook 1990, 1995* (Rome: FAO, 1990, 1995), tables 3, 17, 37.

4. Calculated from *FAO Trade Yearbook 1995* (Rome: FAO, 1995), table 12.

5. Ibid., 1.

6. Walden Bello, Shea Cunningham, and Li Kheng Poh, *A Siamese Tragedy: Development and Disintegration in Modern Thailand* (London and Oakland: Zed Books and Food First Books, 1998).

7. Bread for the World Institute, *Hunger 1998: Hunger in a Global Economy* (Silver Spring, MD, 1997), table 4.

8. International Fund for Rural Development, *The State of World Rural Poverty: A Profile of Latin America and the Caribbean* (Rome: IFAD, 1993), table 4 and page 4.

9. *FAO Trade Yearbook 1990*, table 7. See also the Development GAP, *Structural Adjustment and the Spreading Crisis in Latin America* (Washington, DC: Development Group for Alternative Policies, 1995), part 5.

10. Joseph Collins and John Lear, *Chile's Free-Market Miracle: A Second Look* (Oakland: Food First Books, 1994), 185.

11. The celebrated "Chilean miracle" by 1990 brought per capita output back only to 1970 levels after catastrophic recessions in 1975 and again in 1982. For a complete account of the Chilean miracle, see Collins and Lear, *Chile's Free-Market Miracle*. See also Stephanie Rosenfeld, "The Myth of the Chilean Miracle," *Multinational Monitor* (July–August 1994): 30–32.

12. Ibid., 7.

13. Belinda Coote, *The Trade Trap: Poverty and the Global Commodity Markets* (London: Oxfam, 1992), chapter 11, 144.

14. George Kent, *The Political Economy of Hunger* (New York: Praeger, 1984), chapter 4.

15. The advertisement was reprinted in "Comparative (Dis)Advantage," *Dollars and Sense* 114 (March 1986): 15.

16. G. A. Zepp and R. L. Simmons, *Producing Fresh Tomatoes in California and Baja California: Costs and Competition*, USDA, ESCS Report, February 1980, 32, 37, cited in Steven E. Sanderson, *The Transformation of Mexican Agriculture, International Structure and the Politics of Rural Change* (Princeton: Princeton University Press, 1986), 79.

17. Bernard Wideman, "Dominating the Pineapple Trade," *Far Eastern Economic Review* (July 8, 1974).

18. *Report on Multinationals and Human Rights*, FoodFirst Information and Action Network—FIAN International, Heidelberg, Germany, and *FIAN USA Hotline*, June 17, 1997. FoodFirst Information and Action Network—USA, Oakland, CA.

19. Ibid.

20. David Bacon, "Bitter Strike in Philippine Banana Lands: Dispute Reveals Downside of Market Reforms," *San Francisco Chronicle*, February 16, 1998, A10, A12.

21. Ibid.

22. Dr. Walden Bello, quoted in Bacon, "Bitter Strike in Philippine Banana Lands," A12.

23. FIAN, Heidelberg, 14. The 1 peso rate lasted from 1938 to 1956, but in the latter year a contract was extended for another twenty-five years at comparable rates.

24. On November 10, 1995, Ken Saro-Wiwa and eight other protesters of Shell's environmental destruction in Nigeria were hanged by the government. See "Oil, Shell and Nigeria," editorial, *The Ecologist* 25, no. 6 (November–December 1995): 210–213.

25. Laura Eggertson, "It's Pregnancy Tests—or Else—in Mexico" *San Francisco Examiner*, November 16, 1997, A-26. One company even forced women workers to produce further proof of menstruation and subjected them to palpable inspection for pregnancy.

26. Alan Oxley, *The Challenge of Free Trade* (New York: St. Martin's Press, 1990); see also Jerry M. Rosenberg, *The New American Community* (New York: Praeger, 1992); *Free Trade in the Western Hemisphere*, Special Issue of *Annals of the American Academy of Political and Social Sciences* (March 1993): 526; Joseph Grunwald et al., *Latin American Economic Integration and U.S. Policy* (Washington, DC: Brookings Institution, 1972).

27. For an excellent discussion of globalization and its effects, see *The Case Against the Global Economy: And for a Turn Toward the Local*, ed. Edward Goldsmith and Jerry Mander (San Francisco: Sierra Club Books, 1996).

28. See, for example, Michael E. Conroy, Douglas L. Murray, and Peter M. Rosset, *A Cautionary Tale: Failed U.S. Development Policy in Central America* (Boulder: Lynne Rienner/Food First Development Studies, 1996), 91–92.

29. Don Villarejo, "Labelling Dole: Some Thoughts on Dole Food Company's Expansion in World Agriculture," Fresh Fruit & Vegetables Globalization Network, University of California at Santa Cruz, Working Paper no. 6, 1991, 1.

30. Ibid., 3–4.

31. Conroy, Murray, and Rosset, *A Cautionary Tale*, 98.

32. José Gabriel López, "Agrarian Transformation and the Political, Ideological and Cultural Responses from the Base: A Case Study from Western Mexico," Ph.D. dissertation, University of Texas at Austin, 1990.

33. Conroy, Murray, and Rosset, *A Cautionary Tale*, 99.

34. Ibid.

35. Jeff Faux, "NAFTA's Rules Don't Work: So Why Rush Down a Track to Extend Them to All of Latin America?" *EPI Journal* (Economic Policy Institute, Fall 1997): 1, 6.

36. Peter Rosset, "Bringing It All Back Home: Mexico, the USA, Chiapas and Oklahoma City," *Food First New & Views* 17, no. 57 (Institute for Food and Development Policy, Summer 1995): 1–2, 4.

37. According to a survey commissioned by the Labor Secretariat of the U.S. Commission under NAFTA, threats to shut down operations have been used by over half of the firms in that country. See Public Citizen, et al., "The Failed Experiment: NAFTA at Three Years," *Report by the Public Citizen Economic Policy Institute* (Washington, DC: Public Citizen, 1997).

38. Faux, "NAFTA's Rules."

39. Ibid.

40. Ibid.

41. See Walden Bello with Shea Cunningham and Bill Rau, *Dark Victory: The United States, Structural Adjustment and Global Poverty* (London: Pluto Press/Food First Books/Transnational Institute, 1994).

42. See Conroy, Murray, and Rosset, *A Cautionary Tale*, chapter 3.

43. Martha Honey, *Hostile Acts: U.S. Policy in Costa Rica in the 1980s* (Gainesville: University Press of Florida, 1994), 172–173.

44. Ibid.

45. *FAO Trade Yearbook 1990*, table 5.

46. Honey, *Hostile Acts*, 174, 176–177.

47. Ibid., 176–177.

48. From Conroy, Murray, and Rosset, *A Cautionary Tale*, table 4.2.

49. Ibid.

50. Estimated from figure 2.1 in Conroy, Murray, and Rosset, *A Cautionary Tale.*

51. Ibid., table 4.1.

52. Ibid., figure 4.4.

53. See Bello, et. al., *Dark Victory,* for a thorough discussion.

54. See Chakravarti Raghavan, "Uruguay Round Accord Threatens South's Food Security," Third World Network Features, 1315/95, Penang, Malaysia, 1995.

55. Myriam Vander Stichele, "The Democratic Deficit in the Uruguay Round Negotiations," Working Paper of the Common Agricultural Policy/Third World Working Group of the EECOD (Brussels: European Ecumenical Organisation for Development, 1992).

56. For discussion on these issues, see Coote, *The Trade Trap,* chapter 9; and David Korten, *When Corporations Rule the World* (West Hartford: Kumarian Press/Berrett-Koehler Publishers, 1995), chapter 13.

57. See Jeffery D. Sachs, "Trade and Exchange Rate Policies in Growth-Oriented Adjustment Programs" in *Growth-Oriented Adjustment Programs,* ed. Vittorio Corbo, Morris Goldstein, and Moshin Kahn (Washington, DC: IMF and World Bank, 1987); and Oxfam International, *Growth with Equity: An Agenda for Poverty Reduction,* Oxford: Oxfam International 1997, www.caa.org.au/oxfam/advocacy/equity/index.html.

58. To understand how U.S. pressure was used to undermine those economies, see Bello, et al., *Dark Victory,* chapter 8. For a discussion of how these changes then contributed to the Asian economic crisis that began in late 1997, see Walden Bello, "The End of the Asian Miracle," *The Nation,* (January 12–19, 1998): 16, 18–21.

59. Frances Moore Lappé and Joseph Collins, *Food First: Beyond the Myth of Scarcity* (New York: Ballantine, 1977).

60. See Rone Tempest, "China Stands on Sideline of Asian Financial Chaos," *Los Angeles Times,* November 25, 1997.

MYTH 9: Too Hungry to Revolt

1. Medea Benjamin and Rebecca Buell, *Coalition of Ejidos of the Valleys of Yaqui and Mayo, Sonora State, Mexico* (San Francisco: Institute for Food and Development Policy, 1985).

2. Frances Moore Lappé and Joseph Collins, *Now We Can Speak: A Journey Through the New Nicaragua* (San Francisco: Food First Books, 1982), 106–111.

3. EZLN, *Documentos y Comunicados* (Mexico City: Ediciones Era, 1994), 36.

4. Peter Rosset, "Understanding Chiapas" in *First World, Ha Ha Ha! The Zapatista Challenge*, ed. Elaine Katzenberger (San Francisco: City Lights Books, 1995), 158. For more background on the Zapatista movement, see George A. Collier with Elizabeth Lowery Quaratiello, *Basta! Land and the Zapatista Rebellion in Chiapas* (Oakland: Food First Books, 1994).

5. Mark S. Langevin and Peter Rosset, "Land Reform from Below," *Food First Backgrounder* (Fall 1997): 1.

6. AWEPON, *Women Standing Up to Adjustment in Africa*, A Report of the African Women's Economic Policy Network, July 1996 (The Development GAP, Washington, DC, www.igc.apc.org/dgap/index.html, November 4, 1997), 19.

7. Ibid., 34.

8. Rachel Szego, "Cargill, Incorporated: Controlling the World's Food Supply," FoodFirst Information and Action Network, *FIAN FACT SHEET*, Institute for Food and Development Policy (1997), 4–5.

9. Ibid., 5.

10. Anuradha Mittal, "KFC's Cultural Colonialism," *Food & Water Journal* (Spring 1996): 21.

11. Ibid.

12. Wahidul Haque et al., *An Approach to Micro-Level Development: Designing and Evaluation of Rural Development Projects* (UN Asian Development Institute, February 1977), 15.

13. Lasse Berg and Lisa Berg, *Face to Face* (Berkeley: Ramparts Press, 1971), 154.

14. Willy Randia, *Signes d'Espérance* (Lausanne, 1981), 65–76.

15. Daniel T. Spencer, "Eye Witness: A Week that Shook Port-au-Prince," *Christianity in Crisis* (March 17, 1986): 81–83; and George S. Johnson, "Haiti and Lazarus: The Bible Comes Alive in Port-au-Prince," *Seeds* 9, no. 4 (April 1986): 18–19.

16. For a more complete account, see *Kuala Juru: A People's Cooperative* (Penang, Malaysia: Institute Masyarakat Berhad and Consumer's Association of Penang, undated).

MYTH 10: More U.S. Aid Will Help the Hungry

1. World Bank, *World Development Report 1995* (New York: Oxford University Press, 1995), table 18.

2. The twenty-one rich OECD countries have substantially reduced their aid budgets, which in 1994 reached their lowest point in over twenty years. Earthscan, *The Reality of Aid: An Independent Review of International Aid*. (London: Earthscan Publications, 1996) 17.

3. U.S. Agency for International Development, *Congressional Presentation Fiscal Year 1996* (Washington, DC: USAID, 1995), table AFD_CP.XLS.

4. George Shultz, "Foreign Assistance Request for FY 1986," *Current Policy*, no. 656 (U.S. Department of State, Bureau of Public Affairs, Washington, DC, February 19, 1985).

5. For a discussion of Cold War U.S. aid policies, see the previous edition of this book, Frances Moore Lappé and Joseph Collins, *World Hunger: 12 Myths* (New York: Grove Weidenfeld, 1986), chapter 10; see also Frances Moore Lappé, Rachel Schurman, and Kevin Danaher, *Betraying the National Interest: How U.S. Foreign Aid Threatens Global Security by Undermining the Political and Economic Stability of the Third World* (New York: Grove Press, 1987); and Frances Moore Lappé, Joseph Collins, and David Kinley, *Aid as Obstacle: Twenty Questions about Our Foreign Aid and the Hungry* (San Francisco: Institute for Food and Development Policy, 1981).

6. See Peter Rosset, "Overseas Rural Development Policy" in *Global Focus: A New Foreign Policy Agenda 1997–1998*, ed. Tom Barry and Martha Honey (Albuquerque and Silver City: Interhemispheric Resource Center and Institute for Policy Studies, 1997), 55–56; and Michael E. Conroy, Douglas L. Murray, and Peter M. Rosset, *A Cautionary Tale: Failed U.S. Development Policy in Central America* (Boulder: Lynne Rienner/Food First Development Studies, 1996), chapter 3.

7. *USAID Developments* (Summer 1997), 4.

8. Ibid., 1.

9. U.S. Agency for International Development, *Congressional Presentation Fiscal Year 1996*.

10. U.S. Agency for International Development, *Congressional Presentation Fiscal Year 1996;* calculated with country ranks from U.S. Central Intelligence Agency, *World Fact Book 1995* (Washington, DC: Central Intelligence Agency, 1995).

11. Rosset, "Overseas Rural Development," 54.

12. Conroy, Murray, and Rosset, *A Cautionary Tale,* 70–79.

13. Ibid., table 3.1.

14. Ibid., 76.

15. Ibid., 77.

16. Rosset, "Overseas Rural Development"; Walden Bello with Shea Cunningham and Bill Rau, *Dark Victory: The United States, Structural Adjustment and Global Poverty* (London: Pluto Press/Food First Books/ Transnational Institute, 1994).

17. USAID *Congressional Presentation Fiscal Year 1996.*

18. U.S. Department of Agriculture, U.S. State Department, and U.S. Agency for International Development, *The U.S. Contribution to World Food Security: The U.S. Position Paper Prepared for the World Food Summit* (Washington, DC: U.S. Department of Agriculture, 1996), 4.

19. U.S. Agency for International Development, *USAID Annual Food Assistance Report, 1996* (Washington, DC: USAID, 1996), Budget Annex A-1.

20. See Li Kheng Poh and Peter Rosset, "New Food Aid: Same as the Old Food Aid?" *Food First Backgrounder* (Winter 1995), for definitions of the different kinds of food aid. See also Lappé, Collins, and Kinley, *Aid as Obstacle.*

21. Rachel Garst and Tom Barry, *Feeding the Crisis: U.S. Food Aid and Farm Policy in Central America* (Lincoln: University of Nebraska Press, 1990), 53.

22. USAID, *USAID Annual Food Assistance Report, 1996,* 53.

23. Rachel Szego, "Cargill, Incorporated: Building a Worldwide Presence," *FIAN Fact Sheet* (FoodFirst Information Action Network, 1997): 2–3.

24. See discussions in Lappé, Schurman, and Danaher, *Betraying the National Interest;* and Lappé, Collins, and Kinley, *Aid as Obstacle.*

25. Lappé, Collins, and Kinley, *Aid as Obstacle,* chapter 12, 95.

26. Garst and Barry, *Feeding the Crisis,* 54.

27. Food Security Act of 1985, cited in Ibid., 210–211, n. 50.

28. USAID, *USAID Annual Food Assistance Report, 1996,* Budget Annex, A-9-10.

29. Ibid., A-1.

30. Ibid.

31. Lappé, Collins, and Kinley, *Aid as Obstacle,* 113.

32. Rehman Sobhan, *Agrarian Reform and Social Transformation: Preconditions for Development* (London: Zed Books, 1993), 113–114.

33. Program on Peacekeeping Policy, *United Nations Operations in Somalia, Part II* (Washington, DC: Institute of Public Policy, George Mason University, 1994), 2.

34. See Li Kheng Poh and Peter Rosset, "New Food Aid: Same as the Old Food Aid?"; and Michael Maren, *The Road to Hell: The Ravaging Effects of Foreign Aid and International Charity* (New York: Free Press, 1997).

35. Poh and Rosset, "New Food Aid: Same as the Old Food Aid?" 5.

36. USAID Annual Food Assistance Report: 1996, chapter 3, 20, 26.

37. Michael Maren, "Good Will and Its Limits in Somalia," *New York Times,* August 27, 1993, A29; also, interview with Michael Maren conducted by Li Kheng Poh on May 12, 1995.

38. Lappé, Collins, and Kinley, *Aid as Obstacle,* chapter 15.

39. Poh and Rosset, "New Food Aid: Same as the Old Food Aid?" 4; Tony Jackson with Deborah Eade, *Against the Grain: The Dilemma of Project Food Aid* (Oxford: OXFAM, 1982), chapter 8.

40. Michael Maren, "Good Will," A29. See also Michael Maren, *The Road to Hell.*

41. "Military Aid Legislation," *Arms Sales Monitor,* no. 36 (February 1998): 1; U.S. Agency for International Development, *The USAID FY 1998 Congressional Presentation, Summary* (Washington, DC: USAID, 1998).

42. Congresswoman MacKinney at "Joint Hearing Before the Committees on International Security, International Organizations and Human Rights and International Operations," House of Representatives, Committee on Foreign Affairs, 103rd Congress, November 9, 1993 (Washington, DC: U.S. Government Printing Office, 1994), 4.

43. "Introduction: A Second Chance," pp. 1–7 and Barry and Honey, *Global Focus*, 5.

44. Ibid.

45. David Isenberg, "Arms Trade" in Barry and Honey, *Global Focus*, 94.

46. See Douglas L. Murray, *Cultivating Crisis: The Human Costs of Pesticides in Latin America* (Austin: University of Texas Press, 1994), 110–112.

47. See Joseph Collins with Frances Moore Lappé, Nick Allen, and Paul Rice, *What Difference Could a Revolution Make? Food and Farming in the New Nicaragua,* 2nd edition (San Francisco: Food First Books, 1985); and Peter Rosset and John Vandermeer, *Nicaragua: Unfinished Revolution: The New Nicaragua Reader* (New York: Grove Press, 1986).

48. See Conroy, Murray, and Rosset, *A Cautionary Tale*, chapters 1 and 3.

49. Joint Ministerial Committee of the Boards of Governors of the World Bank and the International Monetary Fund on the Transfer of Real Resources to Developing Countries (also known as the Development Committee), *Aid for Development: The Key Issues* (Washington, DC: World Bank, 1985), 41. In the section of this report entitled, "Aid and the Poor," the Development Committee concedes that "rural development programs have usually been unable to benefit 'the poorest of the poor,' i.e., the lowest 20 percent or so of the rural income distribution."

50. "A Synthesis of AID Experience: Small-Farmer Credit, 1973–1985," USAID Evaluation Special Study no. 41, (Washington, DC, October 1985) 11.

51. Conroy, Murray, and Rosset, *A Cautionary Tale,* chapter 2.

52. Ibid., 37; see also Peter Rosset, "Sustainability, Economies of Scale and Social Instability: Achilles Heel of Non-Traditional Export Agriculture?" *Agriculture and Human Values* 8, no. 4 (1991): 30–37.

53. Conroy, Murray, and Rosset, *A Cautionary Tale,* 39.

54. Ibid., 41.

55. Ibid.

56. Marc J. Cohen, "United States" in *The Reality of Aid 1996: An Independent Review of International Aid*, ed. Judith Randel and Tony German (London: Earthscan, 1996), 194.

57. Erik Leaver and John Cavanagh, "Controlling Transnational Corporations" in Barry and Honey, *Global Focus*, 41.

58. Ibid.

59. World Bank, *World Debt Tables*, 1994–95 (Washington, DC: World Bank, 1996).

60. Ibid.

61. Richard Lawrence, "Clinton's New Plan for Africa" *Journal of Commerce* (February 15, 1996), 6-A.

62. So-called in the U.S. policy document titled *Comprehensive Trade and Development Policy for the Countries of Africa*, quoted in Tetteh Hormeku, "US-Africa Trade Policy: In Whose Interest?" in *African Agenda* (Accra, Ghana: Third World Network Africa Secretariat, 1997).

63. The Growth and Opportunity Bill in the U.S. Congress establishes a series of criteria that condition eligibility of a country to "benefit" from these policies to its performance of a series of "free-market" reforms. These criteria include World Trade Organization membership; promotion of free movement for goods, services, and factors of production in and out of the country; and protection of property rights (Hormeku, "US-Africa Trade Policy," 6).

64. See Hormeku, "US-Africa Trade Policy," 4, 5.

65. See, for example, John William Templeton, "Africa Needs a Seat at the World's Economic Table," *San Francisco Examiner*, June 9, 1997.

66. George Kourous and Tom Barry, "Export-Import Bank" in Barry and Honey, *Global Focus*, 33.

67. Cohen, "United States," 194.

68. Kourous and Barry, "Export-Import Bank," 34–35.

69. Janice Shields, "Overseas Private Investment Corporation" in Barry and Honey, *Global Focus*.

70. For a recent attempt to estimate the magnitude of capital flows from Southern to Northern countries, which far outweigh total North-South

flows, see Martin Khor, "South-North Resources Flows and Their Implications for Sustainable Development," *Third World Resurgence,* no. 46 (1994): 14–25.

71. United Nations, *World Economic and Social Survey 1997* (New York: United Nations, 1997), table A. 36.

72. See Susan George, *A Fate Worse Than Debt: The World Financial Crisis and the Poor,* revised and updated edition (New York: Grove Weidenfeld/Food First Books, 1990).

73. Oxfam International, "Oxfam International Calls for Action on Multilateral Debt," press release (Washington, DC: Oxfam International, February 20, 1996).

74. Debt payment figures from United Nations, *World Economic and Social Survey 1997,* table A. 37; direct foreign investment and development assistance figures from World Bank, *World Debt Tables 1995* (Washington, DC: World Bank, 1995), table 1.

75. *50 Years Is Enough,* 1025 Vermont Avenue, NW, Suite 300, Washington, DC, 20005, USA, wb50years@igc.apc.org.

MYTH 11: We Benefit from Their Hunger

1. Holly Sklar, *Chaos or Community? Seeking Solutions, Not Scapegoats for Bad Economics* (Boston: South End Press, 1995), 36.

2. *Business Week,* November 18, 1994, 164.

3. Sklar, *Chaos or Community?* 41.

4. See Andrew Marshall, "Hunger at Home: The Growing Epidemic," *FIAN Fact Sheet* no. 3 (November, 1996), FoodFirst Information Action Network, Institute for Food and Development Policy, Oakland, CA.

5. Admiral Eugene Carroll, "Peace and Security, Introduction" in *Global Focus: Foreign Policy Agenda, 1997–1998,* ed. Tom Barry and Martha Honey (Albuquerque and Silver City: Interhemispheric Resource Center and Institute for Policy Studies, 1997), 77.

6. Ibid.

7. "Military Aid Legislation," *Arms Sales Monitor,* no. 36 (February 1998), 1.

8. See Carroll, 78. Military aid to Mexico is a case in point. See Peter Rosset, "Let Mexico Decide Its Own Future," *San Francisco Chronicle,* March 10, 1998, A19.

9. On the killing of civilians in El Salvador under the government of President Duarte, see testimony before the Subcommittee on Western Hemisphere Affairs, U.S. House of Representatives, May 14, 1986. For a more general discussion of civilian deaths in Central America, see Richard Garfield and Pedro Rodriguez, "Health and Health Services in Central America," *Journal of the American Medical Association* 254, no. 7 (August 16, 1985): 936–943. According to Garfield and Rodriguez, national registries put violence as the most common cause of death in Nicaragua, Guatemala, and El Salvador between 1980 and 1985 (p. 939). In El Salvador alone, an estimated forty thousand civilians were killed in the U.S.-funded war between 1979 and 1985. See Ruth Leger Sivard, *World Military and Social Expenditures 1985* (Washington, DC: World Priorities, 1985), 10.

10. See, for example, Reed Brody, *Contra Terror in Nicaragua: Report on Fact Finding Mission* (Boston: South End Press, 1985). See also "Affidavit of Former Contra Leader Edgar Chamorro to the International Court of Justice: Case Concerning Military and Paramilitary Activities in and against Nicaragua," *Congressional Record* (January 30, 1986): 1–4; and Joseph Collins, with Frances Moore Lappé, Nick Allen, and Paul Rice, *Nicaragua: What Difference Could a Revolution Make?* (New York: Grove Press/Food First Books, 1986), chapter 14.

11. Kim Moody and Simone Sagovac, *Time Out! The Case for a Shorter Work Week* (Detroit: Labor Education & Research Project, 1995), 8. See also Robert B. Reich, *The Work of Nations* (New York: Vintage Books, 1992).

12. Bennett Harrison and Barry Bluestone, *The Great U-Turn: Corporate Restructuring and the Polarizing of America* (New York: Basic Books, 1988), 71.

13. Robert Greenstein and Scott Barancik, *Drifting Apart: New Findings on Growing Income Disparities Between the Rich and the Poor, and the Middle Class* (Washington, DC: Center on Budget and Policy Priorities, 1990), 6.

14. Center on Hunger, Poverty and Nutrition Policy, *Statement on Key Welfare Reform Issues: The Empirical Evidence* (Medford, MA: Center on Hunger, Poverty and Nutrition Policy, 1995), 13.

15. *San Francisco Chronicle*, March 7, 1995. For a comprehensive study on "wealthfare" spending (that is, the taxpayer money that subsidizes corporations and the wealthiest sectors of society in the United States, see Mark Zepezauer and Arthur Naiman, *Take the Rich off Welfare* (Tucson: Odonian Press, 1996).

16. National Urban League, *The State of Black America 1995* (New York: National Urban League, 1995), 78.

17. Marc L. Miringoff, *1995 Index of Social Health: Monitoring the Social Well-Being of the Nation* (Tarrytown, NY: Fordham Institute for Innovation in Social Policy, 1995), 5.

18. Sklar, *Chaos or Community?* 25–26.

19. *San Francisco Chronicle*, March 20, 1995.

20. *San Francisco Examiner*, September 17, 1995.

21. Moody and Sagovac, *Time Out!* 10.

22. *New York Times*, March 31, 1995.

23. Anthony B. Atkinson, Lee Rainwater, and Timothy M. Smeeding, *Income Distribution in OECD Countries: Evidence from the Luxembourg Income Study* (Paris: Organisation for Economic Co-operation and Development, 1995), 44, 49.

24. Edward N. Wolff, *Top Heavy: A Study of the Increasing Inequality of Wealth in America* (New York: Twentieth Century Fund Press, 1995), 10.

25. Ibid., 2. Zepezauer and Naiman, however, found a different proportion: The total net worth of the top 1 percent equals that of the bottom 90 percent (*Take the Rich off Welfare*, 11).

26. Sklar, *Chaos or Community?* 8.

27. Ibid., 91.

28. National Urban League, *State of Black America*, 306.

29. Frank Levy, "Incomes and Income Inequality" in *State of the Union: America in the 1990s,* ed. Reynolds Farley (New York: Russell Sage Foundation, 1995), 42.

30. See John Cavanagh and Sarah Anderson, "Ten Lessons and Opportunities from the Fast Track Victory," handout from the Institute for Policy Studies, Washington, DC, November 13, 1997.

31. On the shift to the language of competitiveness, see Marc J. Cohen, "From National Security to Competitiveness" in *Hunger 1998: Hunger in a Global Economy,* 24–25, box.

32. See Susan George, *A Fate Worse Than Debt: The World Financial Crisis and the Poor,* revised and updated edition (New York: Grove Weidenfeld/Food First Books, 1990).

33. See Carlos Marichal, "The Vicious Cycles of Mexican Debt," *NACLA Report on the Americas* 31, no. 3 (November–December 1997): 25–31.

34. The experience of Continental Illinois is strong evidence. Robert Lekachman also describes a conversation with financial expert Felix Rohatyn in which Rohatyn confirmed this prediction. See Robert Lekachman, "The Debt Balloon," *Dissent* (Spring 1986): 136.

35. Marichal, "The Vicious Cycles of Mexican Debt"; Walden Bello, "The End of the Asian Miracle," *The Nation* (January 12–19, 1998), 16, 18–21.

36. *Handbook of International Trade and Development Statistics 1994* (New York and Geneva: United Nations Conference on Trade and Development, 1995), table 3.2. Data for food items include beverages, tobacco, and edible oil seeds.

37. *FAO Trade Yearbook 1995* (Rome: FAO, 1996), table 6.

38. See Alessandro Bonanno, Lawrence Busch, William Friedland, Lourdes Gouveia, and Enzo Mingione, eds., *From Columbus to ConAgra: The Globalization of Agriculture and Food* (Lawrence: University of Kansas Press, 1994).

39. Steven Suppan and Karen Lehman, "Food Security and Agricultural Trade Under NAFTA," Institute for Agriculture and Trade Policy, Minneapolis, MN, July 11, 1997 (IATP webpage www.iatp.org).

40. Reggie Brown of the Florida Fruit and Vegetable Association, testifying before the International Trade Commission, quoted in Suppan and Lehman, "Food Security and Agricultural Trade Under NAFTA."

41. Ana de Ita, "Impunidad Local en el Mercado Global: Los Maiceros entre el Filo del Gobierno Mexicano y el Libre Comercio," paper presented at the Annual Meeting of the Latin American Studies Association, April 17–19, 1997, Guadalajara, Mexico.

42. See Katherine Buckley, "Competitive Advantage in Producing Winter Fresh Vegetables in Florida and West Mexico" in *Vegetable Outlook and Situation Report* (Washington, DC: USDA, February 1986), 15.

43. David Weir and Mark Schapiro, *Circle of Poison: Pesticides and People in a Hungry World* (San Francisco: Food First Books, 1981).

44. See Jeffe Gerth and Tim Weiner, "Imports Swamp U.S. Food Safety Efforts," *New York Times,* September 29, 1997, A1, A8.

45. Suppan and Lehman, "Food Security and Agricultural Trade Under NAFTA."

46. Center on Budget and Policy Priorities, *Poverty Rate Fails to Decline as Income Growth in 1996 Favors the Affluent* (Washington, DC: Center on Budget and Policy Priorities, 1997).

47. Interagency Council on the Homeless, Department of Housing and Urban Development, *Priority: Home! The Federal Plan to Break the Cycle of Homelessness* (Washington, DC: Department of Housing and Urban Development, 1994).

48. United States Conference of Mayors, *A Status Report on Hunger and Homelessness in America's Cities: 1994* (Washington, DC: United States Conference of Mayors, 1994), 2.

49. Ibid., 2.

50. *Second Harvest 1993 National Research Study* (Chicago: Second Harvest, 1993), 24.

51. Ibid., 66, 70.

52. United States Conference of Mayors, *A Status Report*, 1.

53. Food Research and Action Center, *Community Childhood Hunger Identification Project: A Survey of Childhood Hunger in the United States* (Washington, DC: Food Research and Action Center, 1995), 14. See also California Budget Project, *Working, But Poor, in California* (Sacramento: California Budget Project, 1996).

54. Ibid., 11.

55. Contact FIAN-USA, c/o Institute for Food and Development Policy–Food First, 398 60th Street, Oakland, CA 94618, USA, fianusa@igc. apc.org and www.foodfirst.org. The international headquarters of FIAN is in Germany and can be reached at fian@fian.org.

MYTH 12: Food vs. Freedom

1. Kathryn Larin and Elizabeth McNichol, *Pulling Apart: A State-by-State Analysis of Income Trends* (Washington, DC: Center on Budget and Policy Priorities, 1997), i.

2. Center on Budget and Policy Priorities, "Poverty Rate Fails to Decline as Income Growth in 1996 Favors the Affluent," *Analysis of 1996 Census Bureau Poverty, Income, and Health Data* (Washington, DC: Cen-

ter on Budget and Policy Priorities, revised October 14, 1997), on the Internet at www.cbpp.org/povday97.htm.

3. Mark Zepezauer and Arthur Naiman, *Get the Rich off Welfare*, (Tucson, Odionian Press, 1996), 7.

4. Ibid., 10.

5. Zepezauer and Naiman, *Get the Rich off Welfare*, 36.

6. Peter Edelman, "The Worst Thing Bill Clinton Has Done," *The Atlantic Monthly* (March 1997).

7. Charles Lindblom, *Politics and Markets* (New York: Basic Books, 1977), 49–50.

8. Thomas Jefferson, *Democracy*, ed. Saul K. Padover (New York: D. Appleton-Century, 1939), 215.

9. Page Smith, *Dissenting Opinions: The Selected Essays of Page Smith* (San Francisco: North Point Press, 1984), 39.

10. Ibid., 40.

11. C. B. MacPherson, *The Political Theory of Possessive Individualism* (New York: Oxford University Press, 1962), 128. Here MacPherson is quoting Henry Ireton, an ally of Cromwell, expressing a view with which the Levellers "had no quarrel."

12. Henry Shue, *Basic Rights: Subsistence, Affluence, and U.S. Foreign Policy* (Princeton: Princeton University Press, 1980), 24–25.

13. For a provocative discussion of the concept of freedom along similar lines, see C. B. MacPherson, *Democratic Theory: Essays on Retrieval* (Oxford: Clarendon Press, 1973).

Beyond the Myths of Hunger: What We Can Do

1. Robert Bellah et al., *Habits of the Heart* (Berkeley: University of California Press, 1985), 289.

2. *Business Week*, March 3, 1986, 62.

3. Robert A. Dahl, *Dilemmas of Pluralist Democracy: Autonomy Versus Control* (New Haven: Yale University Press, 1982). See also Robert A. Dahl, *A Preface to Economic Democracy* (Berkeley: University of California Press, 1985); David C. Korten, *When Corporations Rule the World* (West Hartford, CT: Kumarian Press, 1995); and Kevin Danaher, ed., *Corporations Are Gonna Get Your Mama: Globalization and the Downsizing of the American Dream* (Monroe, ME: Common Courage Press, 1996.)

4. Here in North America there is a movement to change the rules by which corporations operate. By revoking or amending state charters of incorporation, as well as by other tactics, corporations could be forced to follow new rules or else be dismantled. See Richard L. Grossman and Frank T. Adams, eds., "Exercising Power over Corporations through State Charters" in *The Case Against the Global Economy and for a Turn Toward the Local,* ed. Jerry Mander and Edward Goldsmith (San Francisco: Sierra Club Books, 1996); and Tony Clarke, *Dismantling Corporate Rule: Towards a New Form of Politics in an Age of Globalization* (San Francisco: International Forum on Globalization, 1997).

5. See, for example, William Cronon, *Changes in the Land: Indians, Colonists, and the Ecology of New England* (New York: Hill and Wang, 1983).

6. Robert A. Dahl, *Democracy in the United States* (Boston: Houghton Mifflin, 1981), 32.

7. Frances Moore Lappé and Paul Martin Du Bois, *The Quickening of America: Rebuilding Our Nation, Remaking Our Lives* (San Francisco: Jossey-Bass Publishers, 1994).

What We Can Do:
A Resource Guide

The organizations and publications suggested here represent only a small portion of the many resources that can help you to go beyond the myths of hunger and discover effective action for change. Write for more information to those that sound most interesting to you. For more comprehensive lists, refer to the directories at the end of this guide.

Periodicals

Abya Yala News, South and Meso American Indian Rights Center, PO Box 28703, Oakland, CA, 94604, (510) 834-4263, e-mail: saiic@igc.apc.org

Africa News, PO Box 3851, Durham, NC 27702, (919) 286-0747

Catholic Rural Life, 4625 NW Beaver Ave., Des Moines, IA 50310-2199, (515) 270-2634

Community Jobs, 1001 Connecticut Avenue, NW, Suite 838, Washington, DC 20036, (202) 785-4233

Connection to the Americas, Resource Center of the Americas, 317 17th Avenue SE, Minneapolis, MN, 55414-2077, (612) 627-9445, web: www.americas.org/rcta

CounterPunch, PO Box 18675, Washington, DC 20036

Cultural Survival, 11 Divinity Street, Cambridge, MA 02138, (617) 441-5400, e-mail: csinc@cs.org, web: www.cs.org

Dollars and Sense, 1 Summer St., Somerville, MA 02143, (617) 628-8411, e-mail: dollars@igc.apc.org, web: www.igc.apc.org\dollars

Earth Island Journal, 300 Broadway, Ste. 28, San Francisco, CA 94133-3312, (415) 788-3666, web: www.earthisland.org

The Ecologist, S. G. Cowell, The Ecologist, c/o Cissbury House Furze View, 5 Oaks Road, Slinford, West Sussex UK RH13 7RH, Ph. 44-1403-786-726, e-mail: ecologist@gn.apc.org

Texas Association of Community Action Agencies (TACAA), Food Journal, 2512 IH 35 South, Suite 100, Austin, TX 78704, (512) 462-2555, e-mail: HN0163 @handsnet.org

Food Research and Action Center Foodlines, 1875 Connecticut Avenue, NW, Suite 540, Washington, DC 20009, (202) 986-2200

Food First News & Views and Backgrounders, 398 60th Street, Oakland, CA 94618, (510) 654-4400, e-mail: foodfirst@igc.apc.org, web: www.foodfirst.org

Hunger Notes, World Hunger Education Service, PO Box 29056, Washington, DC 20017, (202) 298-9503

In These Times, 2040 N. Milwaukee Ave., Chicago, IL 60647, (773) 772-0100, e-mail: itt@inthesetimes.com, web: www.inthesetimes.com

Labor Notes, 7435 Michigan Avenue, Detroit, MI 48210, (313) 842-0227, e-mail: labornotes@igc.apc.org

Latinamerica Press, Apartado 18-0964, Lima 18, Peru, e-mail: postmaster@acna. org.pe

Left Business Observer, 250 West 85th Street, New York, NY 10024-3217, (212) 874-4020, web: www.panix.com/~dhenwood/LBO_home.html

Monthly Review, 122 N. 27th St., 10th Floor, New York, NY 10001, (212) 691-2555, e-mail: mreview@igc.apc.org

Mother Jones, 731 Market St., Ste. 600, San Francisco, CA 94103, (415) 357-0509, web: www.motherjones.com

Multinational Monitor, PO Box 19405, Washington, DC 20036, (202) 387-8030, e-mail: monitor@essential.org

NACLA Report on the Americas, 475 Riverside Dr., Ste. 454, New York, NY 10115, (212) 870-3146, e-mail: nacla@igc.apc.org, web: nacla@nacla.org

The Nation, 33 Irving Place, 8th Floor, New York, NY 10003-2332, (212) 209-5400, e-mail: info@TheNation.com, web: www.TheNation.com

National Catholic Reporter, 115 E. Armour Boulevard, Kansas City, MO 64111, (816) 531-0538, web: www.natcath.com

New Internationalist, 1011 Bloor Street West, #300, Toronto, Ontario, Canada M6H 1M1, (416) 588-6478, e-mail: nican@web.net, web: www.newint.org

Nutrition Action, Center for Science in the Public Interest, 1875 Connecticut Avenue NW, Suite 300, Washington, DC 20009-5728, (202) 332-9110, e-mail: cspi@ cspinet.org, web: www.cspinet.org

Peacework, American Friends Service Committee, 2161 Mass Avenue, Cambridge, MA, 02140, (617) 661-6130, e-mail: AFSCNERO@igc.apc.org

Political Environments, c/o Population and Development Program, Hampshire College, PO Box 5001, Amherst, MA, 01002, (413) 582-5506

The Progressive, 409 E. Main Street, Madison, WI 53703, (608) 257-4626, web: www.progressive.org

Ram's Horn, 32463 Beaver Drive, Mission, B.C. V2V 5R3, Canada, (604) 820-4270

Seeds, PO Box 6170, Waco, TX 76706, (254) 755-7745

Third World Resurgence, Third World Features, and Third World Economics, Third World Network, 228 Macalister Road, 10400 Penang, Malaysia, (60-4) 229-3511, fax: 229-8106, e-mail: twn@igc.apc.org

Utne Reader, 1624 Harmon Place, Suite 330, Minneapolis, MN 55403, (800) 736-UTNE

Yes! A Journal of Positive Futures, PO Box 10818, Bainbridge Island, WA 98110-0818, (206) 842-0216, e-mail: yes@futurenet.org, web: www.futurenet.org

Why Magazine, World Hunger Year, 505 Eighth Avenue, 21st Floor, New York, NY 10018-6582, (212) 629-8850, e-mail: whyear@aol.com, web: www.igloo.com/why

Z Magazine, 18 Millfield Street, Woods Hole, MA 02543, (781) 251-0755, e-mail: lydia.sargent@lol.shareworld.com, web: www.lbbs.org

U.S. Focus

American Agricultural Movement, 100 Maryland Avenue NE, Box 69, Washington, DC 20002, (202) 544-5750

Building Opportunities for Self-Sufficiency (BOSS), 2065 Kittredge Street, Suite E, Berkeley, CA 94704, (510) 649-1930, e-mail: hn0501@earthlink.net

California Food Policy Advocates, 116 New Montgomery Street, Suite 530, San Francisco, CA 94105, (415) 777-4422, e-mail: cfpa@earthlink.net, web: www.cfpa.net

Center for Living Democracy, 289 Fox Farm Road, PO Box 8187, Brattleboro, VT 05304-8187, (802) 254-1234, e-mail: info@livingdemocracy.org, web: www.livingdemocracy.org

Center on Hunger, Poverty, and Nutrition Policy, Tufts University School of Nutrition, Medford, MA 02155, (617) 627-3956

Center for Rural Affairs, 101 S. Tallman St., PO Box 405, Walthill, NE 68067, (402) 846-5428, web: www.cfra.org

Center for Science in the Public Interest, 1875 Connecticut Avenue NW, Suite 300, Washington, DC 20009-5728, (202) 332-9110, e-mail: cspi@cspinet.org, web: www.cspinet.org

Church World Service, PO Box 968, Elkhart, IN 46515, (402) 665-2429

Coalition on Human Needs, 1000 Wisconsin Avenue NW, Washington, DC 20007, (202) 342-0726, e-mail: chn@chn.org

Community Food Security Coalition, PO Box 209, Venice, CA 90294, (310) 822-5410

Community Nutrition Partnership Council, 202 Ruth Leverton Hall, University of Nebraska, Lincoln, NE 68583-0808, (402) 472-3717, e-mail: wkoszewski@unl.edu

Congressional Hunger Center, 229½ Pennsylvania Avenue SE, Washington, DC 20003, (202) 547-7022, e-mail: nohungr@aol.com, web: www.ghn.org/chc

Californians for Pesticide Reform (CPR), 49 Powell St., 5th Floor, San Francisco, CA 94102, (888) CPR-4880, web: www.igc.org/cpr

Economic Policy Institute, 1660 L Street NW, Ste. 1200, Washington, DC 20036, (202) 775-8810, e-mail: epi@epinet.org, web: www.epinet.org

Farm Labor Organizing Committee (FLOC), 1221 Broadway Street, Toledo, OH 43609, (419) 243-3456

Food & Water, 389 VT Route 215, Walden, VT 05873, (800) EAT-SAFE

Food for Lane County, 255 Madison, Eugene, Oregon 97402, (541) 343-2822, e-mail: food4laneco@earthlink.net

Food Research and Action Center, 1875 Connecticut Avenue, NW, Suite 540, Washington, DC 20009, (202) 986-2200, web: www.frac.org

Henry A. Wallace Institute for Alternative Agriculture, 9200 Edmonston Road, Suite 117, Greenbelt, MD 20770-1551, (301) 441-8777, web: www.hawiaa.org

Inter Church Ministries of Nebraska, 215 Centennial Mall South, Suite 411, Lincoln, NE 68508, (402) 476-3391, fax: (402) 476-9310

Minnesota Food Association, 1916 South Second Avenue, Minneapolis, MN 55403, (612) 872-3298, fax: (612) 870-0729, e-mail: odonn@tc.umn.edu

National Catholic Rural Life Conference, 4625 Beaver Avenue, Des Moines, IA 50310-2199, (515) 270-2634, e-mail: ncrlc@aol.com, web: www.ncrlc.com

National Coaliton Against the Misuse of Pesticides, 701 E Street SE, Suite 200, Washington, DC, 20003-2841, (202) 543-5450, e-mail: ncamp@igc.apc.org

National Coalition for the Homeless, 1012 14th Street NW, Suite 600, Washington, DC 20005-3406, (202) 737-6444, e-mail: nch@ari.net, web: www.nch.ari.net

National Council of the Churches of Christ in the USA, 475 Riverside Drive, Ste. 880, New York, NY 10115, (212) 870-2138, web: www.ncccusa.org

National Farmers Union, 400 Virginia Avenue SW, Suite 710, Washington, DC 20024, (202) 554-1600, e-mail: nfu@aol.com, web: www.nfu.org

National Farm Worker Ministry, 1337 West Ohio Street, Chicago, IL 60622, (312) 829-6436

National Land for People, 35751 Oak Springs Drive, Tollhouse, CA 93667, (209) 855-3710, e-mail: sunmt@psnw.com, web: www.psnw.com\~sunmt

National Student Campaign Against Hunger and Homelessness, 11965 Venice Boulevard, 408, Los Angeles, CA 90066, (310) 397-5270

New York City Coalition Against Hunger, 29 John Street, Suite 708, New York, NY 10038-4005, (212) 227-8480, e-mail: nyccah@juno.com

Pesticide Watch, 450 Geary Street, Suite 500, San Francisco, CA 94102, (415) 292-1486, e-mail:pestiwatch@igc.org

The Preamble Collaborative, 1737 21st Street NW, Washington, DC 20009, (202) 265-3263, e-mail: preamble@rtk.net, web: www.rtk.net/preamble

Public Citizen, 215 Pennsylvania Avenue SE, Washington, DC 20003, (202) 546-4996, web: www.citizen.org

Public Voice, 1012 14th Street NW, Suite 800, Washington, DC 20005, (202) 347-6200, fax: (202) 347-6261

Pure Food Campaign, 860 Highway 61, Little Marais, MN 55614, (218) 226-4164, e-mail: purefood@aol.com, web: www.purefood.org

Research, Education and Action on Poverty, PO Box 50832, Washington, DC 20001, (202) 898-1706, e-mail: reaphq@aol.com

Second Harvest National Food Bank Network, 116 South Michigan Avenue, Suite 4, Chicago, IL 60603-6001, (312) 263-2303, web: www.secondharvest.org

United Farm Workers (AFL-CIO), PO Box 62, Keene, CA 93531, (805) 822-5571, web: www.ufw.org

U.S./International Focus

Agricultural Missions, 475 Riverside Drive, Room 624, New York, NY 10115, (212) 870-2553

American Committee on Africa, 50 Broad Street, Suite 711, New York, NY 10004, (212) 785-1024, e-mail: acoa@igc.apc.org, web: www.prairienet.org/acas/acoa.html

American Friends Service Committee, 1501 Cherry Street, Philadelphia, PA 19102, (215) 241-7000, e-mail: afsc.org, web: www.afsc.org

Amnesty International, 304 Pennsylvania Avenue SE, Washington, DC 20003, (202) 544-0200

Bread for the World, 1100 Wayne Avenue, Suite 1000, Silver Spring, MD 20910, (301) 608-2400, web: www.bread.org

Center for Community Change, 1000 Wisconsin Ave. NW, Washington, DC 20007, (202) 342-0519

Center of Concern, 3700 13th Street NW, Washington, DC 20017, (202) 635-2757, e-mail: coc@igc.apc.org, web: www.coc.org/coc

Corporate Data Exchange, 225 Broadway, Suite 2625, New York, NY 10007, (212) 962-2980, e-mail: txbp07c@prodigy.com

Data Center, World Views Resource Center, 1904 Franklin St., Ste. 900, Oakland, CA 94612, (510) 835-4692, e-mail: datacenter@datacenter.org, web: www.igc.org\datacenter\

The Development Gap (D-GAP), 927 15th Street NW, 4th Floor, Washington, DC 20005, (202) 898-1566, fax: (202) 898-1612, e-mail: dgap@igc.org, web: www.igc.org/dgap

Global Exchange, 2017 Mission Street, #303, San Francisco, CA 94110, (415) 255-7296, e-mail: info@globalexchange.org, web: www.globalexchange.org

50 Years Is Enough: U.S. Network for Global Economic Justice, 1025 Vermont Avenue, NW, Suite 300, Washington, DC 20005, (202) 463-2265, wb50years@igc.apc.org

Focus on the Global South (Food First sister institute), c/o CUSRI, Chulalongkorn University, Bangkok 10330, Thailand, (66-2) 218-7363, web: www.focusweb.org

FoodFirst Information & Action Network (FIAN) USA, 398 60th Street, Oakland, CA 94618, (510) 654-4400, e-mail: fianusa@igc.apc.org, web: www.foodfirst.org

Food for the Hungry Global Hunger Network, 7729 East Greenway Road, Scottsdale, AZ 85260, (800) 2-HUNGER, web:www.ghn.org

Friends Committee on National Legislation, 245 2nd Street NE, Washington, DC 20002-5795, (202) 547-6000, e-mail: fcnl@igc.apc.org, web: www.fcnl.org/pub/fcnl

INFACT, 256 Hanover Street, Boston, MA 02113, (617) 742-4583, e-mail: infact@igc.apc.org, web: www.infact.org

Information Project for Africa, c/o Africa 2000 Media Group, 4938 Hampden Lane, #192, Bethesda, MD 20814, (301) 613-8195, e-mail: a2000@the-hermes.net, web: www.africa2000.com

Interfaith Center on Corporate Responsibility, 475 Riverside Drive, Room 550, New York, NY 10115, (212) 870-2936, e-mail: info@iccr.org

International Alliance for Sustainable Agriculture, 1701 University Avenue SE, Minneapolis, MN 55414, (612) 331-1099, fax: (612) 379-1527, e-mail: iasa@mtn.org, web: www.mtn.org\iasa

The International Center, 731 8th Street SE, Washington, DC 20003, (202) 547-3800, e-mail: ic-nfp@clark.net, web: www.internationalcenter.com

International Forum on Globalization, 1555 Pacific Avenue, San Francisco, CA 94109, (415) 771-3394, e-mail: ifg@igc.org

International Rivers Network, 1847 Berkeley Way, Berkeley, CA, 94703, (510) 848-1155, web: www.irn.org

Institute for Agriculture and Trade Policy, 2105 1st Avenue South, Minneapolis, MN 55404, (612) 870-0453

Institute for Food and Development Policy (Food First), 398 60th Street, Oakland, CA 94618, (510) 654-4400, e-mail: foodfirst@igc.apc.org, web: www.foodfirst.org

Institute for Policy Studies, 733 15th Street NW, Suite 1020, Washington, DC 20005, (202) 234-9382

MAZON: A Jewish Response to Hunger, 12401 Wilshire Boulevard, Suite 303, Los Angeles, CA 90025-1015, (310) 442-0020, web: www.shamash.org/soc-action/mazon/mazon_who.html

National Commission for Democracy in Mexico, USA (NCDM), 2001 Montana, Suite #B, El Paso, Texas 79903, (800) 405-7770, e-mail: moonlight@igc.apc.org, web: www.igc.apc.org/ncdm/

Nicaragua Network, 1247 E Street SE, Washington, DC 20003, (202) 544-9355, e-mail: nicanet.igc.org

Northern California Interfaith Committee on Corporate Responsibility, PO Box 6829, San Francisco, CA 94142, (415) 885-5102

Overseas Development Network, 333 Valencia Street, Suite 101, San Francisco, CA 94103, (415) 431-4204, web: www.igc.org/odn/

Pesticide Action Network, 49 Powell Street, 5th Floor, San Francisco, CA 94102, (415) 981-1771, e-mail: panna@panna.org, web: www.panna.org/panna

Political Ecology Group, 965 Mission Street, Suite 218, San Francisco, CA 94103, (415) 777-3488, e-mail: peg@igc.org, web: www.igc.org/peg

Transnational Resource and Action Center (TRAC) and Corporate Watch, P.O. Box 29344, San Francisco, CA 94129, (415) 561-6567, web: www.corpwatch.org

USDA National Hunger Clearinghouse, World Hunger Year, 505 Eighth Avenue, 21st Floor, New York, NY 10018-6582, (800) GLEANIT, web: www.iglou.com/why/usda.htm

World Hunger Year (WHY), 505 Eighth Avenue, 21st Floor, New York, NY 10018-6582, (212) 629-8850 or (800) 5-HUNGRY, e-mail: whyria@aol.com, web: www.iglou.com/why

Overseas Direct Assistance

American Friends Service Committee, 1501 Cherry Street, Philadelphia, PA 19102, (215) 241-7000, e-mail: afsc.org, web: www.afsc.org

Committee for Health Rights in Central America (CHRICA), 474 Valencia Street, Suite 120, San Francisco, CA 94103, (415) 431-7760, e-mail: chrica@igc.org

Grassroots International, 179 Boylston St., 4th Floor, Boston, MA 02130, (617) 524-1400, e-mail: grassroots@igc.apc.org

International Development Exchange (IDEX), 827 Valencia Street, Suite 101, San Francisco, CA 94110-1736, (415) 824-8384, e-mail: idex@igc.apc.org, web: http://idex.org

Oxfam America, 26 West Street, Boston, MA 02111, (617) 482-1211, e-mail: oxfamusa@igc.apc.org, web: www.oxfamamerica.org

Canadian Organizations

The Council of Canadians, 904-251 Laurier Avenue West, Ottawa, Ontario K1P5J6, (613) 233-2773

IDERA, 1037 W. Broadway, Ste. 400, Vancouver, B.C. V6H 1E3, (604) 732-1496, e-mail: idera@web.net, web: www.vcn.bc.ca/idera

Marquis Project, 711 Rosser Avenue, Brandon, Manitoba R7A 0K8, (204) 727-5675, e-mail: marquis@mb.sympatico.ca, web: www.mts.net/~marquis

Ontario Public Interest Research Group (OPIRG), Provincial Office, 4 Trent Lane, University of Guelph, Guelph, Ontario N1G 2W1, (519) 824-2091, e-mail: opirg@ uoguelph.ca

Oxfam Canada, 2524 Cypress Street, Vancouver, B.C. V6J 3N2, (604) 736-7678, web: www.oxfam.ca

Directories

Alternatives to the Peace Corps: A Directory of Third World and U.S. Volunteer Opportunities, Filomena Giese, editor. Oakland: Food First Books, 1998.

Education for Action: Undergraduate and Graduate Programs That Focus on Social Change, 3rd edition, Sean Brooks and Alison Knowles, editors. Oakland: Food First Books, 1996.

Third World Resource Directory, Thomas P. Fenton and Mary J. Heffron, editors. Maryknoll, NY: Orbis Books, 1995-6.

Who's Doing What? A Directory of U.S. Organizations & Institutions Educating about Development & Other Global Issues. New York: American Forum for Global Education, 1991.

Food First

The Institute for Food and Development Policy

The Institute for Food and Development Policy, also known as Food First, is a nonprofit research and education-for-action center working to expose the root causes of hunger and poverty in the United States and around the world, and to educate the public and policy makers about these problems.

The world has never produced as much food as it does today—more than enough for every child, woman, and man. Yet hunger is on the rise, with nearly 800 million people around the globe going without enough to eat.

Hunger and poverty are not inevitable. Scarcity and overpopulation, long believed to be the causes of hunger, are instead symptoms of the ever increasing concentration of control over food-producing resources in the hands of a few. This deprives many millions of people of the power to feed themselves. Yet real change is possible once we understand the root causes.

In fifty-five countries and twenty languages, Food First materials help free people from the grip of despair, empowering them to work for a more democratic food system, so the needs of all can be met. To serve the public, activists, policy makers, the media, students, educators, and researchers, Food First produces books, reports, articles, films, electronic media, and curricula, plus interviews, lectures, workshops, and courses. Food First participates in activist coalitions and furnishes cogent, clearly written, and carefully researched analyses, arguments, and action plans for people who want to change the world.

Become a Member of Food First

Food First members join us in supporting our work. When you become a member, you receive:

- Quarterly *Food First News & Views* and *Backgrounders*
- A 20 percent discount on most of our books and other educational materials

- An opportunity to receive *Food Rights Watch* by e-mail
- A free one-year subscription to the *New Internationalist* magazine with a donation of $40 or more (new members only)

Individual membership contributions provide more than 50 percent of the funds for Food First's work. Because Food First is not tied to government, corporate, or university funding, we can speak with a strong and independent voice. The success of our program depends on dedicated volunteers and staff, as well as financial support from our activist donors. Your gift now will help strengthen our effort to improve the lives of hungry people around the world.

Become a Food First Intern
Interns, who come from around the world, are a vital part of our organization and make our work possible. There are opportunities for interns in research, advocacy, campaigning, publishing, computers, media, and publicity. Check our web page at www.foodfirst.org for information and application materials, or call 510–654–4400.

Please use these coupons to join Food First or give a gift membership

✂ ---

YES, here's my tax-deductible contribution. Please sign me up as the newest member of Food First.

＿ $30 ＿ $40 ＿ $100 ＿ other

Name ＿＿＿＿＿＿＿＿＿＿＿＿＿＿＿＿＿＿＿＿＿＿＿＿＿＿＿＿＿＿＿＿

Address ＿＿＿＿＿＿＿＿＿＿＿＿＿＿＿＿＿＿＿＿＿＿＿＿＿＿＿＿＿＿

City ＿＿＿＿＿＿＿＿＿＿＿ State ＿＿＿ Zip ＿＿＿ Country ＿＿＿＿

Phone ＿＿＿＿＿＿＿＿＿ E-mail ＿＿＿＿＿＿＿＿＿＿＿＿＿＿＿＿＿

＿＿ Please send me a free catalog of Food First publications

＿＿ Check enclosed

＿＿ Please charge my ＿＿ Visa ＿＿ MasterCard

Card number ＿＿＿＿＿＿＿＿＿＿＿＿＿＿＿＿＿＿ Exp. ＿＿＿＿＿

Food First/Institute for Food and Development Policy
398 60th Street, Oakland, CA 94618, USA
Phone: 510–654–4400 Fax: 510–654–4551
E-mail: foodfirst@igc.apc.org
Website: www.foodfirst.org

✂---

YES, here's my tax-deductible contribution. Please sign me up as the newest member of Food First.

___ $30 ___ $40 ___ $100 ___ other

Name _____

Address _____

City _____ State _____ Zip _____ Country _____

Phone _____ E-mail _____

___ Please send me a free catalog of Food First publications

___ Check enclosed

___ Please charge my ___ Visa ___ MasterCard

Card number _____ Exp. _____

Food First/Institute for Food and Development Policy
398 60th Street, Oakland, CA 94618, USA
Phone: 510–654–4400 Fax: 510–654–4551
E-mail: foodfirst@igc.apc.org
Website: www.foodfirst.org

About the Authors

Frances Moore Lappé is the author of twelve books, including the international best-seller *Diet for a Small Planet*, and co-director of the Center for Living Democracy in Brattleboro, Vermont, www.livingdemocracy.org. In 1975, she and Joseph Collins founded the Oakland-based Institute for Food and Development Policy (Food First), www.foodfirst.org.

Dr. Collins's many books include *Food First: Beyond the Myth of Scarcity*, and *Aid as Obstacle: Twenty Questions About Our Foreign Aid and the Hungry* (both with Lappé), as well as *No Free Lunch: Food and Revolution in Cuba* and *Chile's Free-Market Miracle: A Second Look*. An author, lecturer, and consultant on international development issues, he makes his home in Santa Cruz, California.

Peter Rosset is the executive director of the Institute for Food and Development Policy. He also teaches at Stanford University. Dr. Rosset's many books include *A Cautionary Tale: Failed U.S. Development Policy in Central America*, *The Greening of the Revolution: Cuba's Experiment with Organic Agriculture*, and *Agroecology*.

Luis Esparza is a geographer from the National Autonomous University of Mexico (UNAM), where he authored a widely used geography textbook. Dr. Esparza has been a visiting professor at the University of California at Berkeley.

Index

Acacia trees, 80
Accumulation, unlimited, 165–166
Africa
  aid to, 134
  desert in, 42–45, 189n.15
  exports of, 10–13
  fertility rates in, 26
  and Green Revolution, 59, 80
  hunger in, 17–19, 61, 183n.29
  peasant organization in, 125
  pesticide use in, 54
  private investment in, 143–144, 153
  structural adjustment in, 103
  See also specific countries
African-Americans, 154
African Women's Economic
  Policy Network
  (AWEPON), 125
Agriculture
  traditional vs. industrial, 76–77, 79–80, 100
  See also Farms

Agroecology, 77–82
AgroEvo, 75
Aid. *See* Foreign aid
AIDS, 103
Aid to Families with Dependent
  Children (AFDC), 153
All African Council of Churches,
  125
Altieri, Miguel, 78
Amazon River Basin, 46–48
American Association for the
  Advancement of Science
  (AAAS), 9
Angola, 21
Aquino, Corazón, 112
Arush, Mrs. Faaduma Abdi,
  136
Asia
  fertility rates in, 26
  Green Revolution in, 59
  hunger in, 61
  privatization in, 153
  See also specific countries

Subsistence rights, 168, 169, 172
Sudan
  famine in, 21
  use of farmland in, 11
Supermarkets, 102
Supply–side economics, 153
Sweden, 107

Taiwan
  free market in, 98
  land reform in, 92, 94, 119
Tariffs. *See* World Trade
    Organization
Tenant-operated farms, 87–88
Thailand
  exports of, 110
  family planning in, 37
  fertility decline in, 33
Tobago, 28
Tomatoes, 111, 157
Trachtenberg, Alan, 174
Trade. *See* Free trade; Trade
    liberalization
Trade liberalization, 113–121
Transgenic crops, 75, 217n.103
Trinidad, 28, 52
Tuberculosis, 103
Tungro virus, 71
2020 Vision program, 64

Umehara, Hiromitsu, 73
Unions, 152, 161
United Nations
  Food and Agricultural
    Organization of (FAO), 9,
    17, 64, 80, 88
  population forecast of, 13
  and Somalia, 136
  Universal Declaration of
    Human Rights of, 106–107,
    161

United States
  agroecology in, 81
  demographic transition in, 29–
    31
  desert in, 45
  environmental activism in,
    56
  family planning in, 38
  farming in, 70, 73–74, 86–88,
    89, 90–91, 101–102, 221n.10
  financial bailouts by, 156
  food surplus of, 14
  free market in, 98–102
  Green Revolution in, 69–70
  hunger in, 158–160
  Immigration and
    Naturalization Service (INS)
    of, 158
  imports of, 50, 157
  income distribution in, 154–
    155
  militarism of, 137–138, 151
  and NAFTA, 115
  pesticide use in, 51, 53
  See also Foreign aid, of United
    States
United States Agency for
    International Development
    (USAID), 80, 131–135, 138–
    142
  public relations of, 138–139
Universal Declaration of Human
    Rights, 106–107, 161
University of Nebraska Press
    study, 134
Uruguay Round of GATT, 118–
    119

Vandermeer, John, 29, 33, 48,
    78
Violence, 150–151, 241n.9